SCIENCE WIZARDRY for KIDS

Margaret Kenda and Phyllis S. Williams

D0060621

BARRON'S

For Our Mothers
Dorris Wood Farrar
and
Margaret Mason Secor,
who taught us the wonders of the world
in our own backyards

• • • •

And with special thanks for extraordinary assistance
from Tony Williams, Bethany Williams-Ntacyo,
and Michel Ntacyo; and from Bill Kenda and Mary Kenda

All inquiries should be addressed to:
Barron's Educational Series, Inc.
250 Wireless Boulevard
Hauppauge, New York 11788

Library of Congress Catalog Card No.: 92-26299

International Standard Book No. 0-8120-4766-4

Library of Congress Cataloging-in-Publication Data

Kenda, Margaret.
      Science wizardry for kids / by Margaret Kenda
and Phyllis S. Williams.
          p.   cm.
      Includes index.
      Summary: Includes over two hundred projects
that enable young scientists to make secret
formulas, blow bubbles of all sizes and colors,
grow smart plants, make predictions, and more.
      ISBN 0-8120-4766-4
      1. Science—Experiments—Juvenile literature.
2. Scientific recreations—Juvenile literature.
[1. Scientific recreations. 2. Science—
Experiments.] I. Williams, Phyllis S. II. Title.
Q164.K43   1992
507.8—dc20   92-26299
                                             CIP
                                               AC

PRINTED IN HONG KONG
22 21

CONTENTS

INTRODUCTION

*T*his is your chance to become a science wizard.

Perhaps you didn't know that as a science wizard you can do all sorts of wonderful things. You can play magic tricks. You can concoct a secret formula.

You can write with invisible ink. You can blow bubbles in just about any size or color. You can grow a smart plant that knows its way around or a plant that loves you. You can create moving cartoons.

You can play games with animals, not just puppies or kittens but also other creatures such as ants and fireflies.

As a science wizard, you can draw a map of the moon, or figure out the chances of life on other planets. You can fly a kite or look through your own homemade kaleidoscope. You can float a message out to sea in a bottle. You can predict when you'll do best at sports or on school tests.

You can trick your own eyes, create mysterious color changes, or perform taste-bud tests. You can test for what's in things or measure what's happening to the environment.

You can even give wonderful science parties.

You're the science wizard.

THINK LIKE A SCIENTIST

*J*ust think of something you want to know about the world. Scientists do that—they begin with a question.

Then think of what you expect the answer to your question might be. Scientists do that when they develop a hypothesis. That's a statement of what they believe is the answer.

Then design an experiment to find out if your answer is right. Scientists do the same—they test a hypothesis.

Of course, your hypothesis might turn out to be wrong. Then you have to consider other ideas, just as a scientist would.

But if the first experiment works out, then you may want to know more about the answer to your question. In that case, you might try other experiments.

If, after all the experiments, the hypothesis seems to be correct, it might become a theory. That means that most people accept the hypothesis as true. You may have heard of the atomic theory or of Einstein's theory of relativity.

Sometimes scientists discover new facts, and they have to change a theory. They might even decide to throw out a theory altogether and start over with a new hypothesis.

Or maybe the scientists think up a whole new question, something new they want to learn about the world.

What do *you* want to learn about the world? What's the next question *you* want to answer?

GUIDELINES FOR YOUNG SCIENTISTS

1. *Keep a science notebook.* Write down what you see. Ask yourself questions about the world. Make a statement that seems to explain what you have observed. Then set up an experiment that will help you find the answer.

2. *Have fun with science.* Take your time, and stay relaxed. You don't want to get hurried or frustrated.

3. *Keep things organized.* Before you begin a project, read the steps all the way through. Make sure you understand everything you need to do. Collect all the tools and materials you'll need.

4. *Keep things clean.* Begin with clean materials and clean containers. Wipe up spills right away.

5. *When you're finished, put everything back where it belongs.* Pick up after yourself outside, too. The environment needs your help both inside and outside.

6. *Don't worry about failures.* Every scientist fails at times. Some great discoveries in science started with failures. Even when your experiments don't turn out the way you planned, you're still learning something about the world.

Safety Rules by the Dozen

1. Ask an adult to join your team. You particularly need adult help when you're working with anything that's sharp, hot, or poisonous.

2. Work with a buddy. You need a friend with you when you're near water or out in the woods. Teamwork makes science more fun, anyway.

3. Keep in mind small children and pets. You don't want to leave anything around that could hurt them. Especially keep chemicals and sharp or pointed objects out of the reach of younger children.

4. Put all glues away as soon as you finish using them. They are poisonous, so be sure to keep them out of the way of younger children.

5. Put on labels. You need to know what's in every container, and other people may need to know, too. Make your labels waterproof with clear tape, or paint over them with clear nail polish.

6. Label poisonous chemicals, such as iodine, in bright red letters: **CAUTION: POISON.**

7. Use plastic containers whenever you can. Especially use plastic for carrying from place to place.

    If you must use glass containers, treat them like…glass. Make sure your hands are dry when you're handling glass. If you break a glass container, you'll probably need an adult to help you clean up every little bit. You don't want anyone to get cut.

8. Protect your eyes. Put on goggles or safety glasses when you're working with chemicals or anything else that might splatter or shatter.

9. Wash and rinse all equipment thoroughly before and after you use it.

10. Think safety first outside. Don't look directly at the sun. Wear sunglasses and clothes that protect you from the sun. Use sunscreen even if you have dark skin.

11. Don't touch an insect or a water creature until you've identified it and are sure it can't sting or bite you. Don't go near strange animals. If you think an animal is hurt, go for adult help.

12. Pay attention to your work from start to finish. Don't wander away and forget your project.

PROVE THE INVISIBLE EXISTS

*A*toms are the tiniest particles of matter that cannot be divided without losing their special characteristics. Each element has its own form of atom. An element's atoms will all act the same, but they may vary slightly in weight. Chemists can't separate the atoms of an element into other substances by ordinary chemistry,

Atoms connect or bond together into *molecules*. A molecule can be a new substance, or it can be a common form of an element. For example, oxygen atoms and hydrogen atoms bond to form water molecules. But oxygen gas and hydrogen gas are also molecules, because each contains two atoms.

And atoms and molecules move constantly.

Even though you can't see them, you can prove that they exist. And you can prove that they're moving all the time. Here's how.

· · · · · · · · · · ·

FIND THE INVISIBLE SPACES BETWEEN MOLECULES

· ·

Water is full of invisible holes. That's because the invisible water molecules are moving all the time and leaving invisible spaces in between.

You can prove that the holes exist.

Here's what you need:

1 cup (250 ml) water in a glass 2-cup or 4-cup measure

1 cup (250 ml) rubbing alcohol

Here's what you do:

1. Measure very carefully. You must have exactly 1 cup (250 ml) of water and exactly 1 cup of rubbing alcohol.

2. Pour the cup of rubbing alcohol into the cup of water.

3. Now measure again. You'll find that you have less than 2 cups (500 ml). This is one case where 1 + 1 does not equal 2.

WHY? Rubbing alcohol molecules filled the invisible holes between the water molecules. The shape of the alcohol molecules let them slide right in between the water molecules.

· · · · · · · · · · ·

PROVE THAT INVISIBLE MOLECULES ARE MOVING

· ·

All you need is a glass of water and a bit of food coloring.

Leave the glass of water in a place where no one will disturb it for hours.

Still without disturbing the water, add a couple of drops of food coloring.

At first, the food coloring drops to the bottom.

Come back several hours later. Now the water is all one color.

WHY? *THE MOLECULES ARE MOVING ALL THE TIME. THEY "STIRRED" THE WATER FOR YOU.*

· · · · · · · · · · ·

PROVE THAT MOLECULES MOVE FASTER WHEN THEY'RE HOT

· ·

Molecules move slower when they're cold, and faster when they're hot. Here's one simple way you can tell.

All you need is a cup of hot water, a cup of cold water, and a bit of food coloring.

Put 2 drops of food coloring into each cup.

Time how long it takes for the water in each cup to become all one color.

THE MOLECULES ARE MOVING FASTER IN THE CUP OF HOT WATER, SO THEY MOVE THE FOOD COLORING AROUND MUCH FASTER. THE COLD-WATER MOLECULES WILL PROBABLY TAKE ALL DAY TO DISTRIBUTE THE FOOD COLORING.

MAKE MODELS OF WATER MOLECULES

$\mathbf{Y}$ou can't see molecules separately. A molecule is so small it can be seen only by a powerful electronic microscope. But you can make models of molecules. This is a good project for a creative sort of person.

Each molecule is made from even smaller atoms. Atoms of the 109 elements now known bond to make molecules of just about any shape you can imagine.

And then those molecules bond to form structures in even more sizes and shapes. Think of it. Everything—wood, rocks, air, water, plants, people—is made of atoms and molecules.

A water molecule is a connection of two hydrogen atoms with one oxygen atom. The chemical formula is H_2O. (Kids say the formula looks like Mickey Mouse ears.) The oxygen atom is nearly 16 times larger than the hydrogen atom. In fact, the hydrogen atom is the smallest of all the atoms. (Of course, the molecules you make will not be to scale.)

Here's all you need to make molecule models:

Large marshmallows, to represent atoms

Small, colored marshmallows, to represent smaller atoms

Toothpicks, to represent the bond between atoms

Here's what you do:

1. For the water molecule model, use two small, colored marshmallows for the hydrogen atoms and one large marshmallow for the oxygen atom.

2. Stick them together with toothpicks so that one small marshmallow is on top and the other small marshmallow is at the bottom sticking out at an angle.

 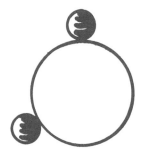

MAKE MODELS OF ICE CRYSTALS

When water freezes, the molecules bond into six-sided ice crystals. The ice crystals look like an artist's designs. Connect up a few of your own.

1. Begin with two water-molecule models. Use toothpicks to connect them at the small "hydrogen" marshmallows. The two water molecules can share a hydrogen, and then each will have one hydrogen bonded just to itself.

   Stick six models of water molecules together to build a sort of six-sided figure. As more and more connect, each can share as many as four hydrogen atoms.

2. The ice structure has depth and is not flat like a drawing of it. To put your "hydrogen" marshmallow in the right place, look down on the marshmallow. You should be able to see three hydrogen atoms at points of an imaginary triangle with equal sides. The fourth hydrogen atom will be in the center, underneath the marshmallow.

3. Stick together as many of these figures as you want. They form a sort of lattice.

ICE CRYSTALS ARE SIX-SIDED FIGURES, ONE AFTER ANOTHER, ON ALL SIDES, AND ABOVE AND BELOW ONE ANOTHER.

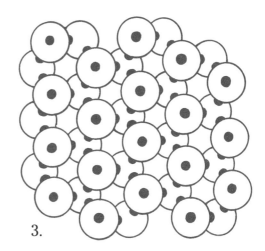

2.

1.

3.

MAKE MODELS OF SALT MOLECULES

A salt molecule is a bonding of one sodium atom and one chlorine atom. The chemical formula is NaCl. (Na stands for sodium. Cl is for chlorine.) The sodium atom is smaller than the chlorine atom.

In water molecules, the atoms share electrons (charged atomic particles that whirl around the nucleus of the atom). In salt molecules, the chlorine atoms actually pull an electron off the sodium atom. But each sodium is attracted to more than one chlorine, and each chlorine to more than one sodium. A salt crystal is really a "giant molecule" of billions of sodium and chloride ions bonded together.

1. To make the model of a salt molecule, just stick one small, colored marshmallow onto one large marshmallow.

2. Keep going to make salt crystals. Use toothpicks to connect small marshmallows ("sodium") with large marshmallows ("chlorine") to form cubes. Remember: Sodium atoms form bonds only with chlorine atoms, not with other sodium atoms.

3. Connect the squares to get an idea of the cube shape of salt crystals.

SALT MOLECULES FORM CUBE-SHAPED CRYSTALS, ONE AFTER ANOTHER, ABOVE AND BELOW ONE ANOTHER.

Now Go On To Design A Molecule From Your Own Imagination.

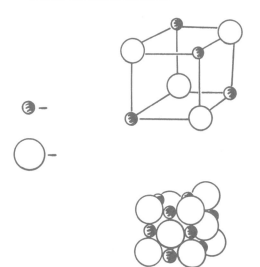

TEST FOR WHAT'S IN THINGS

*Y*ou can use chemistry to find out what's in things.

You can test for acids and bases. And you'll learn a few tricks to show your friends. You can test for starches. And you'll find a way to write invisible messages.

Go into your laboratory, get out your chemicals, and get started.

· · · · · · · · · ·
TEST FOR STARCHES
· ·

Starch is one major kind of carbohydrate. (You could divide food into three basic types: protein, fat, and carbohydrate.)

When you test for starch, you'll see interesting color changes.

The test uses iodine. Iodine is poisonous, so be sure to label your container **POISON**. And keep this experiment away from small children.

Here's what you need:

A small container, such as an empty film cartridge

Tincture of iodine

Water

Samples to test, such as beans, bread, cornstarch, flour, paper (from newspaper to fine stationery), pasta (cooked and uncooked), peas, potato (cooked or uncooked), rice (cooked or uncooked, instant or regular), sugar, vegetables, and fruits

Paper plate, paper towel, or paper mat

A drinking straw

Your science notebook and pen

Here's what you do:

1. Put ¹/₂ teaspoon (2 ml) of iodine into the container.
2. Add 4 to 5 teaspoons (20–25 ml) of water to make a golden-tan solution.
3. Arrange the samples on the paper plate, paper towel, or paper mat. Label each sample on the paper plate or towel.
4. Place one end of the straw in the iodine-water solution. Put your finger over the other end of the straw, and lift. That way you can use the straw as a pipette to transfer drops of iodine onto each sample.

   Caution: This straw is not for drinking!

5. Note the color changes in your science notebook. The food samples with starch in them will turn blue or purple. You can expect that the more starch, the deeper the color change.

Only starch will react to the test. Other types of carbohydrates (such as cellulose or fiber, table sugar, molasses, maple syrup, honey, the sugars in fruits and vegetables) will not react.

This test also works in the opposite way. You can use starches to test for iodine.

TEST AS MANY SUBSTANCES AS YOU LIKE. THEN GO ON TO USE YOUR IODINE SOLUTION TO WRITE SECRET MESSAGES.

WRITE SECRETS TO YOUR FRIENDS

You can write in invisible ink. Use a starch to write a secret message. Then use your iodine solution to read a secret message.

Here's what you need:

A heatproof, nonmetal container

1 teaspoon (5 ml) cornstarch

1/4 cup (60 ml) cold water

An art or lettering pen (the kind with no ink in it), feather pen, or toothpick

Paper

A small sponge

The iodine starch-testing solution

Here's how to write in invisible ink:

1. In the heatproof, nonmetal container, mix the cornstarch and water. Stir until smooth.
2. Put the mixture in a microwave oven. Heat on high for 1 minute. Stir once after 15 seconds. Remove from oven.
3. Dip the pen or toothpick into the cornstarch mixture. Write your message on the paper.

Here's how to read invisible ink:

1. Dip the small sponge into the iodine solution, and lightly wet the paper.

2. Watch the message appear in dark blue. (If the paper contains starch, the paper might turn light blue.)

NOW YOU CAN SEND AND RECEIVE SECRET MAIL.

PLAY A FOAMING TRICK

Try a trick with two liquids that might look like plain water. But you'll know what they really are. You're really mixing an acid and a base.

This can easily spill over, so do the trick on a strain-resistant table, on layers of newspaper, or near a sink.

Here's what you need:

Two clear glasses
Water
Baking soda
White vinegar

Here's what you do:

1. Fill one of the glasses about halfway with water, and then mix in 2 teaspoons or so of baking soda. Stir well so that the baking soda dissolves, and the liquid looks like clear water.

2. Fill the other glass halfway with white vinegar.

3. Now pour the vinegar into the glass of baking soda and water. You'll get quite a reaction. If you're not careful, your magic solution will foam all over the kitchen counter. That's because the base (baking soda) reacted with the acid (vinegar). The result was a salt plus enough carbon dioxide bubbles to foam up and spill.

A CHEMIST WOULD SAY THAT YOU USED THE BASE TO NEUTRALIZE THE ACID. YOU MIGHT SAY THAT YOU PERFORMED A FINE MAGIC TRICK FOR YOUR FRIENDS.

PREPARE A RED CABBAGE TEST FOR ACIDS AND BASES

Every good chemist needs to know the difference between an acid and a base.

Besides their importance in chemistry, acids and bases are necessary for cooking. The right sort of acids add flavor to food. They give food a tangy (or sometimes a sour) taste. Also, acids can help preserve food.

Bases can combine with acids to help with baking. The chemical reaction makes biscuits and cakes rise.

The strongest acids and bases, though, are not foods. Just touching a really strong acid or base can cause a bad burn.

The other word for base is *alkali.*

For your tests, you will need an indicator that will make acids and bases change different colors. Here's how to make an indicator from red cabbage.

Here's what you need:

A red cabbage

A grater

A stainless steel pan

Water

A strainer

A glass jar

A label

Here's what you do:

1. Grate the cabbage into the stainless steel pan. You should get an adult to help you with the grating.
2. Pour in water until you just barely cover the cabbage.
3. Boil the cabbage until it's tender. Before the cabbage is done, it will have lost some of its red color and will look a little bluish. The water will have a color between blue and red.
4. Carefully strain the water into the glass jar. Again, you'll probably want some adult help.
5. Label the jar: INDICATOR. You can use your indicator now, or refrigerate it for later.
6. Don't throw away the cabbage. First, add a little vinegar to turn the cabbage back to a more appetizing red color. Then add a little butter, salt, and sugar. If you wish, stir in chopped apple and a few raisins.

Note: When you add vinegar to the cooked cabbage, you add an acid. That makes the cabbage turn from bluish to bright red.

NOW YOU HAVE A GOOD ACID-BASE INDICATOR.

· · · · · · · · · · ·
TEST FOR ACIDS AND BASES
· ·

Now you're ready to use your cabbage water to test for acids and bases. Think of as many substances to test as you like. Then look on page 17 for more suggestions.

Here's what else you need:

Small glass jars or plastic containers (Clear plastic camera-film containers are perfect.)

A piece of paper, paper towel, or paper place mat for each container

A medicine dropper or drinking straw

Your science notebook and pen

Here's how to test for acids and bases:

1. Put a little of each substance you want to test into a small jar or plastic container. Set each container on a piece of paper, paper towel, paper place mat, or something else you can write on.

2. Transfer a little of the cabbage-water indicator to the substance. Use the medicine dropper or drinking straw. If you use the straw, put one end of it into the cabbage water. Put your finger over the other end, and lift the straw. Release the cabbage water by removing your finger from the end of the straw.

   : *Caution: Don't drink from this* : *straw.*

   To release the water by drops, just move your finger a little bit. When you do that, you allow a tiny bit of air to enter the straw along the grooves on your fin-

gertips. That bit of air pushes out a drop of the cabbage water.

3. Or do your testing another way. Dot the paper towels or place mats with the substances you plan to test. Write the names of the substances right on the paper. Then use the drinking straw or medicine dropper to drop some of the indicator on each substance.

4. You'll see a color change. The cabbage-water indicator turns an acid red, a base blue. Write acid or base on the paper in front of each sample. Then write all about it in your science notebook.

   : **NOW YOU HAVE A COMPLETE**
   : **TEST FOR ACIDS AND BASES.**
   : **TEST AS MANY SUBSTANCES AS**
   : **YOU LIKE.**

ARE THESE ACIDS OR BASES?

Ammonia
Apple juice
Ascorbic acid (vitamin C tablets,
  crushed and dissolved in water)
Baking soda
Banana (mashed)
Coffee
Cola drinks
Cream of tartar dissolved in water
Detergent
Eggshell (crushed and wet)
Egg white
Grapefruit juice
Lemon juice or lemonade
Milk

Milk of magnesia (magnesium
  hydroxide)
Orange or pineapple juice
Rain or seawater
Saliva
Salt dissolved in water
Sauerkraut
Sour pickle juice
Sugar
Tomato juice
Toothpaste
Vinegar
Water from cooking carrots, peas,
  or corn

REMEMBER THE DIFFERENCE BETWEEN ACIDS AND BASES

How can you remember which turns what color when you're using the cabbage juice test? Just match the letters:

aci<u>D</u> - re<u>D</u>
<u>B</u>ase - <u>B</u>lue

PLAY A TRICK WITH RED CABBAGE

You can make something that looks like light blue water turn a mysterious ruby red. Then make it turn blue again.

You're really just showing off how acids and bases change color when you test them with red cabbage water. But your friends may not know that.

Here's what you need:

Two clear glasses
Your red-cabbage-water indicator
White vinegar
Baking soda
Water

Here's what you do:

1. Pour some leftover cabbage water into one glass. The color is bluish.

2. Now pour in a little white vinegar, just until you see a color change. Instantly, the water turns ruby red.
(That's because white vinegar is an acid. You've just "tested" it.)

3. In the second glass, mix some water with 1 to 2 teaspoons (5 to 10 ml) of baking soda.
(If you really want to mystify your friends, mix this ahead of time. The glass will look as if it's full of ordinary water. If the water is cloudy, you've added more baking soda than you need. Add more water.)

4. Pour the baking soda solution into the ruby-red water in the first glass. Instantly, the water foams, and the color turns back to blue.
(That's because baking soda is a base. You've just mixed an acid and a base.)

PREPARE A QUICK AND EASY TURMERIC TEST FOR ACIDS AND BASES

Here's a quick, easy way to test for acids and bases.

Turmeric is a spice that cooks use to add flavor to Indian curries and to give mustard a deep yellow color. You can buy it at the grocery store.

Turmeric is an especially good indicator for acids and bases. You'll like the color changes.

Here's what you need:

Paper towels, coffee filters, or paper place mats

Liquid substances to test (see page 17)

Turmeric

Your science notebook and pen

Here's what you do:

1. Dot the paper towels, filters, or place mats with a sample of each substance you plan to test. Label each substance directly on the paper.

2. Pinch a bit of turmeric between your thumb and forefinger. Drop a pinch on each sample.

3. Watch for a color change. The turmeric stays yellow with acids. With bases, you'll see a range of red colors. Write acid or base on the paper beside the name of each substance you tested.

Then write your conclusions in your science textbook.

PREPARE AN EXCELLENT TURMERIC TEST FOR ACIDS AND BASES

Here's another good way to test for acids and bases. This test gives you especially interesting color changes for bases.

Here's what you need:

A glass jar with a lid
Turmeric
Rubbing alcohol
Labels
A medicine dropper or drinking straw
Paper towels, coffee filters, or paper place mats
Your science notebook and pen

Here's what you do:

1. In the glass jar, mix 1 teaspoon (5 ml) of turmeric in $1/4$ cup (60 ml) rubbing alcohol. Allow the mixture to set until the alcohol turns bright yellow.

2. Label the jar:
   : *WARNING: POISON—TURMERIC*
   : *INDICATOR.*

   Keep the lid on when you're not using the indicator. Keep the jar away from small children.

3. Dot the paper towels, filters, or place mats with a sample of each substance you plan to test. Label each substance directly on the paper.

4. Transfer a little of the turmeric indicator to the substance. Use the medicine dropper or drinking straw.
   If you use the straw, put one end of it into the turmeric jar. Put your finger over the other end, and lift the straw. Release the indicator by removing your finger from the end of the straw.
   : *Caution: Don't drink from this*
   : *straw.*

5. Look for the color changes. Write whether each substance is acid or base. You can expect a reddish change with bases and a less obvious yellow with acids. (The turmeric solution is already yellow.)

   : **NOW YOU HAVE ANOTHER**
   : **INDICATOR FOR ACIDS AND**
   : **BASES. AND YOU CAN USE**
   : **TURMERIC TO PLAY A BLOOD-**
   : **RED TRICK.**

PLAY A BLOOD-RED TRICK

Save a bit of your turmeric indicator to play a blood-red trick.

Just mix 1 to 2 teaspoons (5–10 ml) of baking soda with water in a glass. Then slowly, carefully pour a little of the turmeric indicator down the side of the glass.

Baking soda is a base, so you expect to see a reddish color change.

The yellow alcohol-turmeric solution will float on top of the baking soda solution. That's because it is lighter than the baking soda solution.

Right at the line where the two solutions meet, you'll see a blood-red color change.

: NOW ADD AN ACID LIKE
: VINEGAR, AND SEE WHAT
: HAPPENS. THE SOLUTION
: FOAMS, AND THE COLOR TURNS
: TO PALE YELLOW.

FIND OUT CHEMISTRY SECRETS

*C*hemistry is about change. Chemicals come together and create compounds that are not at all like the original chemicals. Then the compounds can change again to still another, different form.

You can use chemistry to create wonderful changes. Concoct your own secret formula. Change colors, shapes, and forms. Feel as if you're doing magic tricks.

· · · · · · · · · · ·
MIX UP MIXTURES AND SOLUTIONS
· ·

What happens when you try to mix one substance with another? Sometimes the two substances stay separate. They won't mix. Sometimes the two substances dissolve and create a solution somewhere in between the two originals. Sometimes you get a chemical reaction and a whole new substance.

Try some mixing, and see what happens.

Here's what you need:

Small jars and bowls

Water

Cooking oil

Sand

Sugar

Molasses

Baking Soda

Vinegar

Labels

Your science notebook and pen

Here's the mixing to do:

1. Pour a little oil into some water in one of the jars or bowls. Shake the jar.

2. Stir some sand into water. Let it sit a few minutes.

3. Stir a teaspoon (5 ml) of sugar into 2 teaspoons (10 ml)of sand.

4. Pour a tablespoon (15 ml) of molasses into a cup (250 ml) of water. Shake.

5. Put a teaspoon (5 ml) of sugar into a cup (250 ml) of water. Shake.

6. Mix a teaspoon (5 ml) of baking soda into a cup (250 ml) of water.

7. Add a tablespoon (15 ml) of vinegar to a cup (250 ml) of water. Stir.

8. Add 2 tablespoons (30 ml) of vinegar to the mixture of water and baking soda.

9. Label each jar.

Here's how to see the changes:

1. See what didn't really mix evenly. The oil and water separate quickly even though they are in the same container. The sand and water stay separate. The sugar and sand still look like sugar and sand.

   You can easily see the separate ingredients just by looking.

2. See what did really mix. The molasses formed a solution with the water. The sugar formed a solution with the water. So did the baking soda and the water, and the vinegar and the water. These are all examples of homogeneous mixtures or solutions. A homogenous solution shares the characteristics of each of the substances that make up the solution. An example would be mixing white paint with red paint. The result would be pink paint, somewhere between white and red.

In our examples, the molasses becomes more watery. The water with sugar in it becomes slightly sweet. The water with vinegar in it becomes slightly sour.

3. See a chemical change. When a chemical reaction takes place, a new substance is formed that is unlike either of the substances that created it.

   You see that when you mix vinegar and soda. You actually get two new substances. The bubbles are a carbon dioxide gas. The other new substance is sodium acetate, a salt formed by the chemical reaction of vinegar (acetic acid) and soda (sodium bicarbonate.)

   The new substances are chemicals unlike either the vinegar or the soda.

> **NOW THINK OF OTHER MIXTURES AND SOLUTIONS IN NATURE. YOU SEE THEM EVERY DAY.**

· · · · · · · · · ·

MIX UP AN EMULSION (AND MAKE SALAD DRESSING)

· ·

Oil and water won't mix for long. But here's a way you can make them stay together for a while.

Add paprika, and you suspend the oil particles inside the water. The paprika breaks down the oil particles. The result is an *emulsion*. It's not a solution because the oil and water will separate again before long.

Before this happens, make your emulsion into French salad dressing.

Here's what you need:

To make the emulsion:
A small jar
¹/₄ cup (60 ml) vinegar
¹/₄ cup (60 ml) salad oil
¹/₂ teaspoon (2.5 ml) paprika
¹/₂ cup (120 ml)water

To finish the salad dressing:

¹/₄ teaspoon (1 ml) sugar
¹/₂ teaspoon (2.5 ml) basil leaves
¹/₂ teaspoon (2.5 ml) oregano
¹/₂ teaspoon (2.5 ml) garlic salt
¹/₄ teaspoon (1 ml) onion powder
¹/₄ teaspoon (1 ml) salt

Here's what you do:

1. Pour the vinegar and oil into the jar. Add the paprika and water. Shake thoroughly.
   Now look carefully. What difference do you see between this mixture and the plain oil-and-water mixture that you saw before?
2. To finish the salad dressing, add the sugar, basil leaves, oregano, garlic salt, onion powder, and salt. Shake thoroughly to blend the flavors.

   : **NOW YOU HAVE FRENCH**
   : **DRESSING TO USE ON A SALAD.**

THE PAPRIKA KEEPS THE OIL IN SUSPENSION. THE OIL PARTICLES BECAME SO SMALL THAT THEY STAY SUSPENDED IN THE VINEGAR FOR A TIME.

· · · · · · · · · ·

MIX UP A COLLOIDAL MIXTURE (AND MAKE A GELATIN DESSERT)

· ·

A colloidal mixture is a gel. Here's one you can eat.

Here's what you need:

A 2-cup (500 ml) measure

1 package unflavored gelatin

2 ¹/₂ tablespoons (40 ml) sugar

Boiling water

Cold water

2 to 3 tablespoons (30–45 ml) lemon juice

2 or 3 drops yellow food coloring

A covered container

Here's what you do:

1. Put the unflavored gelatin into the 2-cup (500 ml) measure. Stir in the sugar.

2. Pour in boiling water up to the ³/₄-cup (180 ml) mark. Stir.

   : *Caution: You need adult help*
   : *with boiling water.*

3. Add cold water to the 1 ¹/₂ (360 ml) cup mark. Add the lemon juice and yellow food coloring. If you like your desserts especially sweet, add 1 or 2 tablespoons (15–30 ml) more sugar. Taste to see what you like.

4. Pour the mixture into a container. Cover, and put in the refrigerator.

5. Check in about 2 hours, and see how the mixture looks.

   : NOW YOU CAN EAT THIS
   : GELATIN FOR DESSERT.

THE INDIVIDUAL PARTICLES ARE STILL THERE IN A COLLOIDAL MIXTURE, JUST AS THEY ARE IN AN EMULSION. BUT YOU CAN SEE THEM ONLY WITH A POWERFUL MICROSCOPE.

OTHER COLLOIDAL MIXTURES ARE MILK, VARNISH, AND INDIA INK.

. . . .
DISCOVER OXYGEN

. . . .

Fire needs oxygen in order to burn. You can discover if oxygen is present in a closed space by seeing whether fire will burn.

Have an adult assist you with this experiment on finding oxygen.

Here's what you need:

A short candle, such as a food-warmer, scented, or votive candle

A kitchen match

A saucer

Water

A heatproof jar

Here's what you do:

1. Ask your adult assistant to light the candle and set it on the saucer.

2. Pour about $^1/_4$ cup (60 ml) of water into the saucer.

3. Turn the jar upside down, and carefully place it over the candle on the saucer.

4. Look at what happens. In a short time, the candle goes out, and the water moves up into the jar. As the flame burns, the wax reacts with the oxygen, creating carbon dioxide or carbon monoxide. The water replaces the space the oxygen previously occupied.

WHEN THE OXYGEN IS GONE, THE FLAME GOES OUT. FIRE CAN BURN ONLY WITH OXYGEN PRESENT.

COMBINE OXYGEN AND IRON

Create a chemical reaction of oxygen and iron. See what happens.

Here's what you need:

A piece of steel wool
Water
A clear jar
A saucer

Here's what you do:

1. Wet the steel wool.

NOTE: If you are using a steel-wool pad with soap in it, wash out the soap.

2. Push the steel wool into the bottom of the jar.

3. Turn the jar upside down on a saucer.

4. Fill the saucer with water.

5. Set the saucer in a safe place where no one will disturb it. From day to day, check the experiment. As the water evaporates from the saucer, replace it with more water.

6. Notice changes in the steel wool. Also notice changes in the level of the water inside the jar. If you see something red forming on the steel wool and water moving up inside the jar, your experiment has worked.

Here's how you helped create the chemical change:

The iron in the steel wool combines with the oxygen inside the jar. As the oxygen leaves the air inside the jar, water rises into the jar to replace the oxygen. When iron unites with oxygen, the result is a new, rustlike substance, ferric oxide. (Ferric refers to iron. Oxide refers to oxygen.)

GO ON TO USE THE STEEL WOOL AND THE FERRIC OXIDE TO CREATE OTHER IRON COMPOUNDS.

....
MAKE MORE CHEMICAL CHANGES WITH OXYGEN AND IRON
. . . .

You can use the steel wool and the ferric oxide to make other sorts of chemical changes. This experiment uses the combined iron and oxygen to make ferrous acetate and ferric acetate. You'll see color changes that will tell you which is which.

Here's what you need:

The steel wool from the oxygen-and-iron experiment

White vinegar

A saucepan

Two small jars

Labels

A coffee filter or other filter paper

A funnel

A medicine dropper or drinking straw

Hydrogen peroxide

Here's what you do:

1. Pour some white vinegar into the jar with the steel wool. Pour the whole mess into the saucepan, and bring to a boil. Boil for about 5 minutes. Then cool.

   : *Caution: You need adult help*
   : *with boiling water.*

2. Pour a little of the vinegar-steel wool mixture into one of the small jars. Label it "Ferrous Acetate."

3. Put the filter paper into the funnel. Place the funnel in the opening of the second jar. Pour the rest of the mixture into the filter paper, and let a solution drip into the jar.

4. Use the straw to transfer a few drops of the hydrogen peroxide to the solution in the second jar. Put one end of the straw into the hydrogen peroxide. Put your finger over the other end, and lift the straw. Release a few drops of hydrogen peroxide by removing your finger from the end of the straw.

   : *Caution: Don't drink from this*
   : *straw.*

You should see a reddish brown color change. The hydrogen peroxide contains extra oxygen. The extra oxygen creates a new chemical change.

5. Label this solution "Ferric Acetate."

   : NOW YOU'VE CREATED TWO
   : KINDS OF SALT, A FERRIC SALT
   : AND A FERROUS SALT. THE
   : FERRIC ACETATE CONTAINS THE
   : EXTRA OXYGEN FROM THE
   : HYDROGEN PEROXIDE.

Ferric salts tend to be yellow or brown. Ferrous salts are usually light green.

GO ON TO USE YOUR FERRIC ACETATE TO CREATE ANOTHER CHEMICAL CHANGE.

· · · · · · · · · · ·
USE TEA TO MAKE MORE CHEMICAL CHANGES WITH IRON
· ·

You can use tea along with ferric acetate to cause another chemical change. This one creates another compound of iron, ferric tannate.

Here's what you need:

Loose tea or a tea bag

A cup

Boiling water

Two drinking straws

Ferric acetate

A saucer

Here's what you do:

1. Put a teaspoonful (5 ml) of tea or the tea bag into the cup, and pour boiling water over it. Let it sit for a few minutes. Caution: You need adult help with boiling water.

2. Use one of the straws to transfer a few drops of the ferric acetate to the saucer. Put one end of the straw into the ferric acetate. Put your finger over the other end, and lift the straw. Release a few drops by removing your finger from the end of the straw.

   : *Caution: Don't drink from this* : *straw.*

3. Use the second straw to transfer a few drops of tea to the solution in the saucer. See what happens. If the solution turns black, you've created ferric tannate.

Here's how you created the chemical change:

The tea contains tannic acid. The tannic acid combines with the ferric acetate to form a salt, ferric tannate.

Ferric tannate is an astringent. Forms of it are useful in medicine. It has such a strong taste that it would pucker your mouth. If you lean close, you can probably get a sense of what it would taste like without actually tasting it.

And notice that ferric tannate is a precipitate. That means it comes out of solution. You can see it separate.

: **GO ON TO CREATE OTHER**
: **CHEMICAL CHANGES WITH IRON**
: **COMPOUNDS.**
:

USE RAISINS AND CREAM OF TARTAR TO MAKE MORE CHEMICAL CHANGES

You'll find that cream of tartar and raisins are very much alike in one way. They can create the same chemical changes. Use more of your ferric acetate solution for this experiment.

Here's what you need:

Two saucers
Cream of tartar
Water
Drinking straw
Ferric acetate
A cup or small bowl
Raisins
Hot water
A fork

Here's what you do:

1. In one saucer, dissolve ¹/₄ teaspoon (1 ml) cream of tartar into ¹/₄ cup (60 ml) water.
2. Use the straw to add a few drops of ferric acetate solution. Put one end of the straw into the ferric acetate. Put your finger over the other end, and lift the straw. Release a few drops by removing your finger from the end of the straw.

   : *Caution: Don't drink from this*
   : *straw.*

3. Stir. You'll see a greenish color change. The new chemical you're forming is ferrous tartrate.
4. Put about a dozen raisins into the cup or small bowl. Pour a little hot water over them. Mash them with a fork.
5. Pour some of the raisin-water mix into the second saucer. With the straw, add a few drops of ferric acetate. Stir. You ought to be able to see the same greenish color change. Again, you're forming ferrous tartrate. You've discovered that raisins (and grapes) contain tartaric acid. That's cream of tartar. So cream of tartar and raisins create the same chemical change.

COOKS SOMETIMES USE CREAM OF TARTAR ALONG WITH BAKING SODA TO MAKE CAKES AND BISCUITS RISE. AND CANDY-MAKERS USE CREAM OF TARTAR. WHERE DO THEY GET IT? WHEN WINEMAKERS CRUSH GRAPES INTO WINE, THEY HAVE SOME TARTARIC ACID, OR CREAM OF TARTAR, LEFT OVER TO SELL.

CREATE TWO KINDS OF IRON

You've created chemical changes with ferric acetate. Now you can use your solution of ferrous acetate to make two kinds of iron compounds and to create two color changes.

Here's what you need:

Ferrous acetate

A saucer

A drinking straw

Ammonia

Peroxide

Here's what you do:

1. Pour a little of your ferrous acetate solution into the saucer. Caution: Check the label. Don't confuse it with ferric acetate.

2. Use the straw to add a few drops of ammonia. Put one end of the straw into the ammonia. Put your finger over the other end, and lift the straw. Release a few drops by removing your finger from the end of the straw.

   Caution: Don't drink from this straw.

   You'll see a greenish color change. You've created ferrous hydroxide.

3. Now add a few drops of peroxide. Right away, you'll see the color change to rich red. You've created ferric hydroxide.
   You'll see the ferric hydroxide separate out of solution. That means it's a precipitate. It looks like a gel. The red color is from the iron oxide.

   YOU'VE CREATED TWO KINDS OF IRON COMPOUNDS.

· · · · · · · · · · ·

CREATE CARBON DIOXIDE AND PUT OUT A FLAME

· ·

Fire needs oxygen to burn. Carbon dioxide cuts off oxygen, so the flame goes out.

Carbon dioxide actually pushes air up and away from the flame because carbon dioxide is heavier than the air it displaces. Carbon dioxide throws a sort of invisible blanket over a flame. That's how many fire extinguishers work.

You can create carbon dioxide to put out a candle flame.

Perform this experiment in or near a sink. You need an adult to assist you.

Here's what you need:

2 to 4 tablespoons (30–60 ml) baking soda

A heatproof glass or stainless steel mixing bowl

A short, thick candle, such as a food-warmer,

scented, or votive candle

A kitchen match

About 1/4 cup (60ml) vinegar

Here's what you do:

1. Sprinkle the baking soda into the bowl until it covers the bottom of the bowl.

2. Set the candle in the middle of the bowl. Light the candle.

3. Carefully pour the vinegar into the bowl without touching the candle.

Note *how much time goes by before the flame goes out.*

Vinegar is an acid, and baking soda is a base. When you mix them, you set off a chemical reaction. The reaction produces carbon dioxide. And, of course, carbon dioxide smothers flames.

YOUR CANDLE GOES OUT BECAUSE IT HAS NO MORE OXYGEN AROUND IT TO HELP IT BURN.

COVER A NAIL WITH COPPER

You can use a chemical change to cover an iron nail with copper. And you can do this right in your kitchen.

Here's what you need:

A jar
¼ cup (60 ml) vinegar
A pinch of salt
10 to 20 copper pennies
An iron nail
Scouring powder

Here's what you do:

1. Pour the vinegar into the jar. Add the salt.

2. Put the copper pennies into the vinegar. Let them stand for a few minutes.

3. Clean the iron nail with scouring powder. Rinse thoroughly.

4. Drop the clean nail into the vinegar with the pennies. Let it set for about 15 minutes.
   You will find that the nail is coated with copper. And the pennies are bright and clean.
   What happened? The acid of the vinegar cleaned the copper pennies. And the copper formed a compound, with the vinegar. The compound is copper acetate. The copper in the copper acetate covered the iron nail with copper.

NOW YOU HAVE A COPPER NAIL AND SHINY PENNIES.

SEPARATE THE VALUABLE FROM THE NOT VALUABLE

Mining factories need to separate valuable metal from ore, dirt, sand, and other impurities.

A washerwoman came up with the idea of how to do this. She had been watching how laundry floats and turns in the tub. She told a woman chemist her idea. Together they came up with this very valuable method for separating the valuable from the not valuable.

Assume that metal filings or metallic glitter are valuable to you, but sand is not. Here's how you'd get them apart.

Here's what you need:

A jar
2 teaspoons (10 ml) metal filings or metallic glitter
2 tablespoons (30 ml) sand
1 cup (250 ml) water
2 tablespoons (30 ml) oil

Here's what you do:

1. Put the metal filings or metallic glitter into the jar.
2. Add the sand.
3. Add the water.
4. Add the oil.
5. Shake the jar vigorously.
6. Let everything settle.

You should see the filings or glitter float to the top with the oil. The sand will settle to the bottom in the water.

The commercial process goes by the delightful name of froth flotation. The ore, full of valuable metal mixed with not-valuable dirt, churns through water and heavy oil. Air is blown through, forming a froth of oily bubbles. The valuable metal clings to the oil particles. The oil, which does not dissolve in water, floats to the surface. The metal floats to the surface with the oil.

MAYBE WE SHOULD ALL LISTEN TO ALL KINDS OF PEOPLE, AND NOT JUST SCIENTISTS. WE MIGHT LEARN SOMETHING VALUABLE.

Heat Up and Cool Out

*Y*ou can make your own thermometer. You can use the power of the sun or the power of ice.

Use sun power to create a work of art or to brew sun tea. Use ice power to play a magic trick or to make your own ice cream.

· · · · · · · · · ·

MAKE YOUR OWN THERMOMETER

· ·

You can measure temperature with a soft-drink bottle and a straw.

Here's what you need:

Water
Food coloring
A soft-drink bottle
A clear plastic straw
Modeling clay or Play-Doh®
Wax crayons or marking pencils
A pan
Warm water
A glass thermometer
(Either a room or an outdoor thermometer is fine.)

Here's what you do:

1. Color the water with several drops of the food coloring.
2. Fill the soft-drink bottle with the colored water.
3. Mold the clay or Play-Doh® around the straw, about 2 inches from one end.
4. Insert the straw into the bottle, and mold the clay so that you seal the straw in place at the top of the bottle. Do not let the end of the straw touch the bottom of the bottle.
5. The water will rise, probably to about 1/2 inch above the clay seal. Let the bottle sit at room temperature until the water level stops changing.
6. Use a wax crayon or marking pencil to mark the level of the water on the straw. Check the room temperature, either by a room thermometer or a thermostat. Using a different color, write that temperature at your mark on the straw.
7. Fill the pan with warm water. Set the bottle in the pan, and wait for the water level to stop rising. Mark the new level on the straw.
8. Use the glass thermometer to take the temperature of the water in the pan. Label that as the top reading.
9. Now you have two temperatures marked, high and low. Make equally spaced marks between the high and the low temperatures.

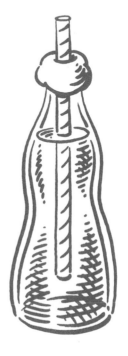

For example, if the low temperature is 70° Fahrenheit (20° Celsius) and the high temperature is 95° Fahrenheit (35° Celsius), make marks for 70°, 75°, 80°, 85°, 90°, and 95° degrees. Or make marks for Celsius: 20°, 25°, 30°, and 35°. (Your straw probably won't be long enough to write in higher or lower temperatures.)
When you've done this, you can say that you have calibrated the thermometer.

10. You can use your thermometer to read temperatures between about 70° and 95° Fahrenheit (20°–35° Celsius). And you can look at the water level to tell when the temperature is below 70°F (20°C) or above 95° (35°C).

Hint: If you want to keep your thermometer, add a drop of glycerine through the straw. The glycerine will help slow the rate of evaporation, so your water will last longer.

: **NOW YOU HAVE YOUR OWN**
: **THERMOMETER.**

When the water rises in the straw, it looks as if the water expands. But that's not really so. Instead, as water gets hotter, the water molecules move faster and faster. The faster the molecules move, the more they spread out. You have the same amount of water in the bottle, but it takes up more space.

· · · · · · · · · · ·

A FAHRENHEIT AND CELSIUS PROJECT

· ·

Knowing two ways of telling the temperature is like knowing two languages. It can be very convenient.

One way to tell the temperature is by the Fahrenheit (F) scale. That's named for Gabriel Daniel Fahrenheit, who invented the first accurate thermometer more than 200 years ago.

The other way is the Celsius (or centigrade, C) scale. Anders Celsius designed it in 1742.

People in the United States mostly use the Fahrenheit scale. But people in other countries, and scientists everywhere usually prefer the Celsius scale.

On both scales, the numbers 0 and 100 are there for a reason. Celsius zero is the freezing point of water (32° on the Fahrenheit scale). Celsius 100 is the boiling point of water (212° F).

On the Fahrenheit scale, zero is the lowest temperature possible for a mixture of salt and water. And Fahrenheit figured that 100° on his scale ought to be the temperature of the human body. (He was just a little bit off. The temperature of human beings is 98.6°—on the Fahrenheit scale, of course.)

Here's how to convert a Fahrenheit temperature into a Celsius temperature:

1. Subtract 32 degrees from the Fahrenheit temperature.

2. Multiply by 5.

3. Divide by 9.

Here's an example:

50°F − 32 = 18
18 x 5 = 90
90 ÷ 9 = 10° C

Here's how to convert a Celsius temperature into a Fahrenheit temperature:

1. Multiply the Celsius temperature by 9.

2. Divide by 5.

3. Add 32.

Here's an example:

10° C x 9 = 90°
90 ÷ 5 = 18
18 + 32 = 50° F

NOW YOU CAN UNDERSTAND BOTH WAYS OF TELLING TEMPERATURES.

CREATE SOLAR-POWERED ARTWORK

Let the sun help you with your artwork. The sun can create silhouettes of your artwork or even of actual objects.

This is a good project for a creative sort of person.

Here's what you need:

Artwork to show in silhouette:
Tracing paper and pencil or
Paper and scissors or
Actual objects
Photographer's light-sensitive paper

Here's what you do:

1. Choose one way to make your picture:
   - Use a pencil to draw a picture on tracing paper.
   - Cut out pictures or shapes.
   - Find objects that you can arrange to make a picture. You'll want interesting shapes that go together well.

2. Arrange your pictures or shapes on the light-sensitive paper.

3. Set the paper in the sun. In just a minute, the light-sensitive paper will turn dark. When you remove your pictures or shapes, you'll see them printed on the paper.

4. Now try something different. Put your pictures on top of construction paper, and leave the paper in the sun for a few days. The construction paper will fade and leave silhouettes of the pictures.

NOW YOU HAVE SILHOUETTES ON PAPER.

Unfortunately, sun-powered artwork doesn't last long. Like the rest of the light-sensitive paper, the silhouettes will turn dark after a while. You can make them last just a little longer by keeping them in a dark place.

BREW SUN TEA

When the weather is really hot, people sometimes try to fry an egg on the sidewalk. Sometimes the sun really is hot enough to fry the egg. Solar cooking is best, though, when you brew your own sun tea.

Here's what you need:

4 cups (1 liter) water

A glass jar with a lid

4 herbal-tea bags, the kind you like best

Here's what you do:

1. Pour the water into the jar.
2. Put in the tea bags. Put the lid on the jar.
3. Let the jar sit in hot sun for 3 or 4 hours.

   SERVE YOUR SUN-BREWED TEA WITH ICE. You may want to add sugar or lemon wedges.

. . . .
WORK WITH ICE POWER
. . . .

Water expands as it freezes. Here's how to see this.

Here's what you need:

A freezer-safe container with a lid
Water

Here's what you do:

1. Fill the container with water to the brim. Set the container in the freezer. Now, add enough water so that the container is full.
2. Lay the lid on loosely.
3. Check the jar when the water has frozen. You'll find the water expanded and pushed up the lid.

NOW YOU'VE SEEN EVIDENCE OF THE POWER OF ICE.

FIND THE FREEZING POINT OF SALT WATER

Plain water freezes at 32°Fahrenheit (0° Celsius). But put salt in the water, and you'll find a different freezing point.

Here's what you need:

Water

A cup

Two freezer-safe containers

Salt

A freezer thermometer, if one is available

Your science notebook and pen

Here's what you do:

1. Turn the freezer to its coldest setting. (First, make sure that your parents don't mind.)
2. Pour 1 cup (250 ml) of water into one of the freezer-safe containers.
3. Pour 1 cup (250 ml) of water into the other container. Stir in 2 teaspoons (10 ml) of salt.
4. Put both containers in the freezer. You might want to label them.
5. Check them every 15 minutes. Note which one freezes first. When the salt water starts to freeze, take its temperature. You'll find that it freezes at a temperature below the freezing point of ordinary water.
6. When you've finished, remember to return the freezer to its usual setting.

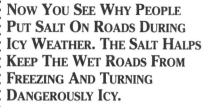

NOW YOU SEE WHY PEOPLE PUT SALT ON ROADS DURING ICY WEATHER. THE SALT HALPS KEEP THE WET ROADS FROM FREEZING AND TURNING DANGEROUSLY ICY.

PLAY AN ICY TRICK

Begin by asking your friends if they can use a string to remove an ice cube from a glass of water. And they have to do this without getting their hands wet.

They may not be able to do this trick. But you can.

Here's what you need:

A glass of water
An ice cube
A piece of string
Salt

Here's what you do:

1. Put the ice cube into the glass of water. Put one end of the string on the ice cube. Hang the other end over the edge of the glass.

2. Sprinkle salt on the ice cube, and let the glass stand for about 5 minutes.

3. Now remove the ice cube from the water just by lifting the string.

   How do you do that? The salt lowered the freezing point of the water below the usual 32° F or 0° C), so the ice melted a little. Then the ice refroze and trapped the string.

YOU SEEM TO HAVE MADE THE ICE COLDER, BUT REALLY YOU SUPER-COOLED THE WATER. IT'S THE WATER, NOT THE ICE, THAT IS COLDER.

· · · · · · · · · · ·

An Ice Skating Experiment Without Skates

· ·

When you ice skate, you're really skating on water, not on ice. Here's how it works.

Here's what you need:

A stack of heavy books

A heavy ruler or yardstick

A piece of thin, strong wire, 8 to 10 inches (20–25 cm) long

A heavy weight such as a small cast-iron frying pan

An ice cube, larger than 1 1/4 inch (3 cm) square

Here's what you do:

1. Stack the books in two piles, each about 12 inches (30 cm) high.
2. Place the ruler or yardstick across the space between the two piles of books, with one end resting on each pile.
3. Loop the wire through the handle of the frying pan. Place the ice cube on top of the ruler. Run the wire over the ice cube, and twist the ends of the wire to form a closed loop. Now the frying pan is hanging in the air between the two piles of books.

Note: *You may want to put a towel under the frying pan to catch drips.*

4. Watch the wire slowly cut into the ice cube. But it doesn't cut the ice cube in two. Instead, the water freezes behind it.

THAT'S HOW ICE SKATES WORK. THE PRESSURE OF THE SKATE BLADE MELTS THE ICE UNDER THE BLADE, SO THE SKATE GLIDES ON WATER. WHEN THE SKATE HAS MOVED ON, THE ICE FREEZES OVER AGAIN.

GROW YOUR OWN CRYSTALS

Since most nonliving substances are crystals, you can find crystals almost everywhere.

They're in sugar and salt, rocks and sand, ice and snow, rubies and diamonds.

You'll like looking at crystals with a magnifying glass because you can see fascinating patterns.

If you like to draw shapes and patterns, you'll find crystals can give you interesting ideas.

Here's your chance to create your own crystals. You can try for the biggest crystal. You can create the most beautiful or the most elaborate crystals.

Or you can create delicious crystals, and serve them up to eat.

GROW A CRYSTAL GARDEN

Crystals are not alive, so they can't really grow. What happens is all due to chemical reactions.

But you'll think there's something magic going on when you see how fast you can make your crystal "garden" spring into being. This is one garden you'll never need to weed.

Here's what you need:

Pieces of charcoal briquets, coal, or brick

A wide, deep soup bowl or similar dish

6 tablespoons (90 ml) laundry blueing

Water

6 tablespoons (90 ml) table salt

1 tablespoon (15 ml) ammonia

Food coloring, if you wish

Here's what you do:

1. Break up the briquets, coal, or brick into pieces about 1 inch long and $1^1/_2$ to 2 inches (4–5 cm) across. (You don't need to be fussy about the exact size.) Place the pieces in the bottom of the bowl.

   : *Caution: You may need adult*
   : *help to break up brick pieces.*

2. If your laundry blueing is in powder form, mix it with 6 tablespoons (90 ml) of water. If the laundry blueing is liquid, mix it with 1 or 2 tablespoons (15–30 ml) of water. If you live in a dry climate, mix in a bit more water.

3. Add the salt and ammonia.

4. Pour the mixture over the pieces in the bowl. (You ought to see undissolved salt covering the brick or charcoal pieces.)

5. If you want your crystal "flowers" in colors, sprinkle drops of food coloring over the mixture in the bowl. Or wait until the crystals start to "grow," and then sprinkle on food coloring.

6. Set the bowl in a place where no one will disturb it. Don't jar or move the bowl.

7. Watch your "garden" grow. If the weather is dry, your garden may start to "grow" within an hour or two. But don't worry if it takes longer to get started. A slow garden is sometimes better in the long run.

: **NOW YOU HAVE YOUR OWN**
: **MAGIC CRYSTAL GARDEN.**

GROW YOUR OWN BIG CRYSTAL

Challenge your family or friends to see who can "grow" the best, biggest crystal. Then use a magnifying glass to look at the crystal structures.

To grow your crystals, you will need alum, an aluminum salt (aluminum potassium sulfate). Alum is an astringent that can help stop bleeding. And alum is good for pickle-making. It helps pickles stay crisp.

Here's what you need:

1 cup (250 ml) water
A clear jar or glass
3 tablespoons (45 ml) alum (You can buy alum in a drugstore or in the spice section of a grocery store.)
Waxed paper or plastic wrap.

Here's what you do:

1. Heat the water to boiling.

   : Caution: You need adult help
   : with boiling water.

   (If you're using a microwave oven, heat the water right in the jar or glass. If you're using a stove, heat the water in a glass, stainless steel, or enamel pan.)

2. Stir in the alum until it dissolves. (You are creating a supersaturated solution. More alum dissolves in hot water than in cold water. As the water cools, the alum stays in solution.)

3. If you heated the water on the stove, rinse the jar or glass with hot water. Then pour in the alum solution.

4. Set the jar or glass in a place where no one will disturb it. Cover it loosely with the waxed paper or plastic wrap.

5. Check the solution every day. Be careful not to shake or disturb it. If your crystal doesn't "grow," try again. Sometimes a bit of other crystal or dust falls into the jar. That can cause the alum to come out of solution as small particles. Then your crystal can't develop right.

: **NOW YOU HAVE YOUR OWN**
: **BIG CRYSTAL TO INSPECT.**

GROW A BEAUTIFUL CRYSTAL

Growing a beautiful crystal takes patience.
But you get a big reward.

Here's what you need:

Alum (You can buy alum at a drugstore or in the spice section of a grocery store.)

Water

A saucer

Two jars (One-pint canning jars or empty peanut butter jars are perfect.)

Thread

Paper coffee filter, cloth napkin, or handkerchief

Cardboard

Scissors

A pencil

Here's what you do:

1. Measure 2 tablespoons (30 ml) of alum. Stir into $1/4$ cup (60 ml) of hot tap water to dissolve.

2. Pour the solution into a saucer, and set aside in a safe place. Over the next day or two, the water will evaporate and leave behind alum crystals.

3. Pick one of the largest, best-formed crystals, and use it as a seed to grow a large crystal.

4. Tie a long thread around the crystal. Set aside in a clean, dry place.

5. Put 4 tablespoons (60 ml) of alum into a clean hot jar. (To make the jar hot enough, just rinse it out with hot tap water.)

6. Heat water in a tea kettle to boiling. Or heat water in a heatproof container in a microwave oven.

   Caution: You need adult help with boiling water.

   Very slowly pour hot water into the jar. Stir until all the alum dissolves. (You are creating a supersaturated solution. More alum dissolves in hot water than could dissolve in cold water. As the hot water cools, the alum stays in solution.)

7. Allow the solution to cool. Some grains of alum should remain on the bottom of the jar.

8. Pour the cool solution through the paper coffee filter, clean cloth napkin, or handkerchief into the second clean jar.

9. Hang the threaded crystal from step 4 in the center of the solution. Here's how:
   - Cut the cardboard into a square slightly larger than the diameter of the jar.
   - With the scissors, cut a slit from one side to the center of the cardboard.
   - Wind the thread around the pencil so that the seed crystal nearly touches the bottom of the jar but does not rest on it.
   - Slide the thread into the slit in the cardboard.

- Place the cardboard and pencil on top of the jar so that the seed crystal hangs in the solution.

10. Put the jar in a cool place where no one will disturb it. You can expect the solution to evaporate slowly, since the cardboard acts as a cover to prevent it from evaporating too fast.

   From time to time, you'll need to add more cooled solution of 4 tablespoons (60 ml) of alum and enough hot water to dissolve it.

   Be patient. It may take a couple of weeks to develop a good crystal.

   Sometimes, instead of "growing," a seed crystal dissolves, usually because the solution got too warm. If that happens, you'll have to start all over again.

11. Store your crystal carefully. Egg cartons make good storage boxes, one little compartment for each crystal.

   You can display your crystals for short periods by hanging them from their threads.

   : **NOW YOU CAN GROW YOUR**
   : **OWN BEAUTIFUL CRYSTAL,**
   : **WORTH WAITING FOR.**

GROW A COLORFUL CRYSTAL

You can grow beautiful crystals in colors. Use the directions for growing a beautiful crystal, but instead of alum, add one of these other salts:

1. For blue, add copper sulfate.
2. For yellow, add potassium chromate.
3. For pale blue-green, add ferrous sulfate.
4. For dark red, add cobalt chloride. You can buy these salts at a drug store, a hardware store, a hobby shop, or a chemical supply company.

NOW YOU CAN COLLECT CRYSTALS IN COLOR.

GROW A SHAPELY CRYSTAL

You can grow clear crystals in various odd shapes, from long needles to double pyramids. Follow the directions for growing a beautiful crystal, but instead of alum, add one of these other salts:

1. Sodium thiosulfate (photographer's hypo)
2. Pickling salt
3. Borax
4. Potassium sodium tartrate

NOW YOU CAN COLLECT CRYSTALS IN ALL SORTS OF PECULIAR SHAPES.

CREATE EDIBLE GLASS

Sugar is made of crystals, and so is glass.

Get together with a friend, and cook up glass. This will be sugar glass that you can eat.

Caution: You will need an adult to help you with the cooking.

Here's what you need:

A buttered baking sheet

1 cup (250 ml) of sugar

A heavy stainless steel or nonstick frying pan

A large wooden spoon

Here's what you do:

1. Place the buttered baking sheet in the refrigerator.

2. Put the sugar in the frying pan. Set the pan on a burner at low heat.

3. Stir the sugar slowly while it is heating. (This takes quite a while, so you may want to take turns with your friend.)

   Gradually, the sugar will turn tan and stick together in clumps. Soon you will begin to see a pale brown melt in the bottom of the pan. Keep stirring.

   As the sugar continues to melt, the lumps become smaller and the sugar begins to turn into a thick brown liquid.

4. When all the sugar has melted, pour the brown liquid into the cold baking sheet.

NOW YOU HAVE SUGAR GLASS READY TO EAT.

The way you created edible glass is basically similar to the way factories produce real window glass. There are a couple of big differences, though, as you might expect. Glass factories use sand, not sugar, for the glass. And the heat needed to dissolve the sand into glass is much higher.

You can use some sorts of sugar glass for decorations. And you could try using it for window panes if you were expecting Hansel and Gretel to stop by. But you'd have one problem. The first rain drops would dissolve the sugar, and your windows would fall in.

· · · · · · · · · ·
CREATE CRYSTAL MODELS
· ·

You'd need a microscope to see the basic shapes of real crystals.

You can put together your own models, though, and then you can see them larger than life.

Many different types of crystals share a basic shape. For instance, salt and diamonds don't seem at all alike but their crystals form in the same basic shape.

The name for a crystal shape is a system.

Here's how to make models of two of the six basic crystal systems.

Here's what you need:

⅛-inch (3 mm) sticks of bass or balsa wood

A craft knife

Pins

Cardboard

All-purpose glue

Here's how to construct two basic crystal systems:

Cut the bass or balsa wood with the craft knife.

: *Caution: Get an adult to help*
: *you with the cutting.*

Put the sticks together by pinning them to a piece of cardboard. Then glue them together permanently.

1. The Cubic System

Crystal examples: salt, diamonds, alum
How to make the model: The shape is a simple cube. Use 12 sticks of the bass or balsa wood, each exactly the same length. (You choose the length.) Set them at right angles to each other.

2. The Tetragonal System

Crystal example: Zircon (sometimes used in jewelry because it can look like a diamond but doesn't cost much)
How to make the model: This is almost like the cubic system. The difference is that the one side is either shorter or longer than the others. Use 8 sticks of bass or balsa wood, each the same length, and 4 other sticks of a different length. (You choose the lengths.)

WHEN YOU CAN STUDY CRYSTALS UNDER A MICROSCOPE, COMPARE YOUR MODELS TO THE REAL THING.

If you wrap your crystal systems in colored plastic, you can use them for Christmas tree ornaments.

 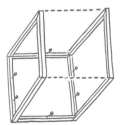

PERFORM LIGHT MAGIC

You can bend light waves to your will.

You can perform magic tricks with light waves.

You can build a kaleidoscope. You can even build your own camera or your own microscope.

· · · · · · · · · ·
MAKE YOUR OWN KALEIDOSCOPE
· ·

A kaleidoscope creates an illusion with mirrors. You'll need an adult to help with some parts of this project.

Here's what you need:

To make the basic kaleidoscope:

Three pieces of mirror, each 1½ inches × 6 inches (4 cm × 15 cm) (Have the mirror cut at a glass company. Our pieces cost only 89 cents.)

A cardboard mailing tube 2 inches (5 cm) across (You can buy this at an office supply store.)

A plastic end to fit the mailing tube (This will be for sale with the tube.)

Electrical, aluminum, or reinforced cellophane tape

Fabric or paper towels

A piece of clear, heavy-duty plastic such as that used in packaging

Clear household cement

Brightly colored construction paper and colored plastic bits

A 14-ounce (500 ml) frosted plastic drinking cup (You can buy this at the grocery store in the department that sells paper cups.)

To decorate the tube:

Construction paper or cotton cloth with a pattern

Clear laminating plastic (the kind used to cover books) or clear acrylic paint or spray coating

All-purpose glue

To use as tools:

A serrated knife or small saw

A ruler

Scissors

Fine sandpaper

Nail scissors or craft knife

Here's what you do:

1. With the serrated knife or small saw, cut a 6½-inch piece (4 cm) from the mailing tube. (See diagram A.) Before cutting draw a guideline around the tube. Be sure the knife or saw is sharp so that the cut will be clean and even.

A.

   Caution: You need adult help with cutting.

   Hint: *You can make five or six kaleidoscopes with one tube.*

2. Tape the edges of the mirrors with narrow strips of the tape. (See diagram B.) (You need to use electrical, aluminum, or reinforced cellophane tape so that the binding will be strong enough.) Keep the tape off the mirrored surfaces.

B.

   Caution: You need adult help with taping the sharp edges of the mirrors.

3. Carefully place the mirrors to form a triangle, with the mirrored surfaces on the inside. Make sure the edges are even, and tape the mirrors together by running strips of tape around them. (See diagram C.)

C.

4. Slide the triangle of mirrors into the mailing tube, so that one end is even with one end of the tube. You should have a half-inch space left at the other end.

5. Use the fabric or paper towels, crumpled, as packing material to cushion the mirrors and keep them tight within the mailing tube.

6. Using the plastic mailing tube end as a guide, cut a circle from the piece of clear heavy-duty plastic. (See diagrams D and E.)

D.   E.

7. Put some of the clear household cement around the end of the mailing tube that is even with the mirrors. This will seal the edge of the cardboard. Allow the cement to dry. This usually takes just a few minutes. Then apply a second layer of cement. Fit the plastic circle over the end of the tube. Press to seal. Stand the tube on end to put pressure on the plastic. Allow it to dry.

8. Cut pieces from the colored construction paper and the colored plastic. They should be tiny triangles, squares, crescents, and other random shapes, no larger than $1/2$ to $3/4$ inch (1–2 cm). You will need quite a few.

9. Cut the bottom from the 14-ounce (500 ml) frosted plastic cup about $1/4$ inch above the point where the cup widens (See diagram F).

F.

10. Put the colored paper and plastic bits into the cut-off plastic cup bottom. Fit the piece over the clear plastic cover on the end of the mailing tube. Holding the tube up to the light, look through the other end. Turn the tube, tap it, and shake it. You ought to see colorful, changing designs. If not, add more colored paper and plastic bits.

11. When you are satisfied that you have enough "confetti" to create good designs, carefully remove the frosted bottom. Apply household cement around a $1/4$-inch (1 cm) strip on the outside of the tube. Put the frosted plastic with the "confetti" in it over the glued edge. Hold tightly in place for a few minutes until the glue has set.

12. Cut a $1/2$- to $3/4$-inch (1–2 cm) hole in the center of the plastic end for the mailing tube. (See Diagram D.) Sand the cut edge with fine sandpaper. You want it fairly smooth and even.

> **Caution: You need adult help with cutting.**

13. Cut a 1-inch (2–3 cm) circle of heavy clear plastic. (See diagram G.) With household cement, glue the clear plastic to the underside of the tube insert to cover the eyehole. Push the insert into the eye end of the kaleidoscope.

G.

Here's how to finish the tube:

1. Cut a piece of the construction paper or patterned cloth to about 6 1/4 inches by 7 1/4 inches (15 × 18 cm).

2. Fit the paper around the tube.

3. With the all-purpose glue, cover the tube. Place the 6 1/4-inch

(15 cm) edge of the paper or cloth along the length of the tube from one end to the other. Using your thumbs, smooth it out. Cut off any excess with the nail scissors or craft knife.

> *Caution: You may need adult help with this.*

4. If you wish to decorate the tube even more, glue on cutouts or designs.

5. Finally, cover the tube with the clear laminating plastic, and smooth it on. Or else coat the tube with the clear acrylic paint or spray.

> **NOW YOU HAVE YOUR OWN HAND-MADE KALEIDOSCOPE. MAYBE YOU CAN WORK LIGHT MAGIC WITH IT.**

··········
LOOK AT LIGHT WAVES FROM A NEW ANGLE
·································

Use a mirror and a flashlight to see how light waves travel.

Here's what you need:

A large mirror
A flashlight

Here's what you do:

1. Turn on the flashlight, and aim it toward the mirror. You can see the flashlight in the mirror. You can also see the point where the light shines on the mirror.

2. Line up those points by pointing the flashlight beam close up and directly at the mirror. The flashlight is shining directly at itself. The light is reflected straight back.

3. Now move the flashlight around any way you wish. You can see:
   - The point where the light hits the mirror
   - The reflection of the flashlight beam in the mirror (as well as a reflection of the flashlight itself)
   - An actual reflection of the light on the wall behind you in the room

4. You're seeing how light waves travel. As long as they're traveling through air, light waves always travel in a straight line. They do not bend around corners. And when light waves hit an object, they bounce back at exactly the same angle as they hit.

Look at the angle from the point where the light touches the surface of the mirror to the spot on the wall. (That is the angle of reflection.) It is the very same angle as the angle at which the light hits the mirror. (That's the angle of incidence.)

Move the flashlight around. You'll see that the two angles may change, but they change together. They're always the same angle.

5. Look at angles the next time you bounce a ball. If you bounce the ball straight down, it bounces straight up again. If you bounce the ball to a friend, you probably aim to bounce it halfway between the two of you. Then the ball bounces up to your friend at the very same angle it bounced away from you.

LIGHT REFLECTS BACK IN JUST THE SAME WAY.

PERFORM A MAGIC COIN TRICK WITH LIGHT WAVES

As long as they're traveling through air, light waves always travel in a straight line. But they change direction suddenly when they leave the air. Light waves bend when they pass from air into water or from air into glass.

You can bend light waves in water, and make a coin appear as if by magic.

Here's what you need:

A coin
A bowl
A pitcher of water
A helper

Here's what you do:

1. Place the coin in the bottom of the bowl.
2. Step back from the bowl until you cannot see the coin.
3. Have your helper slowly pour water from the pitcher into the bowl. Soon the coin will come into view again.

Note: It is important to pour the water slowly to prevent the coin from moving as the water comes in.

The coin seems to move because the light waves changed direction in the water. Show this trick to your friends. If they doubt you, you can have one of them hold the coin down with a finger. As you pour in the water, both the coin and the fingertip will come into view, as if by magic.

LOOK AT YOURSELF UNDERWATER SOME TIME. YOU WILL SEE THAT YOUR BODY LOOKS SHORTER AND FATTER THAN YOU REALLY ARE. AGAIN, THAT HAPPENS BECAUSE THE LIGHT WAVES BEND.

The word that scientists use for this is *refraction* of light waves.

BUILD YOUR OWN CAMERA FROM A CEREAL BOX

Would you like to build your own camera? And would you like to see the world upside down? That's how a camera sees the world.

Light waves travel straight ahead. When they go through the lens of a camera, though, they project an upside-down image.

Our own eyes see in the same way. The light waves enter the lens of the eye and project an upside-down image on the retina, the back of the eye.

So why don't we see everything upside down? Our brains make the correction and turn everything right side up again.

Once, for an experiment, scientists fitted some people with glasses that turned images upside down. After the people wore the glasses for a while, their brains set to work to make things right. Soon the images they saw were all right side up again.

But when the people took the glasses off, they once again faced an upside-down world. Their brains took a while to readjust and turn things right again.

This experiment shows that images turn upside down when you see them through a lens.

Here's what you need:

Scissors
A round oatmeal box
A small piece of aluminum foil
A pin
White tissue paper
Cellophane tape
A candle
A dark room

Here's what you do:

1. With the scissors, remove the cover of the cereal box. In the center of the other end, make a hole about ½ inch (1 cm) across.
2. Cover the hole with the small piece of aluminum foil, shiny side in. Use the pin to make a tiny hole in the center of the aluminum foil.
3. Cover the open end of the box with one thickness of the tissue paper, and fasten with the cellophane tape.
4. With an adult assistant, light the candle in the dark room. Point the pinhole toward the candle. You should be able to see an upside-down image of the candle on the tissue paper.

THAT'S HOW A CAMERA PROJECTS AN IMAGE ONTO FILM.

· · · · · · · · · · ·
USE YOUR CAMERA TO TAKE PICTURES
· ·

The pictures you take with your cereal-box camera might not have the sharp lines of photographs from a regular camera, but some people will think they're very attractive.

This is a good project for a creative sort of person.

Here's what you need:

Black construction paper

Cellophane tape

Removable tape

Black permanent marker

A roll of black and white film (Or buy a 4- to 6-inch [10–15 cm] piece of film from a photo store.)

Lightproof paper, such as the wrapping that comes with a roll of film

A pitch-black room or closet

Here's what you do:

1. Cover the pinhole of your cereal-box camera with a piece of the black construction paper. Tape it at just one edge with the cellophane tape. Tape the other edges with the removable tape. That way you can lift the paper and fold it back to form a flap.

2. Use the black marker to color the inside of the cereal box cover black.

3. Cut six pieces of cellophane tape, each 2 inches (5 cm) long. Stick one end of each to the rim of the box cover. Leave the other ends loose.

4. Take the box, the box cover, and the roll of film into the dark room. Open the film in the dark. If the film is in a cartridge, pull about 4 inches (10 cm) out of the cartridge. At that point, pull the additional film across the back of the box to the other side. Push the cover into place over the film. Cut the film, and tape the edges of the cover in place. Wrap the rest of the film in the lightproof paper to use some other time. Now you're ready to take pictures.

5. On a sunny day, set the camera firmly on a solid base. Aim it at a

scene you would like to photograph. The scene must be still, with the sun shining on it.
If there is any breeze, you will need to prop weights around the camera box.

6. When the camera is all set, fold back the flap and hold it in place with a piece of removable tape.

7. Let the camera sit about 3 seconds to register a picture. Count slowly to 3, and then cover the pinhole.

8. Bring the camera back into the dark room. Remove the film, and place it in lightproof paper.

9. Have the pictures developed at a photo store or in a home darkroom. If your first picture is too dark, expose it longer the next time. If your picture is too light, expose it for a shorter time.

Now You Know How A Camera Works. Expensive, Complicated Cameras Take Pictures Just About The Same Way As Your Own Homemade Camera.

Look Through Your Skin

All you need is a good flashlight to make light waves pass through your hand.

Hold the palm of your hand over the flashlight. You should be able to see your finger bones and joints.

EXPERIMENT TO FIND OUT IF YOU CAN SEE BETTER THROUGH THE SKIN OF AN ADULT OR THROUGH THE SKIN OF A SMALL CHILD.

MAKE THINGS LOOK BIGGER WITHOUT MUCH TROUBLE

Just make a pinhole in an index card. Close one eye, and look through the pinhole with the other eye. Bring a toothpick close to the pinhole. It will look huge.

How does this work? The pinhole cuts down the amount of light that enters your eye. The concentrated light waves make things look bigger than they really are.

TRY LOOKING AT THE STARS THROUGH A LONG TUBE. THEY WILL APPEAR BIGGER AND CLEARER THAN WHEN YOU LOOK AT THEM WITH JUST YOUR EYES.

WAVE AS YOU GO BY

*L*ight waves aren't the only waves in the air. There's a whole spectrum of waves that we can't see. Some of these waves are very useful to human beings. Think of radio and television waves, X rays, and microwaves.

These electromagnetic waves create powerful sources of energy. The waves are invisible, but you can find out their power.

How would you like to use sound vibrations to put out a candle? Or use them to make music. Would you like to create your own electric lemon?

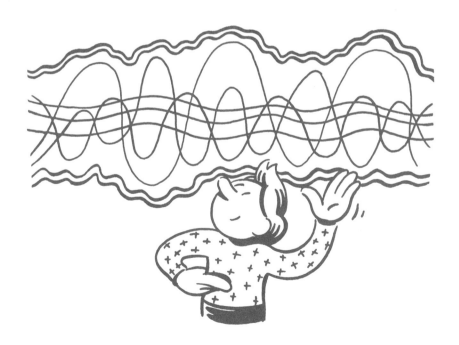

PUT OUT A CANDLE WITH SOUND WAVES

Like light waves, sound waves travel in a straight line. And like light waves, when they hit an object, sound waves are reflected or absorbed.

When sound waves hit an object, they may make it vibrate and send the sound off in all directions.

Did you know that microwaves are a form of sound waves? Microwaves are a type of short, high-frequency radio waves. When microwaves hit an object, they make it vibrate. When microwaves are broadcast inside a microwave oven, they make the molecules of food vibrate against one another. That causes heat, so microwave ovens actually heat food by vibrations.

You can set up your own sound vibrations.

Here's what you need:

A round oatmeal box

Scissors

A candle

Here's what you do:

1. In the middle of the box lid, cut a hole the size of a penny.

2. Set the box on its side with the candle 4 or more inches (10 cm) in front of the hole.

   : *Caution: You need adult help*
   : *lighting the candle.*

3. Lightly tap the other end of the box. The sound is like a drum.

4. You'll see the candle flicker. If you have placed it just right, the flame will go out.

SOUND VIBRATIONS CAN PUT OUT A CANDLE, AND THEY CAN DO MUCH MORE.

MAKE STRINGS SING

Make sound out of vibrations you can see.

Here's what you need:

A piece of strong thread or string about 2 feet (60 cm) long

A large button with two holes

Here's what you do:

1. Put the 2 feet (60 cm) of thread through the holes in the button. Tie the ends together with a square knot.

2. Pull the thread so that you have 6 inches (15 cm) of string on each side of the button.

3. Put your fingers through the loop, and twirl the button around to twist the string.

4. Pull the string in and out. The button will twirl, and you'll hear a humming sound as the string vibrates.

> **YOU CAN THINK OF ANY NUMBER OF OTHER VIBRATIONS THAT CREATE SOUND.**

PLAY A STRAW

Make a little simple music with a drinking straw. You'll hear the music change when the sound waves hit the water at different levels.

Here's what you need:

A glass or bottle
Water
A drinking straw

Here's what you do:

1. Hold the straw up with your thumb toward you. Prop your chin with your thumb joint, and blow across the mouth of the straw. You should hear a high-pitched sound.

2. Fill the glass or bottle with water.

3. Lower the straw into the water. As you move it up and down, the tone changes. The tone is lower near the surface of the water, and higher when the straw is deeper in the water.

4. Try this with containers of different sizes. You'll hear different tones.

TRY TO PLAY A SHORT SONG WITH YOUR STRAW, SOMETHING LIKE MOZART'S "TWINKLE, TWINKLE, LITTLE STAR."

PLAY ON CRYSTAL

The story is that opera singers who hit just the right pitch can break crystal glasses. That's not really true, but it is true that you can make music with crystal.

Crystal vibrates with a clear, ringing sound. You could even form a musical group if you had enough different sizes and shapes of crystal.

Other types of glass vibrate with sound, too. But the sounds are not as clear and bright as crystal music.

Make crystal music with an adult assistant. And be very careful not to break the crystal.

Here's what you need:

Crystal goblets, drinking glasses, or glass bottles

Water

A wooden skewer, a wooden spoon, or a knife

Here's what you do:

1. Line up the crystal goblets, glasses, or bottles. Fill each with a different amount of water.

2. Gently tap the skewer, spoon, or knife near the top of each goblet. You'll hear different bell-like tones. Try picking out a tune.

3. Create a sound like a violin by rubbing a wet finger around the rim of a goblet.

TO STOP THE SOUND, JUST TOUCH YOUR FINGER TO THE RIM. WHEN YOU END THE VIBRATIONS, YOU STOP THE SOUND.

A LISTENING-IN GAME

Find an empty can that's open on one end. Or use a drinking glass.

Just press the can or glass to a closed door, where it will catch the sound vibrations. You can hear sounds inside the room much better this way than you can with just your own ears. You can eavesdrop on what people are saying. Of course, if they open the door suddenly, you may be in big trouble

. . . .
MAKE AN ECHO

. . . .

When sound waves bounce off hard surfaces, they may come back so clearly that the sound is almost unchanged. You can talk to yourself, and an echo will repeat your exact words.

Here are good places to make an echo:

1. In a long hall that has no windows
2. In a large room, especially one with no carpets, no overstuffed furniture, and no people
3. On a hardball court
4. On a cliff, especially when you're surrounded by large, mountainous rocks
5. Over a quiet lake
   Carpets, furniture, and people absorb sounds. Also they interfere with the movement and reflection of sound waves.

MAYBE SOME DAY YOU CAN VISIT A "WHISPERING GALLERY," LIKE THE ONE AT ST. PAUL'S CATHEDRAL IN LONDON. The sound bounces off the walls of the round dome so that you can hear a whisper all the way from one side of the vast dome to another.

. . . .

CREATE YOUR OWN ELECTRIC LEMON

. . . .

You really can make a tiny electric cell with a lemon. This is not powerful electricity, just enough to tingle a bit.

The lemon works like an electric battery. An electric battery needs two kinds of metal plus an acid. A car battery has sulfuric acid. A lemon has just a bit of citric acid.

For an electric lemon, you also need two metals, the bit of steel in a paper clip and the copper in a piece of copper wire.

Here's what you need:

A paper clip

A lemon

A piece of copper wire

Here's what you do:

1. Straighten one end of the paper clip. Insert the paper clip into the lemon.

2. Remove any insulation from both ends of the copper wire. Insert one end of the copper wire into the lemon.

3. Hold the ends of the paper clip and the wire. Touch your tongue to both of them at once. You'll feel a tingling sensation on your tongue. That's caused by the electricity from your lemon. Your tongue acted almost like a switch that turns on a light. You completed an electric circuit between the two metals and the acid in the lemon, and that turned on a bit of electricity. Water conducts electricity, and so can your damp tongue.

AND YOU FEEL THE TINGLE.

Transform Electric Energy into Magnetic Energy

Electric motors actually run on magnetic energy, as well as electricity.

Here's how it works. An electric battery changes chemical energy into electrical energy. In turn, that electrical energy can make another change. It can produce a magnetic field.

A coil of copper wire connected to battery terminals creates a magnetic field inside the coil. And it makes a magnet out of an iron nail.

Make your own iron-nail magnet.

Here's what you need:

A 2-foot (60 cm) length of copper wire
1 long iron nail
A 9-volt battery
Two paper clips

Here's what you do:

1. Wind the copper wire tightly around the nail. Leave about a 4-inch piece (10 cm) of wire at each end.
2. If the wire is insulated, remove the insulation from each end. Make loops of the wire, and fit one loop over each terminal of the 9-volt battery.
3. Hold a paper clip near either end of the nail. You'll feel the magnetic attraction.

> **Look Closely At An Electric Motor, And You'll See The Copper Wiring. The Motor Runs On Magnetism As Well As Electricity.**

CREATE STATIC ELECTRICITY

Static electricity comes from friction. You've probably felt static electricity in the air. You may feel static electricity as a nasty little shock. (Just try walking across a wool carpet in your socks, especially in the winter.)

Here are nonpainful ways to create static electricity:

1. Brush your cat's fur the wrong way. (The static electricity won't hurt the cat.)
2. Brush or comb a piece of fur or wool the wrong way.
3. Brush your own hair in the dark.

SOMETIMES YOU CAN HEAR THE CRACKLING AND SEE THE SPARKS FLY, TOO.

COLOR YOUR WORLD

*W*ould you like to make your own rainbow?

Would you care to mix your own paint colors and create your own very colorful works of art?

And would you like to play games with dazzling colors?

Here are just a few very colorful projects.

HOW IS IT THAT COLORS ARE VERY FAST AND VERY SHORT?

Would you like to discover the colors in a beam of light? Even when a beam of light looks just plain white, the colors are always there. They're just waiting to be found out.

Here's how it works.

A beam of light exists as waves or vibrations.

Light waves travel very fast through space. Can you even imagine something traveling at 186,000 miles (299,000 km) per second?

That speed is why you can't see light traveling. It's just too fast.

At the same time a light wave is very fast, it is also incredibly short. A million light waves can exist in only 1 meter—or just over 3 feet—of space.

(Besides the light waves we can see, there are also invisible waves. Think of X rays, for instance, or the waves that bring us radio and television signals.)

Each color of light vibrates at a different rate. And each is a different length.

When we see a color, we are looking at only one set of light waves. Objects absorb some colors within light waves and not others.

If you'd like to see the colors in a beam of light, look for a rainbow.

Or make your own rainbow.

CREATE YOUR OWN RAINBOW

As light beams travel, the colors can split into the form of a rainbow.

The change can happen when light waves go from air through water or from water into glass. Sometimes light beams separate into rainbows as they travel from warm air through cold air.

The best time to make your own rainbow is the early morning or late afternoon, when the sun is close to the horizon.

Just stand with your back to the sun, and use your garden hose to spray a cascade of water. If you're lucky, you'll see a rainbow right away.

You may see your hose rainbow best if you spray the water upward against a dark background, such as trees or a dark building.

You don't want to waste water. Make your own rainbow when you are already using the hose for something useful like watering the garden.

· · · · · · · · · ·
SPLIT APART A SUNBEAM
· ·

A beam of sunlight begins as white. The white of sunlight is a mixture of colors. So when the light bends, the white color splits into all the colors of the rainbow.

Did you know that the colors of rainbows from sunlight are always the same colors and are always in the same order?

That set of colors in a beam of sunlight is called the visible light spectrum. Here's how to split apart a sunbeam to create your own spectrum of colors:

Here's what you need:

A prism (In place of a prism, you can use a crystal figure, such as a little animal from a glass shop. Or use a crystal from a chandelier, or a crystal glass or goblet.)
A bright, sunny day
White paper

Here's what you do:

1. Set the prism so the sun will shine through it.
2. Hold the white paper behind the prism so that the sun's rays will hit the paper and show you the spectrum of colors.
   You ought to see in your spectrum the same color and the same order of colors that you see in a rainbow.
   At one end you see red.
   Then you see orange, yellow, green, blue-green, blue, and violet. The color red at one end of the spectrum has the slowest vibration and the longest wave. The color violet, at the other end vibrates the fastest and has the shortest wave.

   : **NOW YOU HAVE A SPLIT-APART**
   : **SUNBEAM.**

When you see a rainbow, think about what acted as the prism.

Perhaps you would like to see if you can split apart other sorts of light beams, and look at the colors that form them.

SPLIT APART AN ELECTRIC LIGHT BEAM

Use your prism to see if you can separate the colors in the light from an electric bulb.

Then try for the colors inside a fluorescent light.

If you can, try a "full-spectrum" light bulb and see if it really does contain the whole spectrum of sunlight.

YOU'LL SEE THAT THE COLORS FROM AN ELECTRIC LIGHT ARE NOT QUITE THE SAME AS THE COLORS INSIDE A SUNBEAM. Electric light has less blue and less violet than sunlight.

SEE COLORS SHINE EVERYWHERE

These colors can change around every which way.

First, experiment with how colors look in water and in milk, in clear glasses and in colored glasses.

Be sure to keep notes.

Here's what you need:
Clear glasses or jars
Colored glasses or bottles
Water
Milk
White paper or white tablecloth
Your science notebook and pen

Here's what you do:

1. Hold a clear glass or jar of water up to the light, and look at the colored images you can see through the water.
   What you see may be distorted or backwards. (Try looking through the curved glass near the bottom of a glass jar. You may see one image upside down connected to the same image right side up and backwards at the same time.)

2. Fill a colored glass or bottle with water, and hold it up to the light. What colors do you see? What's different about what you see?

3. Now fill a clear glass with milk, and hold it up to the light.
   Do you see any light shining through the milk? What colors or images can you see?

4. Set all three of these glasses— the clear glass of water, the colored glass of water, and the clear glass of milk—so that light shines through each onto the white sheet of paper or white tablecloth.

5. Hold the white paper directly behind each glass, and see if the colors look different.
   Look carefully before you write down the colors you see.

6. Look at the colors as you pour the water out of the glasses.

   : **NOW LOOK AT YOUR NOTES**
   : **AND SEE HOW COLORS CHANGE**
   : **WHEN YOU LOOK AT THEM IN**
   : **ALL THESE DIFFERENT WAYS.**

Here's part of what you can see when you look at colors through water and milk:

You'll see right through water. That's because water is *transparent*.
But when you look through milk, you'll see only light. That's because milk is *translucent*. Light passes through, but not color or images.

MIX YOUR OWN WATER COLORS

Mix and match your own colored water, and see what happens.

Be sure to take notes again because you may not remember all the colors you are going to see.

Caution: This job can get messy, even though food coloring is washable. You might want to take this job outside, and wear an apron and plastic gloves.

Here's what you need:

Six clear jars or glasses

Water

Small plastic or stainless steel spoons or knives

Red, yellow, and blue food coloring (The paste type used by cake decorators works best.)

White paper

A paper or plastic placemat (one you can write on) or a piece of paper

Your science notebook and pen

Here's what you do:

1. Fill a clear jar or glass with water. Use the spoon or knife to add a small amount of red food coloring to the water. Stir and add the coloring a bit at a time until the water turns a clear crimson-red.

2. Pour a third of the red water into a second jar. Pour another third into a third jar.
   Now you have three jars, each partly full of red water.

3. Fill another clear jar with water. Add a small amount of blue food coloring, and stir. Add the coloring a bit at a time until the water turns a clear indigo-blue.

4. Pour a third of the blue water into one of the jars of red water. Pour half of the rest into another jar. Now you have five jars. Two are partly full of red water. Two are partly full of blue water. And one is a mix of red and blue.

5. Fill another jar with water. Add a small amount of yellow food coloring, and stir. Add the coloring a bit at a time until the water turns a clear, bright yellow.

6. Pour a third of the yellow water into one of the jars of red water. Pour half of the rest into one of the jars of blue water.
   Now you have six jars: one partly full of yellow water, one with red only, one with blue only, one a mixture of red and blue, one a mixture of blue and yellow, one a mixture of red and yellow.

7. Set the jars on the placemat or paper. Write the color or colors in front of each jar.

8. Look at the colors in four different ways. Notice the shadings from one color to another.
   - Look at each jar as it sits on the placemat.
   - Look at each jar as you hold it up to sunlight.

- Place each jar so that the sun reflects through the glass onto a white surface.
- Hold a white paper directly behind each jar and see if the reflected colors look different.

9. Make a color chart on the place-mat or on paper. Then you will have solved the problem of how colors mix.

Here's part of what you can see when you mix colors in water:

Blue and red make violet.
Blue and yellow make green.
Red and yellow make orange.
All the colors together (blue, red, yellow, violet, green, and orange) make black.

When you look at your color mixes in sunlight, you ought to be able to see the final mixed color plus the two original colors.

KEEP YOUR JARS OF WATER READY FOR THE NEXT EXPERIMENT. If you used jars with lids, you can save the water for days.

MIX UP COLORS THAT ARE THE SAME AND DIFFERENT

Here's how water can be different colors all at the same time.

Here's what you do:

1. Pour the blue and yellow water from the last experiment into the jar of red water. The three-color mix will look brown.

2. Now hold the jar up to light, and you'll see a ruby-red color. The light makes the difference.

3. Hold up white paper, and let light shine through. Reflected on the white paper, you'll see brown along with spots of blue, yellow, and red.

4. Now pour the colored water out slowly, and you'll see a bluish color.

WHAT HAPPENED TO ALL THOSE COLORS? Use your color chart to solve the problem.

TELL THE DIFFERENCE BETWEEN BLACK AND WHITE

White is a combination of all the colors of the spectrum.

But if you removed all the colors from a ray of light, you'd get black.

An object that looks white to us is reflecting all the colors of sunlight.

An object that looks black to us is absorbing all the colors of the sunlight.

But if you're talking about paint instead of light rays, you have to look at black and white in another way. When you mix paint, you ordinarily begin with white and then add colors.

And with paint, black is a combination of all colors. If you soaked every color paint into your white shirt, eventually you'd have a black shirt. (Of course, your mother would not think this was a good idea.)

Here's another difference between black and white. Look at the way roads and sidewalks are paved.

Concrete is nearly white. Asphalt is black.

If you put your hand on asphalt on a hot day, you'll feel the heat. You could even get burned, as children do sometimes when they run barefoot across a black asphalt road.

The black asphalt has absorbed the sun's light and heat, as well as its colors.

If you put your hand on concrete, though, you'll be at less risk. Concrete reflects most of the sun's rays, so it looks almost white and stays a lot cooler.

DOT YOUR WAY TO ARTISTIC SUCCESS

A printing press uses only three colors—magenta, cyan, and yellow, with black—to mix every color. But printers don't just smear colors right on top of each other. If they did, they'd be liable to get muddy, ugly colors.

Instead, they put in each color by dots.

For instance, the printer makes green in a picture by first printing blue (cyan) dots and then printing yellow dots in with the blue. When you look at the picture, though, you don't see the blue or yellow dots. You see what looks to be solid green.

Your eyes "mix" the dots into a solid-looking color.

If you look at a printed picture with a magnifying glass, though, you can probably see the dots.

Try creating a picture out of dots. A few very famous painters have done this before you. Some of the world's greatest paintings are made entirely of dots.

Here's all you need:

Colored markers, pens, pencils, or crayons

Paper

Here's what you do:

1. Experiment first to see how the colors of the markers, pens, pencils, or crayons mix into other colors. You don't have to use only the four printer's colors. Mix any colors you like.
2. Then sketch in your picture, and fill in the colors entirely with dots.

STAND BACK AND ADMIRE THE RESULT.

· · · · · · · · · ·

CONSTRUCT YOUR OWN COLOR WHEEL

· ·

Decorators and fashion designers use color wheels to see which colors look best together.

You can have a color wheel, too.

Here's what you need:

A drawing compass

A piece of white posterboard or cardboard

A ruler

Colored markers, pens, pencils, or crayons

Here's what you do:

1. Use your drawing compass to draw a 12-inch (30 cm) circle on the posterboard or cardboard.
2. Draw lines with the ruler so that your circle is divided into 12 equal sections. Now label and color in a color for each section.

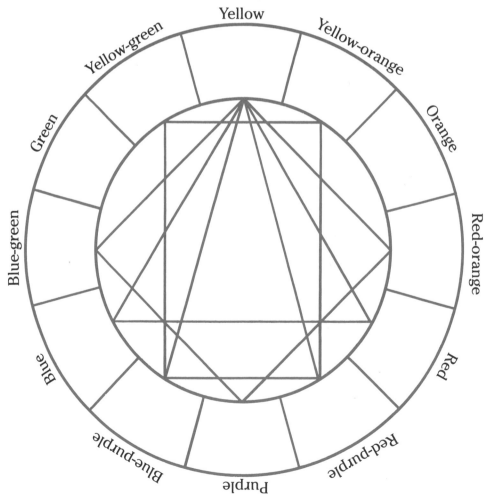

3. Underline the primary colors so that you can remember them: yellow, red, and blue. Then draw a circle around each of the secondary colors: orange, purple, and green. The other colors are combinations of primary and secondary colors: yellow-orange, red-orange, red-purple, blue-purple, blue-green, and yellow-green.

4. To find colors that look good together, use your color wheel like this:

• Pick colors that are directly opposite each other on the wheel. For instance, yellow and purple or blue and orange are supposed to match well.

• Put together colors that are nearly opposite each other on the wheel. For instance, pick red and blue-green, or try a combination of red and yellow-green.

• Pick colors next to each other on the wheel. Blue goes well with blue-green, for instance.

• If you want to put together three colors, select three colors that are equal distances apart on the wheel. Try green, orange, and purple, for instance. Or go for yellow, red, and blue.

> **NOW YOU HAVE YOUR OWN WAY TO CHOOSE COLORS— JUST THE WAY THE EXPERTS USE.**

············
TURN MIXED COLORS BACK INTO BASIC COLORS
·······································

You've tried mixing colors. Now try separating colors. Here's a way you can turn mixed colors back into their primary colors.

Here's what you need:

Strips of paper towels

Felt markers—black, orange, green, purple, and brown (and other colors, if you want)

A glass jar

Water

Here's what you do:

1. On each strip of paper toweling, or paper coffee filter, make a large spot of color with one of the felt markers.

2. Fill the jar with water, and drape each strip of paper toweling over the edge of the jar, with one end in the water. But keep your color spots on the dry end.

3. Wait 20 to 30 minutes while the water gradually moves up the paper strips onto the color spots. You will see a change take place. As the water dissolves the colors, they will separate. You will begin to see the individual colors that make up the beginning color.

For instance, orange separates into red and yellow. Look for the colors that combined to make the green, purple, brown, and the other colors. Black is fun because it separates into several colors. And different brands of black marker will separate into different colors.

: **NOW YOU CAN SEE THE COLORS**
: **INSIDE OTHER COLORS.**

. . . .
COLORS YOU CAN'T SEE
. . . .

Did you know that there are other colors at each end of the light spectrum?

We can't see them, but we know that these colors exist because we know about the invisible light waves.

At the violet end of the spectrum, with even shorter, faster light waves, is ultraviolet.

At the red end of the spectrum, with longer, slower waves, is infrared.

Ultraviolet waves can cause sunburn. When you buy sunglasses or suntan lotion, look for the type that screens out ultraviolet.

Infrared rays are responsible for most of the heat you feel from the sun.

If you don't believe that these colors exist, ask a bee. Bees apparently can see at least a few extra colors just fine.

. . . .

HOW THE COLORS GET INTO FIREWORKS

. . . .

More than a thousand years ago, the Chinese invented fireworks. They filled bamboo tubes with saltpeter, sulfur, and charcoal. The saltpeter and sulfur made for a mostly yellow explosion, and the charcoal created a sparkling, flaming tail.

The Italian people loved the idea, and by the 15th century, they had figured out how to enhance a good story-telling.

They brought on stage figures of wood and plaster. At the right moment, the mouths and eyes of the figures spewed out fire.

In 1613, the English used fireworks to celebrate a royal wedding. If you'd been there then, you could have seen a whole picture done in fireworks. For just seconds, fireworks created an image of Saint George sitting astride a fiery horse and in the act of slaying a flaming dragon.

Chemicals create the special color effects of fireworks. Why?

Each chemical has its own spectrum of colors. When heat hits the atoms or molecules that make up the chemical, they become "excited." The result is a color special to that atom or molecule.

In fact, colors give us a good way to identify chemicals, even from very far away. That's how scientists can tell what the other planets and the stars are made of. They look at the colors. They may even use a prism to split apart a far-away color spectrum, just as you can with a light beam. And then they can tell us the chemicals that exist in outer space.

Fireworks, even small firecrackers, are colorful but very dangerous. You're better off watching fine professional fireworks than creating your own.

But you might like to use some of the same chemicals to create your own colors, even without the fireworks.

MAKE A GIFT OF YOUR OWN FIREPLACE COLORS

You can go to a fireplace shop and buy chemicals that bring out brilliant colors in a fire. Or you can create your own color-creating evergreen cones.

These are perfect gifts for people who like fireplaces.

Here's what you need:

2 plastic pails

1 pound (500 gm) copper sulfate (You can buy copper sulfate at a hardware store or garden center.)

Water

¹/₂ pound (250 gm) boric acid (You can buy boric acid at a drugstore.)

2 large mesh bags (Laundry or onion bags are fine.)

1 bushel (or large bag) evergreen cones

Plastic wrap, preferably colored

Ribbons

Here's what you do:

1. In one of the plastic pails, dissolve the copper sulfate in a gallon of water. In the second plastic pail, dissolve the boric acid in another gallon of water.

2. Fill a bag with half the evergreen cones, and put them to soak in the copper sulfate. Fill the second bag, and put it to soak in the boric acid. You may need to weigh down the bags with rocks.

3. Leave the cones in the solutions for 3 or 4 days.

4. Remove the cones, and spread them to dry in a safe place such as a garage or basement.

5. When the cones are completely dry, wrap several at a time in plastic wrap. (Colored plastic would be fun.) Tie each packet with ribbons, and your gifts are ready.

6. For fiery colors, just toss the gift cones into a fire. The copper sulfate cones will burn with a green flame. The boric acid cones will burn blue-green flames.
   You can make other fireplace colors the same way. Calcium chloride (the same salt you buy to freeze ice cream) burns orange-red. Potassium chloride burns as a violet color.

> **NOW YOU CAN GIVE COLORS FOR CHRISTMAS, HANUKKAH, OR ANY OTHER WINTER HOLIDAY.**

THE OLD-FASHIONED WAY TO PAINT—WITH DIRT, BERRIES, MILK, AND BLOOD

Long ago, people used whatever natural materials they could find for paint.

In fact, the mysterious Red Paint people lived so very long ago that almost all we know about them is their paint.

More than 10,000 years ago, the Red Paint people disappeared from their homes in what is now the northeastern United States and the Maritime Provinces of Canada. They left behind burial grounds and shreds of pottery—all decorated in red paint.

Their red paint came from a kind of reddish brown earth called ocher.

Later people painted with ocher, too, and with other sorts of colored earth.

Children used to pick berries for their colors as well as for their taste. But getting enough berries for dye was a great deal of work. That's why your great-great-grandparents probably didn't have as many colorful clothes as you do. And, unless they were rich, they probably didn't have colorfully decorated houses.

Old-fashioned farmers were so thrifty that sometimes they painted with leftover milk. Any milk they couldn't drink, they could use for paint, particularly if the milk was mixed with something like earth or berry-juice colors. To paint the outsides of their houses, they mixed milk with oil.

Do you know why so many barns were once painted red? The farmers found a cheap source of red color to add to their milk paint.

They added blood.

When the old-fashioned farmers slaughtered animals for food, they had plenty of blood left over.

Milk paint is not much used today (and red paint isn't at all bloody). But once in a while, someone uses milk paint as a trick.

The trick is to paint cheap furniture with milk paint and then put it for sale as if it were old and valuable.

Careless buyers might think they were walking away with valuable antiques, when really they were giving away their money for a bit of milk paint.

JUST FOR FUN, MAKE YOUR OWN MILK PAINT. You might paint with it if you want to give something an antique look.

MAKE YOUR OWN OLD-FASHIONED MILK PAINT

This old-fashioned paint is fine to paint doll houses and doll furniture. Or paint a picture on heavy paper, posterboard, cardboard, or wood.

Here's what you need:

Water

Nonfat dry milk powder (Instant is easiest.)

Plus your choice of coloring materials:

Berry juice (such as cherry or elderberry juice)

Beet juice

Food coloring

Colored earth

Colored paint powder (from a paint or art supply store)

Here's what you do:

1. Mix water and the nonfat dry milk powder about half and half. The liquid should have the consistency of paint.

2. Add your choice of coloring material (juice, food coloring, colored earth, or paint powder) until you get a color you like.

> **NOW BRUSH ON YOUR MILK PAINT JUST AS YOU WOULD ANY OTHER PAINT.**

It takes about 2 hours to dry.

FLOAT SOME, SINK SOME

A small penny sinks, but a giant, heavy ship stays afloat.

A rubber duckie floats, but a pebble sinks.

One sort of vegetable floats, but another sinks.

Would you like to find out why?

Would you like to hold a boat-designing contest? Or perhaps you'd like to experiment on what sort of water keeps boats floating best.

HOLD A FLOATING CONTEST WITH FRUITS AND VEGETABLES

One sort of creature can actually walk on water. Watch a water strider some day, and you can see something about why it doesn't sink.

The water strider is a light little insect, but it would sink if it put all its weight in one place. Instead, its long legs spread its weight over a large area. Also, its legs are formed so that they don't break the surface tension of the water. And it even has waterproof hairs to keep it dry.

Experiment to find out the sizes and shapes that help things float.

Here's what you need:

Your science notebook and pen

A variety of fruits and vegetables

A postage or food scale, if you have one

A dishpan full of water

Here's what you do:

1. In your science notebook, begin a chart. Across the top of the chart, list each fruit or vegetable you have on hand. Along the side of the chart, list the factors that might make a difference in floating or sinking. Here's how your chart should look:

	Fruit or Vegetable				
	#1	#2	#3	#4	#5
Comparative weight					
Comparative size					
Match of size and weight (density)					
Shape					
Other factors (list them)					
Float or sink					

2. Weigh each fruit or vegetable on a postage or food scale. If you don't have the right sort of scale, "weigh" each fruit or vegetable in your hand. Rank each one from heaviest to lightest in comparison to the others. Record the results on your chart.

3. Look at the size of each, and rank each from largest to smallest. Write the comparative sizes on your chart.

4. Compare how the size and weight match. Some fruits and vegetables will seem heavy for their sizes. Others will seem light for their sizes.
That match of size and weight (such as the number of ounces per inch) is the density. Note on your chart which fruits and vegetables seem particularly dense.

5. Look at the shape of each: long, round, flat. Think about other factors that make for floating or sinking, and note them on your chart.

6. Now place each fruit or vegetable in the dishpan of water. Write down which ones sink and which float.

> **NOW YOU HAVE AN IDEA OF THE SHAPES AND SIZES THAT ARE IMPORTANT FOR FLOATING OR SINKING.**

· · · · · · · · · · ·

FLOAT A NEEDLE

· ·

Is it possible to float a needle on water? You can if you know how to use surface tension.

Here is what you need:

A bowl or pan
Water
A small piece of paper, about 1 ½ inches (4 cm) square
A sewing needle

Here is what you do:

1. Fill the bowl or pan with water.
2. Float the piece of paper on the water.
3. Put the needle in the middle of the paper.
4. Carefully push the edges of the paper down into the water. As the paper gets wet, it will sink and leave the needle floating.

Surface tension makes it possible to float the needle on water. The molecules on the surface of water stick close enough together that, under the right conditions, they can make something float that would not ordinarily do so. How can you break the surface tension and make your floating needle sink? Just add 1 drop of laundry detergent. Even 1 drop breaks the surface tension of the water. The water molecules spread apart, and the needle sinks to the bottom.

NEXT TIME, TRY FLOATING A TOOTHPICK.

FLOAT WITH ANCIENT GREECE

Archimedes, one of the world's greatest scientists and inventors, lived in ancient Greece more than 2,000 years ago.

Archimedes thought for a long time about why some things float and some things sink. You can see why that was important for an inventor to know, especially since he was interested in ways to improve shipbuilding. (One of his most famous inventions is a water screw used to pump water out of the holds of ships.)

The story is that Archimedes was sitting in a bathtub when suddenly the answer to a perplexing problem came to him. According to legend, Archimedes leaped from his bath and ran outside shouting, "Eureka! I've got it!"

What is it that Archimedes discovered? He was thinking about how a ship in the ocean or a human body in a bathtub displaces water. Whether the object sinks or floats, it displaces exactly its own weight of water. Then, whether it floats or sinks depends on its shape and density.

Maybe you'll shout "Eureka!" when you find out how much fun this project is. And you can prove Archimedes' theory for yourself.

Here's what you need:

Modeling clay

A postage or food scale, if you have one

A smaller rectangular or square baking pan

A large rectangular or square baking pan

Water

Thin string or button thread

A basting syringe

A measuring cup

Your science notebook and pen

Here's what you do:

1. Mold the clay into a small boat. Make sure your boat can float.

2. If you have a postage or food scale, weigh your boat.

3. Place the smaller pan in the larger pan. Carefully pour water into the smaller pan until it is full to the brim.

4. Cut the string or thread into two pieces, each about 12 inches (30 cm) long. Place each piece under the boat, with the two pieces at right angles. Gently lift the strings and tie the four ends together in a knot over the boat.

5. Holding the strings at the knot, carefully place the boat on the water. Lower your hand enough to let the string go slack. As the boat starts to float, water will

run over the sides of the small pan into the larger pan.

6. Carefully pull up on the strings and lift the boat out of the water. Try not to spill any more water over the side of the small pan.

7. Lift the small pan out of the larger pan without spilling any more water. One way to keep more water from spilling is to use the basting syringe to remove some of the water from the small pan. (Dump the water you remove into the sink, not into the larger pan.)

8. Pour the water in the large pan into the measuring cup. Write down how much there is. That's how much water the clay boat has displaced from the small pan.

9. Dry the clay boat, and squash it into a solid lump.

10. Once again, place the smaller pan in the larger pan. Carefully pour water into the smaller pan until it is again full to the brim.

11. Place the strings under the lump just as you did with the boat. Holding the strings at the knot, carefully put the lump of clay into the water. The lump will sink. Make sure it completely submerges.

12. Carefully lift the lump from the water with the strings.

13. Use the basting syringe to remove enough of the water from the small pan so that you can lift it without spilling any more into the larger pan.

14. Pour the water from the large pan into the measuring cup. Write down how much there is. That's

how much water the clay lump displaced from the small pan.

15. Compare your results. You ought to find that the amount of water displaced was about the same for both the boat and the lump of clay. This experiment may not be exact, though, because of slight variations in filling the pan or other small errors.

16. If you weighed the clay, compare that weight with the weight of the water. (See Page 100 for two ways to weigh water.) Again, you ought to find that the weight of the clay and the weight of the water are just about the same.
That's what Archimedes figured out. A solid body (like the clay boat or the lump of clay) displaces its own weight in water. Thus the body becomes lighter in proportion to the weight it displaces in the water. The clay boat floated because you spread its weight over a large surface of water. And you raised the sides of the boat so that the water did not pour over the top and sink the boat.

: Now You Know Why Boats
: Can Float Even When
: They're Made Of Heavy
: Steel Or Even Heavier
: Concrete.

Wood makes particularly good boats, too, since wood contains a great deal of air in its cells. The air helps the wood float. But when wood soaks for a long time, water replaces the air in the cells. Then the wood becomes waterlogged, too full of heavy water to float.

TWO WAYS TO WEIGH WATER

1. Weigh the empty measuring cup. Then weigh the measuring cup with the water in it. Subtract the weight of the measuring cup alone from the combined weight of the measuring cup and the water:

2. Or you can remember an old saying:

> A pint's a pound
> The world around.

Now all you have to do is remember that a pint equals 2 cups (250 ml), and you can figure the weight of water by knowing the amount of water. If 2 cups (500 ml) of water weigh 1 pound (500 gms) , then:

1 cup = $\frac{1}{2}$ pound (or 8 ounces)
$\frac{1}{2}$ cup = $\frac{1}{4}$ pound (or 4 ounces)
$\frac{1}{4}$ cup = $\frac{1}{8}$ pound (or 2 ounces)
$\frac{1}{8}$ cup = $\frac{1}{16}$ pound (or 1 ounce)

HOLD A FLOATING CONTEST WITH CLAY BOATS

This is a good project for a school group or a group of friends.

Here's what you need:

Modeling clay
A dishpan full of water
Coins

Here's what you do:

1. Design a boat out of modeling clay. If you want to win the contest, design a boat that can hold a heavy load of coins (or pebbles, if you're working outside).

2. Float your boats in the dishpan. Add coins, one by one. The last boat to sink wins.

> **NOW YOU KNOW HOW TO DESIGN FOR FLOATING OR SINKING.**

HOLD A FLOATING CONTEST WITH CARDBOARD BOATS

This is another good project for a school group or a group of friends. And it's a good project for someone who can figure out the best sizes and shapes for floating.

You would think cardboard would always sink. But that's not necessarily so. See if you can design a boat of cardboard and make it float. Prepare your cardboard anyway you want. Cut, fold, and glue it however you like.

Of course, the shape of your boat is most important. But there are a few other additions that could help float your boat:

1. Coat the outside of the boat with plastic spray.
2. Paint the outside of the boat with waterproof paint.
3. Put the boat together with waterproof glue, such as model-making glue, carpenter's glue, or another sort of plastic glue.

THE BOAT THAT FLOATS THE LONGEST WINS.

··········
TEST THE WATER WITH FOIL BOATS
·······································

A body of water naturally pushes upward. That's the water's buoyancy. You can feel buoyancy by pushing the palm of your hand against a water surface.

Some water has more buoyancy than other water. Here's how to find out. You may want to take this job outside. It can get wet and messy.

Here's what you need:

Aluminum foil
A dishpan full of water
Coins
Salt
A large spoon
Sand or cornstarch
Your science notebook and pen

Here's what you do:

1. Shape aluminum foil into several boats. Give each a name so you can remember one from the other.
2. Put the boats in the dishpan. See which boat floats best by adding coins until the boat sinks. Make a record of how many coins each boat can hold before it sinks in just plain water.
3. Carefully lift the boats out of the water, and remove the coins.
4. Pour 1 or 2 cups (250–500 ml) salt into the water in the dishpan. Stir until the salt dissolves.
5. Now see how many coins each boat can carry before it sinks in salt water. Keep a record.
6. Carefully lift the boats out of the water, and remove the coins.
7. Add 1 or 2 cups (250–500 ml) of sand or cornstarch to the water in the dishpan. Stir.
8. See how many coins each boat can carry before it sinks in the salt water with sand or cornstarch in it. Keep a record in your science notebook.

NOW YOU CAN DECIDE WHICH KIND OF WATER HAS MORE BUOYANCY.

BUBBLE, BUBBLE

*Y*ou can almost perform magic with bubbles. And you can have fun with bubbles.

Bubbles are balls of air or gas surrounded by a solid or liquid. The next time you drink a soda, look for the carbon dioxide bubbles. Sometime you might see a glass-blower creating glass bubbles. You might even think of a toy balloon as a kind of bubble.

Soap bubbles are a sort of sandwich of water and soap molecules. The attraction of the water molecules for one another holds the bubbles together. But if there weren't air and soap, the water molecules would hold together so strongly that no bubble could form. A bubble needs air inside to keep it from collapsing right away. And it needs soap molecules to make the water surface stretchy enough to create a bubble.

You can even create a bubble party.

MAKE A BUBBLE MIX

Y ou can save money by turning soap leftovers into the base for a delightful bubble mix. Keep this bubble jar around, and add soap leftovers and water whenever you wish. Leave the lid on, though, so the bubble base doesn't dry up.

Here's what you need:

Ends and leftovers from bars of soap
A large jar with a lid
Water

Here's what you do:

1. Rinse off the soap ends, and put them in the jar with a little water.
2. From time to time, add more soap and water.

SOON YOU'LL HAVE A MESSY LIQUID MASS OF SOAP. THAT'S A PERFECT BUBBLE BASE.

MIX UP YOUR BUBBLES

Use your bubble base to make a solution for blowing bubbles.

Here's what you need:

1/4 cup (60 ml) bubble mix

3/4 cup (200 ml) water

*1 tablespoon (15 ml) sugar or
1 package (about 1/4 ounce [8 ml])
unflavored gelatin or 1 tablespoon
(15 ml) glycerin*

A clean jar with a lid

Note: *The sugar, gelatin, or glycerin helps
the bubbles last longer. These substances
slow down the drying time. When bubbles
dry, they break.*

Here's what you do:

1. Mix the bubble mix, water, and
sugar, gelatin, or glycerin.

2. Pour the solution into the jar.

3. Cover the jar with the lid.

*EXPERIMENT TO FIND OUT HOW
MUCH YOU NEED OF EACH INGRE-
DIENT. Soon you will get just the
mixture you like best.*

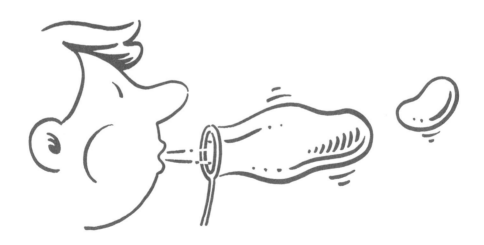

BLOW FINE BUBBLES

Now's the time for some fun with bubbles.
Then try an experiment with a thread.

Here's what you need:

A piece of wire (A fine-wire coat hanger or a large paper clip will do.)
¹/₂ cup (120 ml) of bubble solution
A piece of thread or fine string about 1 ¹/₂ inches (4 cm) long.

Here's what you do:

1. Form the wire into a circle about 1¹/₂ inches (4 cm) across.
2. Dip the wire into the bubble solution, and blow bubbles through it. Or wave the wire in the air to make streams of bubbles.
3. Wet the thread or string in the bubble solution. Roll the ends together between your fingers to form a loop.
4. Dip the wire loop into the bubble solution.
5. Put the loop of wet thread on the soap film inside the wire loop.
6. Break the soap film in the middle of the thread loop, and see what happens.
The loop of thread makes a remarkable hole inside the soap film. The thread loop tends to form an empty circle.

THE THREAD ROLLS AROUND THE WIRE LOOP AS LONG AS YOU MOVE THE LOOP AROUND.

BLOW BUBBLES WITH A STRAW

You can blow big bubbles. You can blow little bubbles. Or you can blow bubbles inside of bubbles inside of bubbles.

To get started, use a drinking straw with your bubble solution.

Here's what you do:

1. Dip the straw into the bubble solution. Blow through the end of the straw to create bubbles. (Listen, and you can hear the air blowing into the bubbles.)

2. Blow quickly to form numbers of small bubbles.

3. Practice blowing slowly to create big bubbles.
   As you practice with the straw, you will see the bubble move away from the straw, so that you are blowing through a little tunnel of film.

4. To blow bubbles inside of bubbles, sit at a table. Wet an area of the tabletop with bubble solution. Dip the straw in the bubble solution.

Blow a large bubble near the table. The bubble will form a dome over the table.
Release the bubble, and insert the straw into it. Blow another bubble inside the large bubble. Notice how the bubbles sometimes come together to form a larger bubble. And notice how a bubble inside a bubble sometimes zooms to one side and seems about to pop right through the large bubble.

KEEP PRACTICING.

BLOW BUBBLES WITH A FUNNEL

Dip the wide end of a funnel into the bubble solution. (The solution needs to be in a dish big enough to get the wide end of the funnel in.) Blow bubbles through the narrow end.

YOU'LL GET SOME INTERESTING RESULTS.

BLOW BUBBLES WITH A BOTTLE

You can blow a bubble and put a marble or a small toy inside it.

Here's what you do:

1. Find a plastic quart or liter bottle, such as a soda pop or liquid detergent bottle.
2. Cut off the bottom. All around the cut-off bottle, cut parallel slits about $1/2$ inch (1 cm) apart and about $1/2$ inch (1 cm) deep. Bend the edges back so that they fan out like a flower.
3. Wet an area of the tabletop with the bubble solution.
4. Dip the fanned-out end of the bottle into the bubble solution. Hold it near the wet tabletop, and blow a large bubble dome onto the table.
5. Roll a wet marble through the bubble. Or try sliding in a small, wet plastic toy.

YOU MAY NOT SUCCEED ON THE FIRST TRY. KEEP TRYING!

BLOW A MASS OF BUBBLES

Blow a mass of bubbles. Here's how.

1. Dip a tea strainer into the bubble solution.

2. Hold the strainer with the open end toward you, and blow gently. Soon you'll see a mass of bubbles hanging down from the strainer. They seem to form angles with each other.

3. See if you can put a wet straw into one of the bubbles. Pick the bubble up with the straw, and blow through the straw to make the bubble grow bigger. Then see what happens.

4. Pop the big bubble. With the end of the straw, you can move the bubbles hanging from the strainer back up to cover the hole.

YOU CAN EXPERIMENT WITH BUBBLES JUST ABOUT FOREVER.

HOLD A BUBBLE PARTY

First, you'll need bubbly decorations. How about balloons with swirling, bubblelike colors?

Bake a bubble cake for the party.
Here's how:

1. Bake the cake in a round mold or in a metal mixing bowl.
2. Frost it smoothly with white frosting. But save 3 or 4 tablespoons of frosting to color with different food colorings. Then swirl the different colors of frosting through the white frosting on the cake, the way colors swirl through a bubble.

Serve other bubbly refreshments:
1. Bubbly punch, with colored round ice cubes floating in it
2. Gelatin made with bubbly ginger ale instead of water
3. Sandwiches of colored bread cut in circles
   Mix a small jar of bubble solution for each of your guests, and give each guest a drinking straw. Wet the top of a table with bubble mix, and give your guests plenty of time to practice.

Then you can hold bubble contests:
1. For blowing the biggest bubble.
2. For creating the highest pile of bubbles in 30 seconds
3. For creating the longest-lasting bubble
4. For creating the prettiest bubble
5. For getting a marble inside a bubble
6. For blowing a bubble inside a bubble

THE PRIZES CAN BE BUBBLE GUM, BUBBLY-LOOKING BALLOONS, OR JARS OF BUBBLE MIX.

MOVE AND ZOOM

You can be a scientist of movement and speed.

You can learn how birds fly, how airplanes take off, how ships sail, how kites catch the wind.

You can figure out how to move heavy loads.

You can make your own paper airplane or your own kite.

How Birds Make It Off the Ground

How come birds can fly but we can't?

When it comes to flying, birds are stronger than we are. The breast muscles that lift their wings are much stronger than even the best-developed human chest muscles. (Chest muscles are called pectoral muscles in either birds or humans. You may have heard a strong man brag about his "pectorals." But those pectorals would be strong for lifting weights, not for flying.)

Birds have less to carry than people do. Because bird bones are hollow, they weigh less than human bones. Yet bird bones are strong. They are reinforced with struts, somewhat like the struts on the wings of early airplanes.

And, of course, birds know all the right moves.

Bird wings push down and forward at the same time. That's important because then the bird has the advantage of air pressure.

Here's how air pressure helps the bird to lift off.

You know that air presses from every direction all the time. Air presses down on a bird, but it also presses up.

To take off, a bird needs more lift from air under the wing than from air pressing down on top of the wing.

One way the bird gets more lift from under the wing is due to the angle at which air hits the wing. When air moves against any flat surface (like a wing), it always exerts pressure at a right angle. That's one way the air pressure pushes upward against the bottom surface of a bird's wing.

Another way that air pressure lifts a bird is due to speed. The forward push of the wings forces air to rush both over and under the bird's wing.

The faster air moves, the less pressure it exerts.

The top, curved surface of a bird's wing is slightly longer than the bottom surface, so the air moves more rapidly over the upper surface than over the bottom surface. The air rushing under the wing is only slightly slower than the air rushing over the wing, but that difference in speed is enough to provide a lift.

The higher pressure against the bottom surface of the wing helps the bird to stay in the air.

YOU CAN MAKE A PAPER WING. Watch how air pressure makes it fly.

FLY A PAPER WING

Airplane wings work a bit like bird wings. You can see how by building your own paper "wing."

Here's what you need:

A rectangular piece of paper
Cellophane tape
A piece of string about 20 inches (50 cm) long
A yardstick or a 3-foot (1 m) dowel

Here's what you do:

1. Hold the paper so that the short side faces you. Bring the end facing you up to the opposite end. Pull it back about 1 inch. Holding it evenly, fold the paper.
2. Turn the paper over, and tape the edges opposite the fold together.
   The top side is longer than the underside, and it curves.
3. Run the piece of string through the folded end. Tie each end of the string to the yardstick or dowel.
4. Wave the stick in the air, and watch the "wing" rise.
   The air going over the curved top of the paper travels faster than the air under the paper. The faster-moving air exerts less pressure than the air moving under the wing. The greater pressure on the bottom surface keeps the wing up in the air.

: **NOW YOU CAN SEE HOW AIR PRESSURE HELPS LIFT BOTH BIRDS AND AIRPLANES.**

· · · · · · · · · ·
MAKE A PAPER AIRPLANE
· ·

This paper airplane will soar. Hold a contest with your friends to see who can design the best flyer.

Here's all you need:

A rectangular piece of paper
Scissors or a straightedge

Here's what you do:

1. Make the paper into a square. You can do this without measuring. Fold the paper diagonally, bringing one corner even with the other side. Use scissors to cut off the extra piece. Or use a straightedge to tear it off.

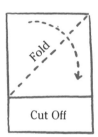

2. Fold the cut-off piece in half the long way. Make overlapping, slanted folds on each side about two-thirds of the length of the paper. Make a hole near the end of the piece. This will be the tail of the plane. Set it aside.

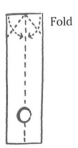

3. Now take the square sheet of paper. Make a second diagonal fold crossing the first. Turn the paper over and fold it in half. Open the paper and fold the paper in half at right angles to the previous fold. Open the paper and turn it over so the diagonal folds are pointing away from you. Now you have a square with two diagonal folds and a horizontal and vertical fold.

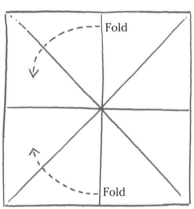

Diagonal folds down
vertical and horizontal
folds point upward

4. Bring the lower right corner and the upper right corner together. Pull the horizontal fold forward as you bring the corners together. Repeat with the left corners.

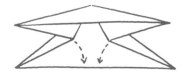

5. Fold the top right and left corners up to the center corner. Leave the bottom left corners flat. They will be the wings of your plane.

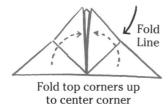

Fold
Line

Fold top corners up
to center corner

6. Fold the corners a second time to the center.

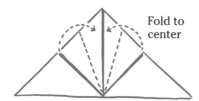

Fold to
center

Leave the bottom corners down.

7. Insert the tail piece all the way to the nose of the plane. Fold the wing flaps downward.

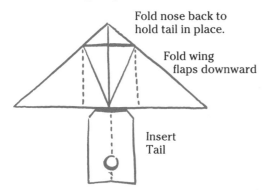

Fold nose back to
hold tail in place.

Fold wing
flaps downward

Insert
Tail

8. Fold back the nose to anchor the tail.

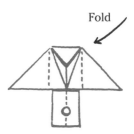

Fold

9. You're ready to launch the airplane. Hold the nose of the plane with your forefinger and have your thumb and second finger under the wings.

: **You Can Create Any Number
: Of Paper Airplane Designs.
: Experiment With A Wider
: Tail Or With More Than
: One Hole In The Tail.**

PARACHUTE POWER

Parachutes are more than 2,000 years old. The ancient Chinese invented them for their acrobats. A parachute could slow down a fall and keep the acrobats from getting hurt.

You have probably heard of the famous 16th-century Italian painter Leonardo da Vinci. (He painted *Mona Lisa* and *The Last Supper*.) Da Vinci had good ideas about just about everything. He believed that a person could jump from a high place and use a "tent of linen" to keep from getting hurt. We don't know whether da Vinci ever tried parachuting himself.

He would probably have liked to try one of the new powerful parachutes.

These parachutes are so powerful that they can stop a moving car. The car can be speeding along, and within seconds, a parachute on the car's back stops it dead. That's parachute power.

....
FLY A KITE

· ·

Soldiers used to construct huge kites to spy on enemy troops. A very brave soldier would ride the kite high enough to see what was happening on the other side.

The ancient Chinese used kites to punish criminals. They'd force the criminal to ride a kite high into the air. Perhaps terrifying criminals made them change their ways.

Benjamin Franklin flew a kite in a lightning storm. He was conducting an experiment on electricity. He attached a metal key to the kite to see if the metal would conduct the electric charges of the lightning. That experiment took courage, too. The lightning could have killed him.

Here's a kite that won't scare you at all. This kite is nothing but fun.

Here's what you need:

6 plastic flexible straws
6 plastic jumbo straws
Tissue paper
Scissors
Household glue or fingernail polish
Frosted cellophane tape
Kite or other strong light nylon string
Water paints and brushes, if you wish to decorate your kite

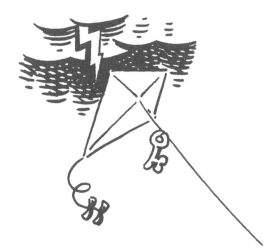

Here's what you do:

1. Cut each flexible straw about 1 1/2 inches (4 cm) on either side of the hinge.

2. Slide one end of each jumbo straw into an end of each flexible hinge piece. Form a six-sided figure with the straws. (A six-sided figure is a hexagon.)

3. Place the six-sided figure on the tissue paper. Cut the tissue paper in the same shape as the figure and about 1/2 inch (1 cm) larger all around.

4. Run a bead of glue or fingernail polish along one of the straws. Bring the tissue paper up over it to glue it in place. Repeat with each straw.

5. Tear off a 4-inch (10 cm) strip of cellophane tape. Tape it around the tissue and straw at the center of one of the six sides. Repeat with more tape at each of the six sides.

6. With the scissors, poke a hole through the tape and paper just inside each straw.

119
•

7. Cut three pieces of the kite string, each about 18 inches (50 cm) long.

8. Poke each end of the three strings through opposite holes. Tie each string in place.

9. Pull the strings up together at the center of the kite. Use the end of the ball of kite string to tie the kite strings together at the center point.

10. If you want to decorate your kite, paint the paper with water colors.

YOUR KITE IS READY TO FLY. THIS IS A GOOD KITE FOR DIPPING AND BOBBING IN THE WIND.

· · · · · · · · · · ·
CONSTRUCT A WINDMILL
· ·

Windmills have been used for centuries to grind flour and pump water. Today they are also used to run machines and to generate electricity.

You can make a simple windmill. It won't do any work for you, but it will be fun to watch.

Here's what you need:

A piece of construction paper or colored plastic

Scissors

Crayons, markers, or paints, if you wish to decorate your windmill

A small hammer

A wire nail

A ¹/₄-inch (6 mm) dowel, 2 to 3 feet (60–90 cm) long

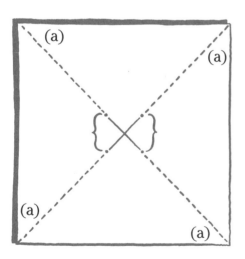

Here's what you do:

1. Cut the construction paper into an 8 ¹/₂-inch (20 cm) square. Or you can make a sturdy windmill from a square of colored plastic. Plastic is especially good if you plan to display the windmill outside.

2. If you wish, use the crayons, markers, or paint to decorate the square on one side. If you plan to display your windmill outside, you can protect it from rain by painting it with acrylic paint.

3. Cut each of the corners of the square toward the center to within ¹/₂ to ³/₄ inch (1–2 cm) of the center.

4. Bring each corner (a) to the center, but don't fold.

5. Use the hammer and the wire nail to tack the corners at the center to the dowel, just below one end.

HOLD YOUR WINDMILL IN THE WIND, AND WATCH IT SPIN.

THROW A CURVE BALL

Scientists used to say the curve ball was impossible.

Baseball players knew they could throw a ball that rises and dips and curves as it flies through the air. But scientists thought the curve was just an optical illusion.

The baseball players were right. Give the ball just the right sort of spin, and it does actually curve. And if it curves just right, it's almost impossible to hit.

Here's how it works.

A baseball is not a perfect round object. It's held together with lines of stitches.

As a baseball spins, the air flows around the stitches. The air flows faster along the bottom of the spinning ball than along the top. Essentially, for the very few seconds that the ball spins between pitcher and batter, the air flowing along the bottom of the ball is holding it up.

Even as the air is holding the ball up, though, gravity is pulling the ball down. As the ball spins, gravity pulls down faster and faster. Of course, the air cannot hold the ball up for very long.

If the curve ball is just right, it breaks downward sharply right over home plate—just in time to surprise and trick the batter.

There are just a few problems with the curve ball.

- A curve-ball pitch is difficult to learn. If you want to pitch baseball, you'll do better to practice your fastball. Developing a good fastball is better use of your practice time.
- And a curve ball is effective only if it curves just right. If it curves right to left, it lines up with the waiting bat, and you've got a home-run in the making.

Overall, it's probably better to be the batter waiting for a curve ball than the pitcher trying to throw one. You need the homeruns on your side.

FIGURE OUT HOW TO LIFT HEAVY LOADS

From ancient times, people have tried to make heavy work lighter. Scientists still wonder how the ancient Egyptians managed to build the great pyramids or how the ancient Britons moved the gigantic stones of Stonehenge.

Perhaps one of the earliest ways to make heavy work lighter was to use an inclined plane. You can try one of your own.

Here's what you need:

A box containing a 10-pound (5 kg) weight, such as a sack of flour

A platform about 2 feet (60 cm) high

A board 4 to 5 feet (1–1 1/2 m) long

Here's what you do:

1. Lift the box to the platform yourself to see what sort of effort you need to move the weight. (Use your legs for lifting. Don't bend over.)

2. Now set the board up so that it slopes from the platform to the floor. You're making an inclined plane.

3. Slide the box up the board to the platform.

NOTICE THAT MOVING THE BOX UP THE RAMP TAKES A BIT LONGER THAN LIFTING IT YOURSELF. BUT THE WORK TAKES ONLY ABOUT HALF THE EFFORT. That really makes a difference if you are moving very many or very heavy weights.

CONSTRUCT A LEVER TO LIFT HEAVY LOADS

Over centuries, levers have helped move the immovable. Even if you're not building a pyramid, you will find that a lever can cut the effort in half.

When you see an old stone wall around a farm, picture the farmer using levers to move heavy stones out of the fields.

You can construct a lever and see how it works.

Here's what you need:

A small rock

A large rock or heavy object to move

A heavy wooden board, pole, or long steel bar.

Here's what you do:

1. Place the small rock near the heavy load. The rock is the part of a lever called the fulcrum.
2. Push the board, pole, or bar as far as you can under the large rock or other heavy object you want to move.
3. Push the small rock you plan to use as a fulcrum as far under the bar as you can.

4. Push down on the bar. You can hope the load will begin to move. A seesaw or teeter totter is a lever. If you are riding a seesaw with a person much heavier than you, how can you lift that person into the air? Move the seesaw board far toward your side, so that the board acts as a lever. Then a small person can keep a bigger person in the air.

WATCH AN OLD MOVIE ABOUT THE MIDDLE AGES SOME TIME, YOU'LL SEE SOLDIERS THROW HEAVY ROCKS ACROSS THE WALLS OF AN ENEMY TOWN. SOMETIMES THEY EVEN THROW THEMSELVES OVER. WHAT DO THEY USE FOR A CATAPULT? A LEVER, OF COURSE.

TELL THE TIME

*H*ere's your chance to tell time without looking at a plain old clock.

You can build a clock that tells time by the sun. You can measure the speed of the earth in just minutes.

You can design a clock that tells you what time it is all around the world.

You can even make yourself into a swinging pendulum.

FIND OUT HOW FAST THE EARTH TURNS

It's a wonder we can stand at all when the ground beneath us is whirling at such high speed. Of course, we are all used to the earth spinning, or else we would certainly fall down.

How fast is the earth spinning?

Here's how to find out.

Here's what you need:

A bright, sunny day

A piece of white paper

Tape

A magnifying glass or the round convex lenses on glasses (such as reading glasses)

A watch with a second hand

Your science notebook and pen

Here's what you do:

1. Put the piece of white paper on a flat place outside where the direct sun will hit it. You may need to tape it down or hold it in place with rocks.

2. Secure the magnifying glass or other lenses a few inches above the paper. Or lean the glass against something. Tilt it so that the light from the sun shines directly through the lens onto the paper. Slant the magnifying glass until the sun creates a circle no more than $1/2$ inch (2 cm) wide on the paper. Be sure the glass does not move.

3. Draw a circle on the paper outlining the circle of light from the magnifying glass. Note the exact time.

4. Now wait until the sunlight leaves the circle, and time exactly how long that takes. The sunlight leaves the circle quickly because the earth is moving quickly.

Here's how to figure the earth's speed:

The earth turns fast enough that the light probably left your circle in about 2 minutes.

During that time, the earth moved $1/2$ degree of its 360-degree rotation. Here's how you can figure that:

Since the earth rotates 360 degrees in 24 hours, you can find the number of degrees it rotates in 1 hour by dividing 360 degrees by 24, the number of hours in a day. The result is 15 degrees, the earth's rotation in 1 hour.

360 degrees ÷ 24 hours = 15 degrees per hour

To find how many degrees the earth rotates in 2 minutes, divide 15 by 30, the number of 2-minute periods in 1 hour. That gives you 0.5 or $1/2$ degree.

15 degrees ÷ 30 = $1/2$ degree

: NOW YOU KNOW HOW FAST
: THE EARTH SPINS.

OUTRUN THE EARTH

Could an airplane outrun the earth? Figure it out.

If it's 12 noon in New York, it's only 9 o'clock in the morning in California. That's 3 hours' time difference—and 3 hours' difference in the position of the sun. While the sun is high in the New York sky, it's still low in the morning sky out west in California.

That's not because the sun is traveling so fast, but because the earth is turning so quickly.

Let's say you want to go from New York to California. Could your plane leave New York at 12 noon and get to California by 12 noon on the west coast?

You plane would have only 3 hours to travel about 3000 miles (5,000 km). To travel as fast as the earth, your plane would have to fly at 1000 miles (1600 km) per hour.

So the answer is yes and no.

You couldn't go that fast on an ordinary airplane.

But you might be able to go that fast on the very fastest Air Force jet. Your plane could even get fuel in the air from another airplane.

Of course, you couldn't go that fast for too long because eventually your plane would need maintenance. And you'd be pretty tired yourself.

THINK HOW OUR EARTH TURNS THAT FAST ALL THE TIME. LUCKY FOR US, OUR PLANET HAS NOT EVER STOPPED OR WORN OUT.

BUILD A SUN CLOCK

Before people had watches or mechanical clocks, they had sun clocks. You ought to know how to tell time by the sun. It's the natural way.

Build a sun clock for your yard.

Here's what you need:

Scissors
Two pieces of heavy cardboard
A drawing compass
A pen
A ruler
Household glue
Masking tape
A directional compass
A watch or clock

Here's what you do:

1. With the scissors, cut one piece of heavy cardboard into a square 12 inches by 12 inches (30 cm × 30 cm).

2. Use the drawing compass to draw a half circle. Place the point of the compass at 6 inches (15 cm), the midpoint of one side of the 12-inch (30 cm) square.

3. Draw a triangle on the second piece of cardboard. Here's how. Measure 12 inches (30 cm) up from one corner, and make a mark. Then make another mark 12 inches (30 cm) over from the same corner. Use your ruler to draw a line from one mark to the other, and back to the first mark. Now you have a triangle that is 12 inches (30 cm) by 12 inches (30 cm) by just under 17 inches (43 cm) .

4. Cut out the cardboard triangle.

5. Use the glue and masking tape to secure a 12-inch (30 cm) side of the triangle upright across the center of the cardboard square. Secure the triangle so that it divides the half circle in two.

6. Take your sun clock outside on a bright day. Use the directional compass to position the sun dial so that the cardboard triangle points directly north.

7. As soon as your watch or clock reaches an hour mark, note where the shadow falls on your sun clock. Label that hour. Then come back in an hour and label the next hour. As the shadow moves, label each hour until you have all the hours of the day.

: NOW YOU CAN TELL TIME BY
: THE SUN.

· · · · · · · · · · ·
CREATE YOUR OWN WORLD CLOCK
· ·

Make this time machine so that you can always tell the time anywhere in the world. You'll especially like this project if you are an artistic and creative type of person.

Here's what you need:

Scissors

Two pieces of posterboard or card-board

Ruler

Drawing compass

A full-circle or half-circle protractor

Colored markers

A two-pronged fastener

Here's what you do:

1. With the scissors, cut one piece of the posterboard or cardboard into a square 15 inches (75 cm) by 15 inches (75 cm) .

2. Make a mark in the exact center of the square. The easiest way to find the center is to draw lines from the opposite corners of the square. Where the two lines come together is the exact center of the square. Punch a small hole at that spot.

3. Open your drawing compass to 6 inches (15 cm). Use it to draw a circle, 12 inches (30 cm) in diameter, on the second piece of posterboard or cardboard.

4. Make a mark in the exact center, and punch a small hole. Cut out the circle.

5. Divide the outside rim (the perimeter) of the circle into 24 equal parts. You are making a clock, but this clock has 24 hours instead of 12 hours. Look on page 132 for two easy ways to mark the 24 equal parts.

6. Write in the hours all around the clock. Begin with 12 noon at the top. At the bottom will be 12 midnight (hour 24).

7. Divide your circle clock in half. Color one side black for the nighttime hours (6 p.m. to 6 a.m.) and the other side white for the daytime hours.
   If you feel creative, draw moon and stars in the nighttime half of the clock, and a sun in the daytime half. (Of course, place your drawings so you can still see the number of the hours clearly.)

8. Fasten the clock to the cardboard square by inserting the two-pronged fastener through each of the small center holes. The clock ought to move easily after you fasten it. Turn the clock until 12 noon is right at the top.

9. On the square, write the names of cities all around the world, and match each one to the right time. Look on page 133 for some places and times that may interest you.

10. When it is 12 noon in Chicago and 1 p.m. (hour 13) in New York, what time is it where you live? Write in your answer opposite the right place on the clock, and draw a special picture for you and your own hometown.

11. Note the times for other places in the world that interest you, too. You really ought to make special drawings for the places where your grandparents and penpals live, for the birthplaces of your ancestors, and for the countries you especially want to visit.

12. If you feel creative, draw pictures around the square to show something about the places. Or paste on pictures from old magazines. You might want to decorate your world clock with flags of countries around the world. Or show what people in different countries are doing, what they are wearing, what they are eating.

13. Think about the times. When you are having breakfast in the United States, what meal might people in Africa or New Zealand be eating? At the time you're in school, what might kids in China or India be doing?

: **NOW YOU CAN TURN YOUR**
: **WORLD CLOCK TO KNOW**
: **WHAT TIME IT IS ALL AROUND**
: **THE WORLD.**

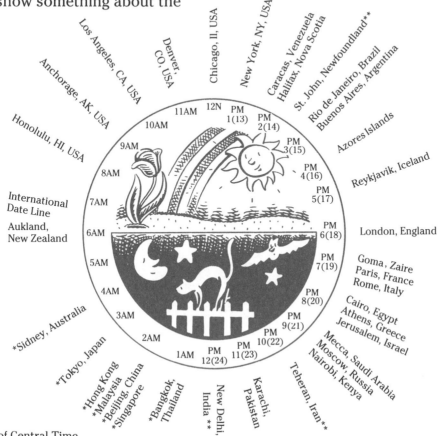

‡ day ahead of Central Time
*half-hour zone

THREE WAYS TO MARK THE 24 HOURS ON YOUR WORLD CLOCK

Here are three easy ways to mark the 24 hours on your world clock:

1. A simple way is to use a full-circle protractor. Place the protractor so that its exact center is over the center mark of the circle. Starting with 0 at the top, make pencil marks around the outside rim at these degrees:

   0, 15, 30, 45, 60, 75, 90, 105, 120, 135, 150, 165, 180, 195, 210, 225, 240, 255, 270, 285, 300, 315, 330, 345

2. Or you can use a half-circle protractor. Mark the first 12 numbers. Then move the protractor to the other half of the circle, and mark 12 numbers again.

3. Or you can use a ruler. Place the ruler on the outside rim of the circle. Adjust it so that it intersects the circle at $1^9/_{16}$ inches or at 4 centimeters. Move to that mark, and measure to the next marks. Make a mark at each spot all around the circle. When you finish, you should have exactly 24 marks.

PLACES AND TIMES FOR YOUR WORLD CLOCK

Here are the names of some places around the world that you might like to write on your clock:

Chicago, USA	12 noon
New York, USA	13 (1 P.M.)
Caracas, Venezuela	14 (2 P.M.)
Rio de Janeiro, Brazil	15 (3 P.M.)
London, England	18 (6 P.M.)
Paris, France	19 (7 P.M.)
Rome, Italy	19 (7 P.M.)
Cairo, Egypt	20 (8 P.M.)
Athens, Greece	20 (8 P.M.)
Jerusalem, Israel	20 (8 P.M.)
Moscow, Russia	21 (9 P.M.)
Dubai, United Arab Emirates	22 (10 P.M.)
Karachi, Pakistan	23 (11 P.M.)
* New Delhi, India	23:30 (11:30 P.M.)

* Bangkok, Thailand	1 A.M.
* Beijing, China	2 A.M.
* Hong Kong	2 A.M.
* Tokyo, Japan	3 A.M.
* Sydney, Australia	4 A.M.
* Auckland, New Zealand	6 A.M.
International Date Line	6 or 7 A.M.
Honolulu, Hawaii, USA	8 A.M.
Anchorage, Alaska, USA	9 A.M.
Los Angeles, USA	10 A.M.
Denver, USA	11 A.M.

Note: The places starred are on the other side of the International Date Line. So it's not only a different time there, it's also the next day. When it's still Sunday in the United States, for example, it's already Monday in Asia and Australia.

SWING IN TIME

You'll find this hard to believe, but each swing of any pendulum of the same length takes the same amount of time. That's true no matter how high the pendulum swings. And it's true no matter how heavy the weight on the end of the pendulum.

That's why a pendulum is good for telling time.

Try an experiment on the playground.

Here's what you need:

A swing

Two people of different weights

A stopwatch or a watch with a second hand

Paper and pencil

Here's what you do:

1. Have one person swing slowly. The other person uses the watch to time the exact number of swings in 1 minute. To be sure the count is right, count just at the top of the forwards motion of one full swing. (You may need a third person to help make sure you count the correct number of swings during exactly 1 minute.) Be sure to write down the result.
2. Now have the same person swing hard and fast. Count the number of swings in 1 minute again.
3. Have a second person swing slowly. Since this person is a different weight, you might think the number of swings would be different. Count the number in 1 minute to see.
4. Now count the number of swings in 1 minute when the other person swings hard and fast.

Number of Swings per Minute
Lighter person swinging slowly
Lighter person swinging fast
Heavier person swinging slowly
Heavier person swinging fast

IF YOU COUNT THE SWINGS RIGHT, YOU FIND THAT ALL THESE NUMBERS ARE THE SAME. EACH SWING OF THE SAME PENDULUM TAKES THE SAME AMOUNT OF TIME— EVEN WHEN THE WEIGHT ON THE PENDULUM IS HUMAN.

· · · · · · · · · ·
STRING TOGETHER A PENDULUM
· ·

You can keep track of time without a clock. String together a pendulum, and find out how.

Here's what you need:

Weights of various sizes (We suggest you use washers. But you can use just about anything that you can tie to the end of a string.)

String lengths from 30 inches to 40 inches (75 cm to 150 cm)

A hook in the ceiling (Some kind person may let you remove a hanging plant so that you can use the hook for a while.)

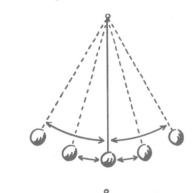

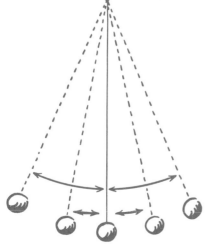

Here's what you do:

1. Tie a weight to one end of a length of string. Tie the other end of the hook. Your string can be any length, but there's a special reason you might want to try a 39-inch (1 meter) length first. Then try other lengths as well.

2. Start your pendulum swinging. Count the swings for 1 minute.

3. Now tie on a different weight, and count the swings in 1 minute again.

4. Keep trying different weights with different lengths of string.

Here's what you should discover:

1. The shorter the pendulum (in this case, the string), the shorter the distance it swings. Because a short pendulum does not have to swing far, it swings more times in 1 minute than a long pendulum does.

2. Different weights do not change the number of swings of the pendulum. You can see that, when a pendulum is moving slowly, it moves a shorter distance in all. When it moves faster, it moves a longer total distance.

   You can see a pendulum in a grandfather clock.

The pendulum in a grandfather clock is always 39 inches (1 meter) long. (That's why we told you to use a 39-inch string in step 1.) A 39-inch pendulum swings 60 times a minute, so it's convenient to count off 60 seconds every minute.

Of course, a 39-inch (1 meter) pendulum makes for a very tall clock. Some fine old grandfather clocks are so tall that they won't fit in modern houses.

SEE IF YOU CAN MAKE A 39-INCH (1 meter) STRING SWING 60 TIMES A MINUTE.

FORECAST THE WEATHER

*Y*ou can learn a lot about the weather on television.

But television tells you about weather all over the place. Perhaps you'd like to forecast the weather right in the spot where you are now.

You can build your own weather forecasting station, complete with your own homemade devices.

You can build a rain gauge for your weather station.

You can construct your own wind vane to tell the direction of the wind. You can make an anemometer to measure how fast the wind is blowing.

You can add a barometer. You can even construct a device to measure the moisture in the air.

With your weather station, you can tell people how comfortable they will feel on a hot day. You can warn people when a dangerous storm is approaching. You can be on top of the weather.

Weather forecasting is most fun if you have a weather notebook. Then you can keep a record of weather ups and downs. And you can compare weather from one season to the next, or one year to the next.

· · · · · · · · · ·
HELP WITH TELEVISION WEATHER REPORTS
· ·

Most local television stations welcome weather reports from people at home. Call in your report, and you might get to be an official weather watcher. You might even hear your name on the air.

· · · · · · · · · ·
ALASKA AND HAWAII TOGETHER
· ·

The hottest temperature ever recorded in Alaska is 100°F (38°C). The hottest temperature ever recorded in Hawaii is 100°F.

As you might expect, though, Alaska wins as the coldest place in the United States. In 1971, for instance, the temperature at Prospect Creek, Alaska, sank to 79.8° below zero (or minus 62.1°C).

That's so cold that you couldn't use a regular thermometer to record the temperature. The mercury in the thermometer would freeze.

What you might not guess is that the rainiest places in the United States are in Hawaii. Mount Waialeale on the island of Kauai can average 460 inches (11 m) of rain a year. And some years, Kuki on the island of Maui gets more than 578 inches (14 m) of rain. Imagine if that happened in New York City, where people are used to about 44 inches (110 cm) of rain in a year.

What's the average rainfall where you live?

Keep Up with the Hot and the Cold

Find out if the temperature where you are is different from the reports on radio or television. And find out if your high and low readings are different from temperature listings in the newspaper.

Here's how to find the average daytime temperature where you are right now.

Here's what you need:

An outdoor thermometer
Your weather notebook and pen

Here's what you do:

1. Write the outdoor temperature each hour for 10 hours. (You can keep track for however many hours you want. But you need a good long sample of highs and lows.)

2. Add up all the temperatures in the 10 hours, and divide the sum by 10. Now you have the average temperature.

3. Or find the average of the temperatures at 1 particular hour every day for 1 week.

4. Note the highest temperature and the lowest for the day. Then the next day, check newspaper listings of high and low temperatures.

: **Now You Know The**
: **Temperatures Where You**
: **Are.**

Temperatures are different from one place to another, even when the two places are very close.

FIND OUT HOW THE SUN TRANSFERS HEAT

The sun warms up air, soil, and water—but all at different rates.

The smooth, shiny surface of water reflects the rays of the sun. The rough, dark surface of the ground tends to absorb the rays of the sun. So the sun takes longer to heat water than to heat the soil. Here's how to make sure.

Here's what you need:

A bright, sunny day
Two identical cups or jars
A thermometer
Water and soil
Your weather notebook and pen

Here's what you do:

1. Fill one cup or jar with water, and fill the other with soil. Insert the thermometer into each, and note the temperatures.

2. Set the two cups in a sunny place.

3. After 15 minutes, note the temperatures again.

4. After 30 minutes, note the temperatures a third time. Which heats more quickly—the water or the soil?

5. Put both cups in the refrigerator, and check the temperatures after 15 minutes. Then note the temperatures again after 30 minutes. Which cools more quickly—the water or the soil?

You'll find that, although the water heats more slowly than the soil, it holds the heat longer. That's the reason the air is cooler near oceans or lakes in summer than it is away from water. And in winter, the ocean or lake air is warmer.

NOW YOU KNOW WHY, ON A HOT SUMMER DAY, YOU HAVE MORE CHANCE OF COOLING DOWN BY SWIMMING IN WATER THAN BY ROLLING IN DIRT. AND YOU LOOK BETTER CLEAN.

Do Something About Sun Power

A shiny surface reflects the rays of the sun. A dull, rough surface soaks up the rays of the sun.

Colors make a difference, too. Light surfaces reflect. Dark surfaces absorb.

Here's how to tell:

Here's what you need:

A bright, sunny day

A white cup or jar

A black cup or jar, the same size

Note: You can color paper cups. Or cover glass jars with black and white construction paper. Or cover one jar with aluminum foil and the other with black paper.

Water

A thermometer

Your weather notebook and pen

Here's what you do:

1. Fill each cup with an equal amount of tap water (of the same temperature). Cover each with a lid or with a piece of paper. Set the cups in a sunny window.

2. After 30 minutes, measure the temperature of the water in each cup. The water in the white cup ought to be cooler than the water in the black cup.

> **Now You Know Why You Have More Chance Of Keeping Cool On a Hot Summer Day If You Wear White Clothes. And You Can Keep Warmer In Winter If You Wear Dark Clothes.**

MAKE YOUR OWN RAIN

You get rain just at dewpoint. That's the point at which water vapor begins to condense into liquid raindrops. You can create dewpoint in your own kitchen.

Here's what you need:

A large pot of water boiling on the stove

A second, smaller pot

Ice cubes

A little cold water

Caution: You need adult help with boiling water.

Here's what you do:

1. As water in the large pot begins to boil, fill the small pot with ice cubes and add a little cold water.
2. Hold the smaller pot over the larger pot.

   Caution: The steam from the boiling water condenses and changes back into drops of water on the bottom of the small pot. As the drops get larger and too heavy to cling to the bottom of the small pot, they will rain back into the boiling pot.

NOW YOU HAVE YOUR OWN PERSONAL RAIN. YOUR OWN RAIN WORKS A BIT LIKE NATURE'S RAIN.

Water in the atmosphere is constantly changing its form. Water goes back and forth from vapor to liquid to ice or snow.

Water vapor evaporates from lakes, oceans, rivers, or even small puddles. As water vapor rises into the colder atmosphere, it cools and forms clouds. Cool air cannot hold as much water as warm air does. When the air gets too cool to hold all the water vapor, even in the form of clouds, the water becomes rain or snow.

Then it falls back to earth to form lakes, river, and puddles. The cycle starts all over again.

MEASURE RAINDROPS

Measure the sizes of raindrops. Maybe you can find out if raindrops are different sizes in different circumstances.

Here's what you need:

A rainy day or evening
A piece of cardboard
A ruler
Your weather notebook and pen

Here's what you do:

1. Put out the piece of cardboard when it first starts to rain. Be sure to bring the cardboard in quickly before the rain soaks it. If that happens, you will not be able to see the size of the drops.

2. Using the ruler, quickly measure the raindrops. The size can vary from $1/100$ inch up to $1/4$ inch. (That's between 4 and 50 millimeters.)

3. Check the size of raindrops at other times of the rain.

4. Keep a chart in your weather notebook. Write down the raindrop sizes, and decide if you see a pattern. Here are factors you might consider:

   - The date and season of the year
   - The size of the raindrops
   - The outside temperature
   - The length of the rain shower
   - Beginning, middle, or end of the rain shower—when you collected the raindrops
   - The kind of rain—heavy or light

   - The way the rain fell—quickly or slowly
   - The wind, if any
   - The type of clouds

Here's a hint about one rainfall pattern you may find. Did you know that tiny raindrops may take as long as an hour to reach the ground? They weigh so little that they blow around in the air currents. Heavy raindrops travel more quickly.

> NOW YOU CAN FIND OUT THE DIFFERENT SIZES OF RAINDROPS. AND THAT CAN HELP YOU DECIDE ABOUT WEATHER PATTERNS.

LOOK AT THE CLOUDS FOR WEATHER CHANGES

You can tell a lot about the weather by looking at the clouds. Here are a few of the major types:

1. Cirrus clouds are high, thin, and wispy. They mean fair weather.

2. Cumulus clouds are flat at the bases, and then billow up high and fluffy. They can mean light rain showers.

3. Nimbus clouds lie in straight layers. Sometimes they look enough like fish scales that people describe them as "a mackerel sky." Nimbus clouds usually forecast a change in weather. They can mean that a long period of rain is on the way.

4. Towering cumulonimbus clouds are large and tall, dark and threatening. (The name of these clouds shows you they are a combination of "cumulus" and "nimbus.") They often bring heavy storms with thunder and lightning.

LOOK UPWARD FOR A QUICK WEATHER FORECAST.

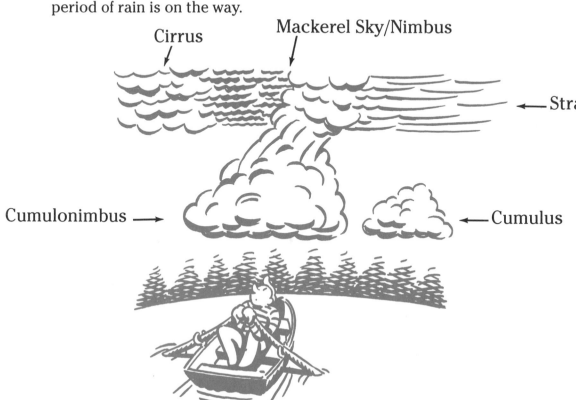

Cirrus

Mackerel Sky/Nimbus

Stra

Cumulonimbus →

← Cumulus

MAKE YOUR OWN RAIN GAUGE

A rain gauge is a must for your weather station. You'll want to measure how many inches of rain fall in your garden.

Here's what you need:

A #10 can (or a large glass jar with straight sides and a mouth as large as the bottom)

A ruler

Your weather notebook and pen

Here's what you do:

1. Set the can or jar where it won't tip over. Find a place where extra rain won't splash into the can and where bugs and leaves won't get into it. You might try putting it up high or protecting it by packing sand around it.

2. After a rainfall, measure the depth of the water in the can with the ruler, and write down the number of inches. Be sure to pour out that rainwater before you start again.

YOU CAN MEASURE THE AMOUNT OF RAIN IN ONE RAINFALL, OR YOU CAN KEEP TRACK OF THE RAIN OVER A LONG PERIOD OF TIME. Rainfall measurements from the past help forecast future amounts of rain.

MAGNIFY BEAUTIFUL SNOW CRYSTALS— EVEN IN THE SUMMER

Of course, it's most fun to look at real snow crystals. But you can also scrape some frost from a freezer and look at those crystals.

If you are an artistic sort of person, you'll particularly like drawing snow crystals.

Here's what you need:

Snow or frost crystals
A magnifying glass
Paper and pen or pencil

Here's what you do:

1. Look at a snow or frost crystal under the magnifying glass. You will see that it is not solid. Instead, it is like a lace doily with six sides.

2. Now look at another snow crystal. As far as anyone knows, each snow crystal is different from every other, though they all have six sides.

3. If you wish, draw pictures of snow crystals.

NOW YOU HAVE YOUR OWN ARTISTIC SNOW CRYSTALS.

Like rain, snow forms from fine water droplets in the clouds. But these water droplets become supercooled to below the freezing point.

When the supercooled droplets of water collide with tiny dust particles, snow crystals begin to form.

Did you know that snow crystals can form in the skies when it's very hot on the ground below? Of course, the crystals will melt before they reach the ground.

TELL THE DIFFERENCE BETWEEN RAIN AND SNOW

One inch of rain is about the same as 5 to 12 inches (12 to 30 cm) of snow. You can tell by letting your rain gauge fill with snow and then melting the snow. You'll see the gauge is much less full when the snow turns to water.

Why? Crystals are filled with air. When the snow melts, the air is freed, and so the melted snow takes up much less room.

WHICH WAY IS THE WIND BLOWING?

We describe the wind by the direction it blows from, not the direction it blows to. A north wind is blowing from the north. A south wind is blowing from the south.

Wind direction can help forecast the weather. In the northeastern part of the United States, for instance, a winter wind from the northeast can mean a blizzard. In summer, an east wind may bring rain with it.

Do you remember Christopher Robin sitting with his Pooh Bear and thinking about the north wind blowing in snow? Even a Pooh Bear can forecast weather by watching the wind.

BUILD A WIND VANE

You'll want a wind vane for your weather station.

With a wind vane, you can always tell from what direction the wind is blowing. But keep this one out of the rain and away from extremely strong wind.

Here's what you need:

Scissors

A piece of light cardboard

A plastic drinking straw

A pencil with an eraser on top

Light wire (Picture-hanging wire works well.)

A straight pin

A small container, such as a plastic margarine tub or a plant pot

Play-Doh® or modeling clay, or something else to fill the container, such as sand, soil, or beans

Directional compass

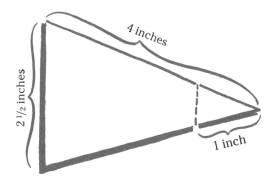

Here's what you do:

1. With the scissors, cut the cardboard into a triangle with two 4-inch (10 cm) sides and one 2 1/2-inch (6 cm) side.

2. Mark 1 inch (3 cm) back from the tip where the two 4-inch (10 cm) sides come together. Then draw a line straight across.

Note: You can use the diagram as a pattern.

3. Cut on the line you just drew, so that you have two pieces of cardboard remaining, one triangular piece and one four-sided piece. The triangular piece will serve as the arrow pointer, and the other piece will be the tail. If you're feeling creative, you can paint or color both the arrow pointer and the tail.

4. Make a slit about 1 inch long at the end of the straw. Insert the cardboard tail into the slit. Make a slit about 1/2 inch (2 cm) long in the other end of the straw (in the same direction), and insert the arrow pointer.

5. To fix directions for your wind vane, cut the wire into two pieces, each about 20 inches (25 cm) long.

At either end of one length of wire, form an N and an S. Form and E and a W at either end of the other length of wire.

Then wind the center of each piece of wire around the pencil twice, just below the eraser.

Be sure to get the wind directions in the right order: north, east, south, west.

6. Put the pin through the straw about 2 inches (5 cm) from the tail. Insert the end of the pin into the eraser.

7. In the small container, put about 1 1/2 to 2 inches (4–5 cm) of the Play-Doh® or modeling clay. Or put in sand, soil, or beans. Insert

the pencil, point down. Make sure the clay holds it firmly.

8. Find a good, windy place outside for your wind vane. Make sure there is room for it to turn freely.

9. Use a directional compass to find out which way is north. Then set your wind vane so that the "N" wire points north.

> Now You Have A Wind Vane To Tell You The Direction Of The Wind. Put It Out Only On Good Days.

· · · · · · · · · · ·
MEASURE THE WIND
· ·

You can build a device to measure how fast the wind is blowing. You'll want one of these for your weather station.

Here's what you need:

Four paper cups with handles

A plate, rigid plastic or heavy paper

A stapler

A long pin or nail

A 1-inch-diameter (3 cm) (dowel or other long, thin stick

Here's what you do:

1. Color or mark one of the paper cups so that it stands out from the others.

2. Mark the exact center of the plate. Punch a hole there. Staple the handles of the four cups to the edge of the plate, so that the openings in the cups all face in the same direction.

3. Insert the long pin or nail through the hole in the plate, then into the dowel or stick. Secure the stick in dry ground.

4. Watch the cups turn in the wind. Use the marked cup to help you count the turns. The number of turns per minute tells you how fast the wind is blowing.

> NOW YOU HAVE A WAY TO
> MEASURE THE SPEED OF THE
> WIND. THE FANCY NAME FOR A
> DEVICE OF THIS SORT IS
> ANEMOMETER.

HOW TO NAME A HURRICANE

When people first started thinking up names for hurricanes, they seemed to settle on the first word that came to mind. There was a hurricane, for instance, named "Dog." Some names, like "Blustery" or "Windy," at least made sense.

The person who named a hurricane "Easy" was probably guilty of wishful thinking, since hurricanes are anything but easy.

World War II pilots began a tradition of naming storms after their wives and girl friends. They even named one Bess, after Mrs. Truman, the wife of the President. When President Truman objected, they named one Harry after the President himself.

In the 1950s, the Weather Bureau began issuing an alphabetical list of women's names for the hurricanes they expected each season.

But that wasn't fair. Women are not like hurricanes. Many women felt a little insulted at the idea.

By the late 1970s, the Weather Bureau began naming hurricanes after both men and women.

Now men can feel offended at hurricane naming, just the same as women, presidents, and maybe even dogs.

What's the Difference Between a Watch and a Warning

A *weather watch* means the meteorologist is worried that dangerous weather is near.

A weather warning means the dangerous weather is already here.

Find out what you should do to protect yourself during different sorts of dangerous weather.

Count How Far Away Lightning Is Striking

Where there is thunder, there is always lightning.

Why? Bolts of lightning are actually huge (and dangerous) electric sparks jumping from cloud to cloud or to the ground.

As the lightning zigzags through the air, it creates heat and a sudden space where there is no air.

Air very rapidly expands to fill the gap. When the air comes together, that causes the boom of the thunder.

Sound travels much more slowly than light, so you see the lightning before you hear the thunder. In fact, since light travels at 186,000 miles (299,000 km) per second, you see the lightning almost immediately. By contrast, sound takes about 5 seconds to travel 1 mile (1.6 km).

So you can tell how far away the lightning is by counting the seconds between the flash and the boom. (Count slowly. A second is just a little longer than you might think.) Then divide by 5. That's the number of miles away the lightning is.

Here's a sample: You hear the thunder 10 seconds after you see the lightning. Divide by 5. The storm is 2 miles (3.2 km) away.

. . . .
MEASURE WATER IN THE AIR
. . . .

Your weather station needs a device that measures moisture in the air. That information will help you predict how comfortable you'll be in the heat.

The amount of water in the air is the humidity. Although humidity is invisible, it makes a difference in how you feel.

When the humidity is low, you usually feel good even if the temperature is high.

But when the air is already full of water, drops of sweat stay on your skin and cannot evaporate easily. You feel sticky all over—and very uncomfortable.

Here's how to measure the humidity in the air.

Here's what you need:

Two standard thermometers

Two rubber bands, one heavy, one light

Wet cotton gauze (or a scrap of wet cotton 2 or more inches [5 cm] long)

A tall bottle or wooden stand to which you can attach a thermometer

A cup of water

Your weather notebook and pen

Here's what you do:

1. Keep track of the temperature outside on one of your thermometers. You may already have one installed somewhere in a window.

2. Use the light rubber band to wrap the bulb of the other thermometer in the wet gauze. Leave an end of gauze sticking out.

3. Use the heavy rubber band to attach the wet-bulb thermometer to the tall bottle or wooden stand. Then put the gauze end into a container of water. The water will travel up through the gauze to keep the bulb wet.

4. Soon you will see a difference in the two temperatures. If the humidity in the air is low, the air can accept more water. So water will evaporate rapidly from the wet-bulb thermometer. As the water evaporates, it carries heat with it. In that case, the temperature on the wet-bulb thermometer will read lower than the temperature on the dry thermometer.

5. If the humidity in the air is high, though, the air does not easily accept more water. So water from the wet-bulb thermometer will not evaporate rapidly, and the temperature will remain closer to the temperature of the air. The greater the difference between the two temperatures, the more humidity is in the air.

> NOW YOU HAVE A WAY TO
> MEASURE THE AMOUNT OF
> HUMIDITY IN THE AIR. AND ON
> A HOT SUMMER DAY, YOU CAN
> PREDICT HOW COMFORTABLE
> YOU WILL BE.

MAKE AIR HOLD UP WATER

. . . .

Air is so powerful that it can keep water from spilling. This experiment shows how air presses from every direction. Air presses down, but it presses up, also, with the same power.

Here's what you need:

A thin skewer or ice pick

A 1-pint (500 ml) plastic bottle with a plastic cap (A disposable soft-drink bottle will do.)

Water

Here's what you do:

1. Use the skewer or ice pick to make a small hole in the base of the plastic bottle and another small hole in the center of the plastic cap.

   : *Caution: You need adult help*
   : *with this.*

2. Do the rest of this experiment over a sink. Holding your finger over the hole in the base, fill the bottle with water. Screw the plastic cap onto the bottle. Hold your finger over the hole in the cap, also.

3. Turn the bottle upside down. Remove your finger from the hole in the cap. What happens?

4. Still holding the bottle upside down, remove your finger from the hole in the base, and see what happens.

5. Put your fingers back over the hole in the cap and the hole in the base, and turn the bottle right side up. Remove your finger from the hole in the base. What happens?

6. Now remove your fingers from both holes, and see what happens.
   Pressure from the air keeps the water from pouring out of the bottle when only one hole is open. Air presses all around, whether the bottle is upside down or not.
   When you open the second hole, air can enter and equalize the air pressure. Then the water drips out.

7. Now cover the hole in the cap with your finger, and shake the bottle slightly. Some water will come out of the hole, and you ought to see a bubble of air rise up in the bottle. The air replaces the water you shook out and equalizes the air pressure.

   : **NOW YOU SEE HOW YOU CAN**
   : **MAKE AIR HOLD UP WATER.**

··········
PERFORM AIR PRESSURE MAGIC
·······························

Here's a dramatic way to make air hold up water. Maybe your friends will think you're a magician.

Here's what you need:

A glass with a smooth rim
Water
A piece of stiff cardboard

Here's what you do:

1. Do this experiment over a sink. Fill the glass partly with water.
2. Place the piece of cardboard over the opening in the glass.
3. Holding the cardboard tightly in place, turn the glass upside down.
4. Remove your hand from the cardboard. What happens?

IF YOU HAVE DONE THE EXPERIMENT CORRECTLY, THE CARDBOARD WILL STAY IN PLACE OVER THE MOUTH OF THE GLASS. THE WATER WILL NOT POUR OUT. The upward pressure of the air holds the cardboard in place.

MAKE YOUR OWN BAROMETER

A barometer measures air pressure, and the measurement helps predict the weather. On clear days, air pressure is usually high.

When the air pressure lowers (and your barometer drops), a storm may be on the way.

Every good weather station needs a barometer

Here's what you need:

Scissors

A balloon

A small jar, such as a peanut butter jar

A heavy rubber band or strong thread

A large, empty thread spool

A pen

A small index card

A small rubber band or thread

A drinking straw

Household glue

Your weather notebook and pen

Here's what you do:

1. With the scissors, cut a piece of balloon large enough to cover the mouth of the jar and extend over the sides. Secure the balloon piece with the rubber band or strong thread. Be sure the entire mouth of the jar is covered so that no more air can enter the bottle.

2. Roll up the index card so that it will fit over the pencil. Secure the ends with the small rubber band or thread. Slide the rolled-up index card over the pencil, and support the pencil in the thread spool.

3. Cut the straw slant-wise to create a point. With the pointed end

sticking out, glue the other end of the straw to the center of the balloon piece.

4. Set the jar on a shelf with the spool and index card. With your pen, mark on the card the exact place the straw points. That will be your starting point. As the air pressure changes, the straw will move up and down.

5. Watch your barometer from day to day. When the air pressure is high, it will press hard on the air in the bottle, and the other end of the straw will point higher. When the air pressure lowers, the air pressure in the bottle will push up, and the point of the straw will go down.

NOW YOU HAVE ONE WAY TO KEEP TRACK OF AIR PRESSURE.

. . . .

TELL THE TRUTH ABOUT WEATHER SAVINGS

. . . .

Can you tell which of these weather sayings are true?

1. A bee is never caught in the rain.
   That's true. Bees are sensitive to humidity in the air. As the humidity rises and rain is near, bees seem to know that it's time to head back to the hive.

2. Red sky at night, sailors delight. Red sky in the morning, sailor take warning.
   There's truth in this one, too. In the evening the sunset may look unusually red because the sunlight is passing through dust particles—but only if the weather is dry and fair, with no rain in sight. If faraway storm clouds blocked the sunset, the sky would be gray, and a storm might be moving eastward.
   At sunrise, on the other hand, a deep red sky may mean that rain and clouds are still to the west and may be about to move eastward. Rain might be on the way.

3. A ring around the moon means rain or snow.
   That's another true saying. Clouds in the atmosphere, which may bring rain or snow, cause the moonlight to spread out, and so we see what appears to be a ring around the moon.

4. Dew on the grass in the morning means a fair day.
   People used to call dew-specked cobwebs "fairy wash." Yes, dew can mean a fair day because dew forms when the ground is warm and damp but the air above is cool and dry.

5. If you don't like the weather, wait a few minutes.
   Mark Twain said this about the ever-changing weather of New England. It's true in many other places, too.

6. The wind on the day of your birth might tell your fortune if you believed the folklore.
   According to the folklore, an east wind foretells wealth. A west wind is a sign of poverty, alas. A south wind means interesting friends. A north wind indicates a life of war. And no wind at all foretells a life of foolishness. But don't believe a word of it.

7. Drink from a river just at the point where a rainbow shines through the water, and you will instantly change sex.
   Now how could we possibly find out if this were true?
   Anyway, we'd rather look for the pot of gold at the end of the rainbow.

TRAVEL TO THE MOON AND BEYOND

Would you like to set foot on the moon or travel to other planets?

Even before you become a space traveler, you can find out something about what's out there. You can stand right here on earth and calculate the size of the moon. You can tell at a glance the difference between a planet and a star.

You can spot satellites and maybe even an unidentified flying object (UFO). Who knows? You may be on your way to out-of-this-world travel.

· · · · · · · · · ·

CHART THE PHASES OF THE MOON

· ·

Why can't you always see a full moon?

The sun shines on the moon, just as it shines on the earth. At any given time, half of the moon is in daylight, and it's night on the other half.

But as the moon rotates around the earth, we see only portions of its daylight half. So each night (or day) of the month, we see a slightly different phase of the moon.

You can have a beautiful experience keeping track of the phases of the moon.

Here what you do:

1. Consult an almanac or calendar to see the phase of the moon as you begin. Then go out every night (or day) to see how the moon has changed. (In each of its phases, the moon rises at different times.)

2. Draw a picture each night. Most nights you will be able to see at least a small change in the phase of the moon.

3. Keep notes for 29 nights so that you can see the whole cycle of the moon. Of course, you'll miss a few nights when clouds get in your way. On those nights, you could draw a picture of the phase you think the moon has reached. Keep notes on how clouds, rain, and snow change the look of the moon, or make it disappear altogether.

Here's how to label the phases of the moon:

- New moon (when the moon is invisible)
- Waxing crescent (the first thin sliver of moon)
- First quarter (a half moon)
- Waxing gibbous (a three-quarter moon)
- Full moon
- Waning gibbous (back to three-quarters)
- Last quarter (back to half moon)
- Waning crescent (the last thin sliver before the next new moon)

> **NOW YOU CAN ALWAYS KNOW HOW THE MOON IS SHINING.**

HOLD A NEW MOON CONTEST

Once a month, the moon is invisible.

Who can catch the first glimpse of the crescent moon returning?

This is a contest where no one can lose. The first glimpse is so beautiful that it is worth seeing even if someone else sees it before you.

Here's what you do:

1. Consult an almanac to learn the exact hour of the new moon. That's when you cannot see the moon at all.

2. Soon after that hour, look for your first glimpse of the returning moon.

   Usually you cannot see even the thinnest crescent moon until at least 30 hours have passed since the new moon. But occasionally, in very clear weather, you can see the first thin shine in just over 20 hours.

   The moon sliver will show itself first in mid or late afternoon. You'll see it trailing after the sun, just a bit higher in the sky than the sun is.

   : *Caution: Do not look directly*
   : *at the sun.*

   You may have specially good luck with your sighting in springtime.

NOW YOU CAN LOOK FOR SOMETHING BEAUTIFUL EVERY 28 DAYS.

(And you can look for something beautiful in nature all the other days, too.)

LOOK FOR EARTHSHINE ON THE MOON

Sometimes you can see the unlit part of the moon shining softly.

That soft shine is a sort of double reflection. Our own earth reflects the light of the sun onto the moon, and the moon (sometimes) reflects it gently back toward us. This lovely glow goes by the name of earthshine.

The fanciful explanation for earthshine is that you are seeing the old moon in the young moon's arms.

LOOK FOR BLUE MOON

You've heard the phrase "once in a blue moon" to describe something that doesn't happen very often. Certainly you don't see a blue moon very often.

During unusual conditions in the atmosphere the moon can sometimes shine through as blue. But, of course, that happens only "once in a blue moon."

Another sort of "blue moon" is a full moon that falls twice in the same month. Then a full moon shines about the first of the month and again at the very end of the month. But that's rare, too.

You'll probably have to wait a long time to see a blue moon. Look at the calendar to see if the second kind of blue moon will shine any time this year.

· · · · · · · · · ·
DRAW A MAP OF THE MOON
· ·

Just standing here on earth, you can see markings on the moon, evidence of the mountains, the craters, and the flat territories called marias. (*Maria* is the Latin word for seas, although really the marias of the moon have no water.)

Try drawing a map of what you see on the moon.

This is a good project for an artistic sort of person.

Here are some hints for moon map-making:

1. Draw your map at sunset, rather than during the day or in full dark. You will see the markings better when the moon is not quite full and not totally bright.

2. Don't let your sketch show just a bright circle with deep, dark shadings. Try to sketch in the lighter shadows of the moon as well.

3. This is a good project to do with friends. When you each draw your own map, you can compare what you saw. Draw your maps at the same time and place, and give yourselves the same time limits.

4. Don't look at a professional map of the moon until you have tried your own. You want to discover what you can see, not what someone else tells you to see. Your own map may be more beautiful anyway.

5. But after you finish your own map, you'll want to look at a professional map. You can read the strange names of all the places on the moon. Then you may be able to look at your map and label some of the moon mountains and marias.

Particularly, look for the Sea of Tranquillity. That's where Neil Armstrong first set foot in 1969.

6. Use your imagination to look for shapes on the moon. You can probably see what people call "the man in the moon." His face seems to show a crooked grin, a tiny nose, and big, tearful eyes. Look at the top of a full moon, and you may be able to see the shape of a long-eared rabbit. The ancient Aztec people thought they saw a rabbit that a god had thrown against the moon. The ancient Chinese saw a rabbit or a toad. The ancient Greeks had an interesting idea about the markings on the moon. They thought the moon might act as a mirror to reflect the oceans and continents of the earth.

> **NOW YOU HAVE YOUR OWN MOON ART. AND NOW YOU KNOW WHO "THE MAN ON THE MOON" REALLY IS**

What other shapes can you see when you look at the moon?

SEE 59 PERCENT OF THE MOON

Did you know that the moon revolves around our planet, Earth, so that it always turns the same face toward us? Standing here on Earth, we cannot see the other side of the moon.

You'd think that would mean that we can see only that one side of the moon. Actually, we can see a little more.

The moon orbits Earth so that it is sometimes closer and sometimes farther away. And its speed varies. As a result, the moon wobbles a bit.

Because of the wobble, astronomers on Earth have been able to look at about 59 percent of the moon's surface.

And now, of course, we can send spaceships to take photographs of the dark side of the moon. So we are on our way to solving moon mysteries.

LOOK FOR THE MOON ILLUSION

The moon might be tricking our eyes.

The trick is called the moon illusion.

Look at the full moon when it is low on the horizon. It will appear huge and its color will be bright, sometimes even reddish. Look at the full moon high overhead, and it appears small and much lighter in color.

The moon can look twice to four times as big on the horizon as it does overhead.

No one is sure why this happens.

One theory is that, when the moon is low on the horizon, the layers of the atmosphere distort our view of it. They make it seem larger than it appears when we see it overhead.

A new theory is that our eyes are tricking us. The large moon is just an illusion—but an illusion that we all share.

Here's a way to figure out your own explanation.

MEASURE THE SIZE OF THE MOON— WITHOUT MATH

Since no one knows for sure what causes the moon illusion, why don't you try to find out?

Develop your own theory.

Here's what you need:

A clear night with a full or nearly full moon in view

A penny, dime, or quarter

Here's what you do:

1. Go out early in the evening when the moon is close to the horizon. Hold the coin at arm's length. See how large the moon looks in comparison. Now compare the size of the coin to the stars in the same part of the sky. And compare the coin to the sizes of trees and buildings nearby. You may get a sense of how your eyes have been tricking you about the size of the moon.

2. Go out later in the evening, and use the coin to compare how the moon looks when it is high overhead.

3. Keep notes at different times and on different nights.

Here's what you may see:

1. You may notice that we often see the moon as larger than it really is in comparison to objects on earth such as trees and houses—or coins.

2. If you keep notes, you may be able to tell the positions of the moon or the weather conditions that make it look larger or smaller. Sometimes even the angle at which you look can make a difference.

> NOW YOU CAN HAVE YOUR OWN IDEAS ABOUT HOW THE MOON TRICKS OUR EYES.

· · · · · · · · · · ·
MEMORIZE THE PLANETS WITHOUT REALLY TRYING

· ·

Here's an easy way to remember the planets of our solar system, beginning with Mercury, closest to the sun, and going all the way out to Pluto, farthest from the sun.

Just remember this sentence:

MOTHER VERY ENTHUSIASTICALLY MADE A
JELLY SANDWICH UNDER NO PROTEST.

This silly sentence gives clues to the order of the planets:

MERCURY, VENUS, EARTH, MARS, ASTEROIDS,
JUPITER, SATURN, URANUS, NEPTUNE, AND PLUTO

NOW YOU KNOW A MNEMONIC, AN EASY WAY TO JOG YOUR MEMORY ABOUT THE PLANETS. (When you say mnemonic, don't pronounce the "m.")

DRAW THE SOLAR SYSTEM

This is a good project for several artistic people to work on together.

Unless you have a very long place for display, you can't keep your drawings of the solar system in proportion to the real solar system. The distances are just too great. Also, the sun is too big in proportion to the planets. (If you pictured our Earth, for instance, as 1 inch across, you'd have to draw a sun more than 9 feet across! If the Earth were 2.5 cm, then the sun would be 3 meters.)

But you can make splendid pictures of the planets and moons, and you can get an idea of sizes and distances.

Here's what you need:

Several pieces of posterboard or art paper

A ruler

Pens, fine markers, or pencils of many colors

A good place to display your solar system (An ideal place is a long corridor at school, a gymnasium, or an outside wall. But go ahead even if you don't have a lot of space.)

Here's what you do:

1. We suggest that you draw just a part of the sun, a flaming curve at one edge of your first drawing. Or picture a small, sun, and label it at 865,000 miles (1,392,530 km) in diameter.

2. You may be able to display your solar system on a long corridor (or gymnasium or playground) to give an idea of distances. If so, draw each planet on a separate piece of paper.
   If you don't have a lot of space, you can just label the distances between planets.

3. You may want to try wiring your planets together as a mobile. If so, draw the planets on the posterboard or cardboard and then cut them out.

4. Look on the next pages for suggestions on how to draw the planets.

SUGGESTIONS FOR YOUR SOLAR SYSTEM DRAWINGS

1. **MERCURY:** Scale Mercury at $1^3/_4$ inches (4 cm) from the sun and $^3/_4$ inch (2 cm) in diameter. Label Mercury as 35,964,590 miles (57,900,000 km) from the sun and 3030 miles (4,870 km) in diameter.

   Draw in mountains, ridges, and hard lava "wrinkles." Mercury keeps one side turned toward the sun at all times, so divide the planet in half and draw in a daytime half and a nighttime half.

2. **VENUS:** Scale Venus at $3^1/_4$ inches (8 cm) from the sun and 2 inches (5 cm) in diameter. Label Venus as 67,200,000 miles (108, 150,000 km) from the sun and 7520 miles (12,104 km) in diameter.

   Draw in dense clouds of brownish yellow sulfuric acid. Venus is mostly flat territory, but you could also draw a few high mountains and a volcano or two.

3. **EARTH:** Scale Earth at $4^1/_2$ inches (11 cm) from the sun and 2 inches (5 cm) in diameter. Label Earth as 92,900,000 miles (149,500,000 km) from the sun and 7930 miles (12,756 km) in diameter.

   Draw in the blue oceans, brown and green continents, and swirling white clouds. At this scale, though, no sign of life would show, not even a large city.

Don't forget to use white for the ice at the north and south poles.

MOON: Draw the moon as close to the earth as possible and at $^1/_2$-inch (1 cm) diameter. Label the moon at its closest to Earth, 221,468 miles (356,410 km) from Earth and as 2160 miles (3476 km) in diameter.

If you can squeeze them in, draw mountains, craters, and maria on the moon.

4. **MARS:** Scale Mars at 7 inches (17 cm) from the sun and 1 inch (2.5 cm) in diameter. Label Mars as 128,005,000 miles (206,000,000 km) from the sun and 4215 miles (6787 km) in diameter.

   Draw pink sand dunes and pink dust swirling in the air. Sketch in red lines for the "canals." Put in craters, canyons, and volcanoes. Add white ice caps at the north and south poles of Mars. Add two tiny moons, Phobos and Deimos.

5. **ASTEROIDS:** Between Mars and Jupiter, draw in a belt of many asteroids of different sizes.

6. **JUPITER:** Scale Jupiter at 25 inches (62 cm) from the sun and 20 inches in diameter. Label Jupiter as 483,300,000 miles (777,800,000 km) from the sun and 88,210 miles (142,000 km) in diameter.

   Jupiter is not quite round, but a little flattened at the poles. Draw in bright white clouds and orange and brown belts all around the planet. Put in 16 moons, and label four large moons as Europa, Ganymede, Calisto, and Io.

7. **SATURN:** Scale Saturn at 44 inches (110 cm) from the sun and 18 inches in diameter. Label Saturn as 886,100,000 miles (777,800,000 km) from the sun and 74,130 miles (119,300 km) in diameter.
Saturn is not quite round, but a little flattened at the poles. Draw multicolored rings all around Saturn with gaps in some of the rings. Saturn should look something like a colored phonograph record. Put in 20 moons, and label one large moon as Titan.

8. **URANUS:** Scale Uranus at 89 inches (225 cm) from the sun and 8 inches (20 cm) in diameter. Label Uranus as 1,783,135,000 miles (2,869,500,000 km) from the sun and 32,190 miles (51,800 km) in diameter.
Draw 11 multicolored rings all around Uranus and 15 moons.

Label five large moons as Miranda, Ariel, Umbriel, Titania, and Oberon.

9. **NEPTUNE:** Scale Neptune at 140 inches (3.5 m) from the sun and 7 inches (17 cm) in diameter. Label Neptune as 2,793,000,000 miles (4,494,900,000 km) from the sun and 30,760 miles (49,500 km) diameter.
Draw an icy, rocky surface. Put in one large moon, Triton, and one very small moon, Nereid.

10. **PLUTO:** Scale Pluto at 183 inches (5 m) from the sun and 5/8 inch (1 cm) in diameter. Label Pluto as 3,670,000,000 miles (5,906,300,000 km) from the sun and 1500 miles (2,400 km) in diameter.
Draw an icy, rocky surface. Add one moon, Charon, and make it big enough so that Pluto looks almost like a double planet.

IF YOU WANT TO IMAGINE LIFE ON THESE PLANETS AND MOONS, LOOK AT THE "DESIGN YOUR OWN SPACE ALIEN" PROJECT ON PAGES 174–177.

· · · · · · · · · ·
WRITE THE STORY OF A TRIP THROUGH THE SOLAR SYSTEM
· ·

Here's a way to understand the distances between planets without trying to comprehend millions and millions of miles and kilometers.

Suppose when you were ten, you took it into your head to travel the whole solar system. You jump into a very fine, fast spaceship, and you start your journey, leaving from the sun.

Write a story about what you would do during your journey and what it would be like at each stop.

- Getting from the sun to Mercury takes only 3 months.

- When you reach Mercury, you'd be 10 years and 3 months old.

- When you reach Venus, you'd be 10 years and 8 months old.

- You'd reach Earth at age 11 years 6 months. (And wouldn't you want to stay awhile?)

- You'd be over 12 years 4 months old when you got to Mars.

- By the time you reach Jupiter, you'd be over 18 years old.

- By Saturn, you'd be almost 25.

- Go all the way to Uranus, and you'd be nearly 40 years old.

- At Neptune, you'd be celebrating your 56th birthday.

- And when you reached Pluto, you'd be 70—a senior citizen.

: **NOW YOU CAN HAVE YOUR**
: **OWN AUTOBIOGRAPHY OF A**
: **TRIP THROUGH THE SOLAR**
: **SYSTEM.**

· · · · · · · · · ·
TELL THE DIFFERENCE BETWEEN A PLANET AND A STAR
· ·

Most newspapers list the planets that are shining on any particular night and tell you where to locate them in the sky.

Here's a way to check on what you're seeing.

Usually, when you look directly at a star, it twinkles. A planet doesn't. That's because stars are much farther away than planets. Light from distant stars is usually not as steady as light from nearer planets.

If you don't see any twinkling at first, cover one eye or look at the star from a different angle. If you see twinkling then, you're looking at a star.

Some stars even seem to twinkle with different colors.

SEE THE STARS DURING THE DAY

Once in a very long while, you might be able to see stars during the day. (The stars are always there. You just can't see them when the sun is out.)

Sometime when you're visiting a pioneer cabin or a very old house, look up the chimney. The very long chimney narrows your focus on the sky and closes out much of the daylight. Chances are you'll be able to see stars.

(You can't look up a modern chimney because a damper blocks your way.)

LOOK FOR A SATELLITE

Satellites circle the earth by the dozens these days. They bring in telephone and television signals, and they help the military.

How can you tell when you see one? They shine like little stars in the sky.

But there is one major difference. Although planets and stars move across the sky, you can't see them move in just the few minutes that you stop to look.

You can see satellites move, though. They're unmistakable.

But don't confuse a satellite with a shooting star. Shooting stars are meteors that flash by so fast you don't have time to tell someone else to look. They're gone in a split second. Satellites are fast, but they're not that fast.

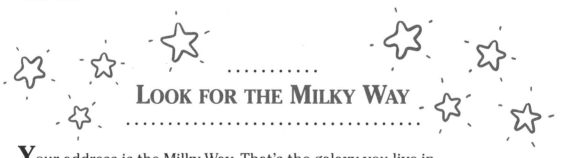

LOOK FOR THE MILKY WAY

Your address is the Milky Way. That's the galaxy you live in.

When you look overhead, sometimes you can see the glow of the Milky Way, millions of faraway stars that seem to stretch over our sky like a band of eerie white milk. You can see the glow, but it's difficult to pick out individual stars.

To see the Milky Way, you'll have to wait for a very clear night. And you'll need a dark place to watch, away from city lights.

FIGURE LIFE ON OTHER PLANETS

*Y*ou can probably do better than the movie-makers at inventing ideas for life on other planets.

Old movies show aliens as people built like us—only with green skin or with no pupils in their eyes.

Or maybe they're just like the apes on earth, only smarter and with better manners.

A few are nice teddy-bear-like creatures. Others are big, disgusting, badly behaved lumps.

Do space aliens exist at all?

Here's how to figure it.

IS THERE LIFE ON OTHER PLANETS?

What are the chances that there is life on other planets?

So far, we have not found any.

The Viking spacecraft that landed on the planet Mars found nothing, not even one little bacterium.

The Pioneer spacecraft that orbited the planet Venus took no photographs of E.T.—or of anyone else—smiling back at us from there.

If there is life on a moon, it is not our moon.

(Scientists still hold out a faint hope for life on one of the moons of Saturn or perhaps on a moon of Jupiter. It looks as if conditions on some of these moons may be less extreme than those on the other planets.)

So how can we know whether life exists on other planets?

1. We can look at the numbers. Our sun is a star, with planets circling around it, including, of course, one special planet, Earth, teeming with life.

   The number of stars, is so vast that other life forms are at least possible.

   Besides our sun, we think there are 100 billion trillion other stars in the universe. (That's a 1 with 23 zeroes after it.)

   We can guess that planets revolve around at least a few of these stars, perhaps a few billion planets in all.

   Some of those planets may have conditions right for life. On just a few thousand of those planets, life may begin to grow.

   On far fewer planets, maybe numbering in the dozens, we can imagine forms of intelligent life—possibly even intelligent enough to have telescopes and spaceships.

   No one has any real evidence yet. We are still just imagining that all those trillions of stars mean there is a chance of the right conditions for life somewhere.

2. We can consider the chemicals. Sometimes, from a far distance, we can study the chemicals on other planets. We can look particularly for the chemicals that make life on Earth possible—carbon, oxygen, hydrogen, and nitrogen, for example.

   Of course, these chemicals make up life only as we know it. For all we know, different chemical orders could exist in outer space.

3. We can listen for radio signals from outer space. So far we have heard only random noises from space. But someday we may hear something that sounds organized and deliberate.

4. We can send radio messages and hope for a reply.

AS WE LOOK FOR LIFE ON OTHER PLANETS, MAYBE SOMETHING OR SOMEONE OUT THERE IS LOOKING FOR US.

FIGURE OUT A MESSAGE TO SEND TO OUTER SPACE

If you were sending a signal to outer space, what message would you send?

We are already sending messages from Earth. A gold-plated record is traveling deep into space on our Voyager spacecraft.

And radio signals go out into space from radio telescopes on Earth.

Here's what is already on its way:

1. Greetings in 60 human languages

2. Music

3. The songs of other important earthlings, the humpback whales

4. The sounds of the body of a human woman: indication of her brain activity, her heartbeat, the movement of her muscles

5. A map of the positions of Earth and our solar system

6. A diagram of a man and a woman standing together

7. An indication of how tall people are and of how many people inhabit our world

8. A diagram of the DNA molecule, the "building block" of life on Earth

9. The atomic numbers of our most important chemicals, the chemicals that our bodies (and our planet, Earth) are made of, such as carbon, oxygen, hydrogen, nitrogen, and phosphorus

WOULD YOU LIKE TO SEND A MESSAGE ABOUT YOUR OWN WORLD AND ASK QUESTIONS ABOUT THE OTHER WORLDS OUT THERE? WHAT WOULD YOU SAY?

········
DESIGN YOUR OWN SPACE ALIEN
······························

You'll like this project if you're a creative sort of person. You'll like it even better if you organize a creative group of friends to work together.

On pages 175–177, we describe four planets. Select one you like, and then design a living thing that could live there.

You can draw a picture of your space alien or just describe it in words.

Or you can create a truly trashy space alien. Instead of throwing away things like used boxes, paper, foil, or plastic, make them into an HCA. (That's a Highly Creative Alien.)

Think about all your creature's features:

1. The space alien can breathe and eat whatever you say.

2. It can survive in whatever climate you decide is right.

3. It can grow to whatever size and shape you like best. Its chemicals can be whatever you think is best suited for its own planet.

4. You can decide how it gets around and how it protects itself against its enemies. You decide what it sees—or even if it can see anything at all.

5. Best of all, you can decide its thoughts.

6. But you mustn't let your space alien get too human. The best life forms for other planets might be entirely different from us.

Perhaps your space alien would survive best as a cloud of molecules or as a giant intelligent plant or as a living but nearly invisible shell.

CONCOCT A REALLY DIFFERENT SPACE ALIEN.

LIFE FOR MERCURY

Think up a Mercury person.
   Here's what you have to keep in mind:
1. The planet Mercury is the smallest planet and closest to the sun. Mercury has no air at all.
2. Mercury is very, very hot—and very, very cold. On the side of Mercury facing the sun, the temperature can reach 780° Fahrenheit (415° C). On the side turned away from the sun, the temperature plunges to –340° Fahrenheit (–170° C).
3. The ground is hardened lava with many hills, ridges, and "wrinkles."

LIFE FOR VENUS

If you design a Venusian, keep these facts in mind:
1. The atmosphere on Venus is heavy, thick, and gloomy. Being on Venus would be like being in a submarine deep at the bottom of the ocean, except that you'd look out at a brownish yellow sky.
2. The air is carbon dioxide gas with clouds of sulfuric acid.
3. Venus is red hot. Venus is the hottest of all the planets, with temperatures around 880° Fahrenheit (470°C).
4. Choose a flat, rocky place for your Venusian to live. Or perhaps it would prefer one of the mountains of Venus—or maybe even a volcano.

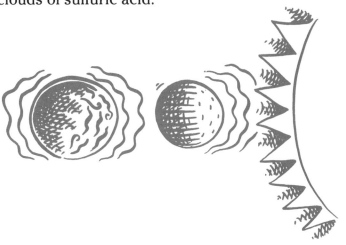

LIFE FOR MARS

Here on Earth, Martians are by far the favorite space aliens (though hardly anyone believes they really exist). Your Martian would have to live in an environment like this:

1. The air on Mars is almost all carbon dioxide. The pressure of the atmosphere is only about $1/100\text{th}$ the Earth's pressure, so the air is very thin. Mars is close to having no air at all.

2. The force of gravity is not nearly as strong on Mars as we are used to on Earth. You'd weigh much less on Mars than you do on Earth, and you could throw a ball much farther.

3. Mars has warm and cold seasons, a bit like our seasons on Earth, although the year on Mars is about twice as long as ours.

4. The daytime temperatures are not quite so extreme as on other planets. Occasionally, the daytime weather of Mars could be downright pleasant, if you were in the right place at the right time. Still, survival would not be easy. At night, the temperature can drop far below freezing, averaging −170° Fahrenheit (−75° C).

5. Depending on where you were on Mars, the ground might be pink sand dunes. The air would be full of pink dust, and the sky would look pink. And you might see craters, mountains, and volcanoes.

LIFE FOR JUPITER

You'd probably like life on one of Jupiter's moons better than on Jupiter itself. Try to imagine a really weird creature for Jupiter.

This is what the planet is like:

1. The day is short, only 9 hours and 55 minutes. Jupiter rotates so quickly that its middle bulges.

2. So many moons circle Jupiter that the planet almost has a solar system of its own. From Jupiter, you might be able to see as many as 16 moons. You could see signs of gases and meteorites. And you could see brilliant white clouds of icy ammonia, with other layers of orange and brown clouds.

3. Strong winds blow constantly, pushing the clouds—and anything else—around the planet.

4. There's no place to stand on Jupiter. The planet is almost all gases, mostly hydrogen and helium. The surface, where there is one, is an ocean of silvery liquid, like nothing we have ever seen on Earth.

5. Gravity is much stronger on the largest planet than on our little planet. If you weighed 100 pounds (45 kg) on Earth, on Jupiter you'd weigh about 250 pounds (115 kg). Even then, the winds could carry you away. And you'd be bombarded constantly with radiation.

EXPLORE YOUR OWN
PLANET EARTH

*Y*ou can really find your way around your own planet, Earth. Would you like to examine a sample of soil to see if any tiny creatures live in there? Would you like to collect rocks or fossils?

Would you like to make your own fossil? Or perhaps you'd like to make your own active volcano.

The planet Earth is yours.

RESEARCH DIFFERENT TYPES OF SOIL

Look at a cross section of soil. You may see more in it than you supposed.

The purpose of your research is to find out how soils differ. Then you'll be able to discover how plants vary when they grow in different soils.

You may need an adult associate to help you with this experiment.

Here's what you need:

A few inches of grass from a place where you have permission to dig (You should promise to repair any damage.)

A garden spade

A cardboard box

A ruler

Your science notebook and pen

Here's what you do:

1. Find a spot where the grass is thick and green. Don't worry about ruining the grass. You can replace your soil sample when you finish your observations.

2. Use the spade to cut out a sample of grass about 4 inches (10 cm) deep and 2 inches (5 cm) wide by 4 inches (10 cm) long. Here's how to do it:
First stick the spade straight down into the soil.
Lift the spade, and insert it into the soil again for each of the other three sides of your sample.
As you insert the spade for the final side of the square, pull back on the handle to loosen the soil. Use the spade to lift the square sample out of the ground.

Place the sample in the box so that it rests on one side.

3. Observe the sample. Look for the soil layers, and take notes about them in your science notebook.

4. First, observe the top layer (the topsoil) with the grass growing in it.
Take some of the top layer into your hand and squeeze it. It should be loose and come apart easily. It will probably feel a little damp in your hand, since this top layer of soil is good at holding moisture. It should be the layer of soil darkest in color. This top layer is loam, the best part of the soil for growing plants. The "ingredients" of your sample of loam are probably sand and clay. If the soil was ever near running water, there might be a deposit of silt. Probably the most valuable "ingredient" of loam is humus. Humus is made of decayed roots, plants, and animals.

5. With the ruler, measure the depth of the loam and note it in your science notebook. Also note the color. The deeper and richer the loam is, the better it will support plant life.

6. Now observe the next layer down. This is the subsoil. This subsoil can be either clay or sand. Take some of the subsoil in your hand and squeeze it. When you squeeze clay subsoil, you'll find that it holds together. If it's wet, it will feel slippery. If it's dry, it will feel hard and packed. You will notice that the color varies from gray to reddish. Clay soil contains fine, tightly packed particles, and it holds water for a long time. Water does not drain easily from clay soil. When the clay does dry though, it becomes hard. Plants have a difficult time sending roots deep down into it.

When you squeeze sandy subsoil, you'll find that it flows through your fingers easily. It will feel rough or gritty, almost like sand on the beach. Sandy soil contains larger particles. That's why it feels rough or gritty to the touch. In sandy soil, unlike clay soil, roots have room to grow. On the other hand, water flows through the sand very quickly. The roots of plants might not find enough water or enough of the nutrients that water brings with it.

7. Write in your science notebook the color, feel, and type of the subsoil in your sample.

8. When you finish your observations, replace the soil sample in the hole. Carefully tamp it back into place.

9. Now do comparisons. Your soil sample was growing thick, green grass. So you know that was good soil. Look for some other sorts of soil. You'll especially want to look in places where you can see the subsoil. Here are a few suggestions:
- Look at places where digging is going on.
- Look at banks along rivers or at the edges of hillsides.
- Look at places where trees have been uprooted.

In your science notebook, describe the soil layers, their colors, and their feel. Take a measurement of the topsoil. Then observe the plants that grow in each of these places.

> **NOW YOU CAN COMPARE YOUR OBSERVATIONS OF DIFFERENT SORTS OF SOIL.**

You'll have an idea of how different soils create differences in plants.

TEST FOR THE BEST

Suppose you want to plant a garden. Where can you find the very best soil? Here's how to figure out the answer.

Remember that the couple of inches of soil that lies on top of the ground is precious. You can't grow a good garden without it.

Yet nature can take 300 years to create just 1 inch of topsoil.

And topsoil can disappear all too easily.

Here's what you need:

Soil to test
Water
A pencil

Here's what you do:

1. First, test the soil for color.
   The best topsoil is dark. Dig just a couple of inches, and you come to lighter colored subsoil.

2. Next, test for humus. Humus is the part of soil that's made of decaying plants and animals. It's especially good for growing plants.
   Just put some of each soil sample in water. See if any part floats to the top. That part is likely to be humus, especially if it is dark in color compared to the rest of the soil.

3. Third, test for how packed down the soil is. Soil that is light and full of air is better for growing plants than hard-packed soil. Push the pencil into the soil every 6 inches (15 cm) or so, and note how far the pencil goes in (without hurting your hand). Where the soil is light and full of air, the pencil will push in easily.

But it will hardly go an inch into packed-down soil, such as the soil in the middle of a path.

4. Finally, test the soil for its ability to hold water.
   Pour on water, and see if the water soaks into the soil.
   If the soil is poor and packed down, the water may just run off. If the soil is sandy and lacks humus, the water will run right through. Or the water may sit on top of the soil without soaking in. The best soil holds water and lets it soak in gradually.

> **NOW YOU KNOW HOW TO TEST FOR THE VERY BEST TOPSOIL.**

Go on for other ways to test soil and water.

TEST HOW SOIL HOLDS ONTO WATER

Of course, water is necessary for the living organisms in soil. And, naturally, you need moist soil to grow plants.

Topsoil must be able to hold water for another reason, too. If it can't, rain or flood water can wash away the best, fertile topsoil. The loss of topsoil can ruin a farm or destroy a garden. Or it can erode away a hillside.

Find out which soil holds water the best.

Here's what you need:

Several empty cans, all the same size
A watering can
Water
A watch

Here's what you do:

1. Remove the tops and bottoms of the cans.

2. Look for soil to test. You'll want to try several types of soil, especially bare soil, soil with grass growing in it, and soil on a steep hill.

3. Just push one of the cans into each type of soil. Pour in water, and record how long it takes the water to disappear.
   You'll probably find that the best soil for holding water is grassy soil on flat land. The worst is bare soil on a steep hill. That's the sort of soil that is in danger of eroding away.

YOU MAY DISCOVER A GOOD PLACE TO PLANT A GARDEN. YOU MAY FIND A PLACE THAT NEEDS WORK TO CONSERVE THE SOIL.

CONDUCT A SOIL AND RAIN TEST

How do you go about keeping topsoil in place as rains and floods hit it? One way is to plant grasses and help hold down the soil. Some ways of planting are smarter than others. Find out which method is best.

This job can get messy. You may want to take it outside.

Here's what you need:

Three shallow foil or plastic pans
Potting soil
Seed for grass, oats, wheat, or barley
Water

Here's what you do:

1. Fill each pan with potting soil.

2. Leave one pan unplanted, with no seeds. This is your test pan.

3. In the other pans, plant seed in two different ways. In one pan, plant the seed straight across in rows. In the other pan, plant the seed in up and down rows. Water both pans lightly.

4. Now set each pan at an angle as if it were on a hillside. (A 30-degree angle is just right.)

5. Let the seed grow for several days until the grass is about 2 inches (5 cm) high.

6. Now you're ready for the rain test. Get out your watering can, and make it rain hard on each of the three pans. See what happens to the topsoil, and decide which way of planting is best.

NOW YOU HAVE AN IDEA OF ONE WAY TO KEEP TOPSOIL SAFE.

FIND LIVING ORGANISMS IN SOIL

If creatures from outer space came down to Earth, they'd find life everywhere. Even in the deepest arctic ice, they would at least find bacteria.

You're bound to find signs of life in any sample of soil you try, even if you don't see it at first. Here's how to find life.

The name for this sort of life-finding device is a Berlese funnel.

Here's what you need:

Light wire or a heavy rubber band
A small piece of wire screen or netting
A large funnel
A wide-mouthed glass jar
A random sample of topsoil
A lamp

Here's what you do:

1. Use the light wire to attach the small piece of wire screen over the narrow end of the funnel. Or use a rubber band to attach the netting.

2. Set the funnel in the wide-mouthed glass jar.

3. Carefully pour the soil sample into the funnel. The idea is that the screen or netting at the narrow end of the funnel prevents the soil from going into the jar. Small organisms, though, might get through.

4. Now turn the lamp so that it will heat the soil in the funnel. Leave the lamp on for several hours or overnight.
   The lamp will dry out the soil and heat it, so that any small organisms will be motivated to leave. Soon you'll find them in the jar.

    NOW YOU SEE LIFE EVERYWHERE.

Be kind and put the little creatures back into cool, moist soil.

START A ROCK COLLECTION

Rocks make a good collection. First of all, you can collect rocks anywhere. You can find interesting rocks on vacation, but you can find them at home, too. You can even buy unusual rocks from around the world. They don't cost much, either.

And rocks come in many different colors and odd shapes. Your collection can look impressive even when you're just getting started.

Another good reason to collect rocks is that they are the oldest possible things to collect. You can collect real antiques, some of them millions of years old.

When you find an interesting rock, try to identify it the way a professional geologist would:

1. Look at the colors in the rock.

2. Consider how hard the rock is. Professional geologists classify hardness on a scale of 1 to 10. The softest rock, number 1 on the scale, is talc. One form of talc is so soft that you can turn it into powder just by squeezing it in your hand. Other rocks are soft enough that you can scratch them with a fingernail. On the other end of the scale, at number 10, are diamonds. Diamonds are the hardest form of rock. (Of course, you won't find a diamond just lying around, waiting to go into your collection. Diamonds are rare, and that's one reason they're valuable.)

3. Look for layers and streaks in the rock.

4. Look at the rock's luster. Is the rock dull or shiny?

5. Write down where you found the rock. The location and the other types of rocks in the same place give clues about how to identify a particular rock.

6. Get out your magnifying glass, and look for marks and prints. If you're lucky, you may find a fossil, the print of a plant or animal from long, long ago.

7. Look in an encyclopedia, or find a book about rocks. See if you can identify your rocks by name. Then you can label each rock in your collection.

8. Store small rocks in egg cartons. Keep bigger rocks in cardboard boxes with dividers.

NOW YOU CAN HAVE A COLLECTION THAT WILL LAST FOREVER.

Your children and grandchildren can add their own rocks to the collection you started.

FIND A FOSSIL

If you're lucky, you may find a fossil imprint in the rocks you collect. Or you can go out on purpose to collect fossils.

Fossils were once living plants or animals. The once-living thing leaves its imprint in clay or mud, and then the clay hardens over time and preserves the print.

Or sometimes fossils are actual petrified plants or animals. People love to look for dinosaur fossils (or giant dinosaur footprints).

Here's where to look:

1. Look in old stone walls or piles of rocks left from clearing fields. (Be sure to ask the owner's permission.)

2. Look in places where you can see different layers of rock. For instance, look where roads have been cut through hills or mountains.

3. Look along streams and rivers. Look along a beach. Fossil shells look just like real shells, except that they've turned to rock.

4. Look at sedimentary rocks, especially limestone. Natural chalk almost always has fossils. But look with a magnifying glass. These fossils might be too small to see at first glance.

MAYBE YOU'LL FIND A SPECIAL FOSSIL.

MAKE YOUR OWN FOSSIL

Use shells, leaves, or flowers to make your own, up-to-date fossil imprint.

This is a good project for a creative sort of person.

Here's what you need:

A shallow box or pan (Heavy cardboard or foil will work.)

Modeling clay

Shells, leaves, or flowers

Plaster of paris

Water

A stick or knife

Shortening or other cooking grease

Here's what you do:

1. Fill the shallow box or pan with modeling clay, and smooth over the surface.

2. Press in shells, leaves, or flowers. Your "fossil" can be almost anything as long as it was originally part of a plant or animal. You could even try imprinting a pet's pawprint or your own handprint. Then remove your "fossil" (especially if your pet is anxious to leave).

3. Sprinkle about 3 cups of plaster of paris over about 2 cups of water. Mix until you have a thick sort of soup. Pour a thin layer over the clay, and let it set until hard.

4. Now carefully remove the box and the clay. You'll find a "fossil" imprint in the hard plaster. This is a negative imprint, something like the negative of a photograph. Everything is backwards.

Use the stick or knife to clean off any bubbles or rough edges.

5. If you wish, make a positive imprint of your fossil. Put the negative imprint back into the box or pan. Mix up more plaster of paris with water. With the shortening, grease the top of your negative imprint, and pour on a second layer of plaster. Let it set until hard.

6. Separate the two pieces of plaster, and you'll find a positive imprint of your fossil.

7. If you are feeling especially creative, make several fossil imprints, paint them, and arrange them artistically.

NOW YOU SEE HOW NATURE WORKS TO MAKE A FOSSIL.

Fossils are not that rare. Chances are that some day you'll find the real fossil of an ancient animal or plant.

MAKE YOUR OWN ERUPTING VOLCANO

Construct your own small volcano, and make it erupt.

Here's what you need:

A shallow box or pan

Three colors of modeling clay in natural-looking colors such as green, brown, dark gray, black, or red

A container such as the small cover from a spray can, if you wish

¹/₄ cup (60 ml) water

1 tablespoon (15 ml) baking soda

A few drops of red food coloring

A few drops of liquid dishwashing detergent

¹/₄ cup (60 ml) vinegar

Here's what you do:

1. Use the shallow box or pan to hold your volcano.

2. Use the modeling clay to model your volcano. You may want to use green clay to indicate grass growing on the good soil at the base of the volcano.
   Make the body of the volcano a natural-looking color such as brown, dark gray, or black. Next, use dark red or dark brown modeling clay to create the lava flowing down the sides of the volcano.

3. Scoop out a hole at the very tip of the volcano. If you wish, put in a container.

4. Pour the water into the hole or into the container at the tip of the volcano. Stir in the baking soda, red food coloring, and liquid dishwashing detergent.

5. Just as you're ready for your volcano to erupt, pour in the vinegar. The base (baking soda) and the acid (vinegar) combine to produce a good bubbling-over effect.

   NOW YOU HAVE YOUR OWN ERUPTING VOLCANO.

How many people can say the same?

SAVE THE ENVIRONMENT

*W*ouldn't you like to do what you can to save the environment? You don't want to live in a world that's suffocating in trash, where the water is dirty and the air polluted.

You can experiment on getting rid of trash. You can analyze packaging. You can set up a recycling center. You can even learn how to clean up water.

You'll be creating a better world to live in.

PUT OUT A POLLUTION CATCHER

Some air pollution you can see. Some air pollution you can smell. But some air pollution you can recognize only by what happens because of it.

Here's how to test for air pollution where you live:

1. Wait for a dry, sunny day. Put a coffee filter paper or paper towel outside. Choose a place where the paper won't get dirty in any other way than from the air. And put the paper in a place where it won't blow away.

2. Come back at the end of the day, and see whether the paper collected dirt particles.

3. Now try putting papers in other places. See if papers in different locations catch different sorts of air pollution.

JUST LOOKING AT THE DIRT YOU COLLECT IN ONE SMALL PLACE CAN GIVE YOU SOME IDEA OF THE PROBLEM OF AIR POLLUTION.

LOOK FOR AIR POLLUTION

Where air pollution is bad, you may see it on your skin or on your handkerchief when you blow your nose.

You might be able to see or smell some obvious kinds of air pollution.

Here are other ways to tell:

1. Watch the newspaper or listen to weather reports for air pollution warnings. Sometimes air pollution is so bad that people who already have breathing problems need to stay inside.

2. Look for reports of acid rain. Factories sometimes do incomplete burning, and acid fumes float up into the atmosphere. The acid dissolves in the water vapor of clouds, and then wind carries it, sometimes very far away. The acid can come down with rain hundreds of miles away.

3. Look for smog. That's a combination of smoke and fog. Fog is natural. Air pollution is not. You can often see smog as yellowish or gray air. It can make your eyes water or give you a headache.

4. Smell for air pollution. Sometimes bad smells have natural sources, like the smell from an angry skunk. These smells usually don't last long. But other smells might come from a polluting factory or a paper mill. Or bad smells can come from water pollution, from a dying lake, from open sewage.

5. When you see factory smoke stacks, you might be seeing air pollution even if the air looks clear.

When you see hundreds of cars and trucks on a highway, you know there's air pollution, even if it's invisible.

Unfortunately, you can't see or smell some kinds of air pollution. Those factory smokestacks might be releasing carbon monoxide into the air. Cars and trucks give off carbon monoxide as their engines run.

The gas carbon monoxide has no color or smell, even though it's poisonous. It can combine with red blood cells so they can't carry oxygen to the brain. Too much can kill. (That's why it's dangerous to be in a closed garage with a car engine running.)

WHAT CAN YOU DO ABOUT AIR POLLUTION? Plant a tree. Trees give off oxygen, and they help "clean" the poison out of the atmosphere. Get interested in saving forests, especially rain forests.

And if you think major air pollution is going on, tell someone. Write a letter to the editor of a local newspaper. Young people can make a difference, especially if they work together.

Working against air pollution is a good project for a school or family group.

· · · · · · · · · ·
LOOK FOR WATER POLLUTION
· ·

When you come upon water pollution, your nose often tells you first.

Here are other ways to tell:

1. Look for what ought to be there but isn't. You ought to see lots of fish, birds, and insects around water.

2. Look for trash floating in the water—ugh!

3. Look for green algae. Algae are little plants that spread over the surface of polluted water. Algae can build up as a result of water pollution. They can prevent air from getting into the water. Eventually, nothing else can grow. Algae are the sad sign of a dying body of water.

4. Look for other odd colors besides green in the water. You may not see a factory dumping pollutants into the water, but you can see the effect downstream.

5. Look for soapsuds on the water. Huge amounts of detergent can spill into water. Soap gets water dirty, not clean. Soap can kill water plants and creatures. And, of course, it makes water taste bad.

6. Look for multicolored, shiny spots on the surface of the water. They could be oil.

7. Smell for bad odors, especially the rotten-egg odor of sewage.

WHAT CAN YOU DO ABOUT WATER POLLUTION? Carry your own trash away with you. You might even pick up other people's trash.

If you think major pollution is going on, tell someone. Rivers and lakes have keepers these days, people who work hard to keep pollution away.

Or write a letter to the editor of a local newspaper. Other people ought to know that you're concerned.

· · · · · · · · · ·
COUNT UP YOUR TRASH
· ·

If you're an average sort of person, you throw away 5 or 6 pounds of trash in a day.

This means that a family of four throws away something like 150 pounds of trash a week, including trash at home, at school, and at work.

Keep track of your trash for 1 day.

This is a good project for a school or family group.

Here's what you do:

1. Make a chart showing what's in your trash. You'll need to look at each item, and decide on a category for it. Write the number of items in each category:

   Newspaper
   Paper or cardboard
   Plastic
   Paper/plastic combinations
   Aluminum (cans, foil, foil packaging)
   Glass (bottles)
   Metal
   Wood
   Old clothes or other cloth items
   Other

2. For a day, put the "clean" trash (the kind you don't mind touching) in a separate place. Weigh the trash at the end of the day. If you wish, put the messy garbage in a separate trash bag, and weigh it, too, at the end of the day.

3. Figure out the percentage of your trash (by item) that falls in each category.

4. Perhaps you can find out which of your trash items might be recycled or used again. Check them off on your chart.

You might even be able to return bottles and get some money back. That's better than cluttering up our one and only planet, Earth.

5. If your state does not allow you to recycle bottles and cans, complain. Write a letter to the editor or to your favorite politician. Kids can make a difference. Perhaps your local newspaper would like to print an article about your trash analysis.

> **NOW YOU KNOW HOW MUCH YOUR TRASH WEIGHS ON AN AVERAGE DAY. AND YOU KNOW SOMETHING ABOUT WHAT'S IN YOUR TRASH.**

Try this project for a whole week.

· · · · · · · · · · ·
ANALYZE PACKAGING
· ·

This project is fun. Go through groceries, and prepare to hand out an award for the worst packaging and an award for the best..

This is a good project for a school or family group.

Here's what you do:

1. For the worst packaging award, look for unnecessary packaging. Often, you can find package within package within package. Perhaps a loaf of bread is wrapped in layers of both plastic and paper, with a plastic tab to seal it.
   Or you can find candy wrapped in little papers inside layers of cardboard inside a plastic box inside a plastic/paper wrapping. For the best packaging award, look for minimum packaging. Perhaps you'll find bread wrapped in only a paper sleeve or candy in just a paper bag.

2. Look for packaging that cannot be recycled. That includes plastic/paper combinations.
   For the best packaging award, look for packaging made of recycled paper. You may see a recycling symbol on the box. Or you may notice gray paper or cardboard inside. That's the usual color of recycled paper.

3. Look for packaging that is dangerous to wildlife.
   The plastic rings that hold together six packs of drinks can end up on land that birds visit. Or the rings can end up in water. Those plastic rings can strangle birds or fish. The birds and fish cannot get them off, and the plastic never wears away.
   When "Styrofoam" plastic gets into water, it breaks up into little plastic balls. Water creatures such as turtles think the plastic looks like food. But when they swallow the plastic, it has a disastrous effect.
   The light plastic may force a sea turtle to float to the surface. Then the turtle cannot dive for food. Or the plastic can clog up intestines. Then the poor animal cannot eat real food, and it could starve to death.

> **NOW YOU CAN FIGURE OUT WHAT KIND OF PACKAGING POLLUTE.**

Write to companies that make these products and tell them about your "awards." Usually, you'll find their addresses on the side of the boxes, or you can ask a librarian.

Or write a letter to the editor of your local newspaper.

FIGURE THE COST OF PACKAGING YOU DON'T NEED

. . . .

You can prove to yourself that elaborate packaging costs an elaborate amount of money. You could be paying more for a fancy package than for the food that's inside.

Here's how to figure packaging costs:

1. Choose several packages of the same type of food. For instance, look at cookies packaged in different sorts of bags, boxes, and cans.

2. Rate the packaging as to how earth-friendly it is. You can give the packaging any grade from A+ to F. Here are two questions to ask:
   - Is the packaging simple or unnecessarily complicated?
   - Can the packaging be recycled? Rate packaging very high if you know that it can be used again. For instance, you might keep an attractive cookie can to hold your own homemade cookies. You can return some bottles and cans for recycling and get back your deposit money.
   Rate packaging fairly high if you know you can recycle it. Plain paper or glass bottles, for example, can be easily recycled.
   Rate packaging very low if you know that it will never be used again. Plastic/paper combinations cannot be recycled. "Styrofoam" plastic cannot be recycled, and it's dangerous to wildlife.

3. Write down the price of each package.

4. For each package, divide the total price by the number of ounces (or pounds, quarts, liters). That gives the unit price. Now you can see how the prices compare per unit.
   For instance, a large package of cookies may cost more than a small package of cookies, but each cookie in the larger package may cost less.

5. Consider other factors that may add to the cost of the food. For example, one kind of cookie may taste better or have better ingredients than another kind.

6. Make a chart on your packaging grades, the unit prices, and the other factors:

7. Look at your chart, and judge how the packaging added to the cost of the food. You can't tell the exact amount, but you can guess when you're paying for packaging you don't need.

· · · · · · · · · · ·
FIGURE OUT FAST-FOOD WASTE
· ·

You can help save the environment at fast-food restaurants. Or look at waste in your own school cafeteria.

Here's what you do:

1. Decide if the restaurant or your school cafeteria uses unnecessary food packaging.
   People at a few restaurants and schools are aware of the problem. They're cutting down on layers and layers of packaging.

2. Figure out how much food packaging the restaurant or cafeteria uses. If you can, take the packaging home and weigh it. Also figure out how much space it takes up. Keep a record.
   See if you can tell which fast-food restaurants use the most packaging by weight.

3. Find out if the restaurant or cafeteria recycles its food packaging. Some encourage people to put waste paper in recycling bins. Someone has just invented the ultimate in recyclable fast-food packages—a bag to hold French fries. The bag itself is made of French fries, and you can dip it in catsup and eat it.

4. See if the restaurant or cafeteria uses packaging that is dangerous to wildlife, such as "Styrofoam" containers. Many schools, churches, and temples no longer use "Styrofoam."

LET PEOPLE KNOW ABOUT YOUR FINDINGS. Write a letter to the editor of your local newspaper. Or write to the president of the restaurant chain. The people working behind the counter can give you an address for headquarters. Write to the State Department of Education about your school cafeteria. That is usually the department that has the power to create changes.

DECIDE ON PAPER OR PLASTIC

At some supermarkets, the clerks ask if you want paper or plastic bags. In the morning, when you get ready for school, you may have to decide between a plastic and a paper lunch bag. How do you choose?

Plastic bags are made from oil. When you use plastic bags, you're using up the world's oil supply. Oil cannot be replaced. That's bad.

Paper bags are made from trees. When you use paper bags, you're helping to destroy forests. One tree makes 700 paper bags. That's enough for only half an hour of bagging at one busy supermarket. That's bad. But trees can grow again, and oil can't.

So what do you decide?

Here are suggestions:

1. Use bags more than once. Bring back sandwich and lunch bags you took to school. They'll do for a second lunch.
   Encourage your parents to take back to the supermarket the bags you saved from the last time you shopped for groceries. You can use them over again for this week's groceries.

2. Recycle bags.
   Bring old bags back to the recycling center at school or the supermarket. (If your store doesn't have a recycling bin, talk to the manager.)

3. Use "bags" you never throw away. Bring a lunch box to school, instead of using a new lunch bag every day. Pack your sandwiches in reusable plastic containers instead of sandwich bags.
   When you shop for groceries, bring your own bag, preferably a sturdy canvas bag.

4. Don't use unnecessary packaging. Take apples and bananas for lunch at school. They're good for you, and they come in their own natural wrappers.
   Ask the clerk at the supermarket not to use bags inside bags to pack your groceries.
   And don't take a bag if you don't need one. If you buy just one or two items, you may not need a bag at all.

> **MAKE A DECISION: PAPER, PLASTIC, OR SAVING THE ENVIRONMENT.**

· · · · · · · · · · ·
CREATE A LANDFILL IN A JAR
· ·

Find out how long it takes things to return to nature. This will be your own special, tiny landfill.

Here's what you need:

Two gallon-size (4 liter) glass jars
Potting soil
Outside soil
Garbage or trash
Water
Your science notebook and pen

Here's what you do:

1. Fill one of the gallon jars with the potting soil. Fill the other jar with the soil you dug up outside.

2. Bury the same type of garbage or trash in each jar. You might like to use the remains of a lunch, perhaps an apple core or part of a sandwich you didn't eat. Also put in something you can't eat, like a sandwich wrapper or a paper lunch bag. Be sure the types of refuse in the two jars are the same.

3. Water well.

4. Put the jars in a dark closet or cupboard.

5. Look in the jars once a week, and record what has happened in each. See what's disappeared, and what has stayed the same. You'll probably find that most refuse disappears faster from the jar with the outside soil. There are more organisms in that jar than in the sterile potting soil.

The organisms help break down the refuse. It's food to them.

: **NOW YOU KNOW WHAT**
: **HAPPENS IN A LANDFILL. MOST**
: **GARBAGE GOES TO LANDFILLS,**
: **WHERE MACHINES PLOW IT**
: **UNDER SOIL. SOME OF THE**
: **GARBAGE GOES BACK TO**
: **NATURE. SOME STAYS JUST**
: **ABOUT THE SAME FOR YEARS.**
:

Go on to see if refuse breaks down faster or slower in a "backwards" garden.

· · · · · · · · · ·
DON'T GROW A BACKWARDS GARDEN
· ·

If you have a bit of land outside, you can "plant" a garden that doesn't grow. This garden is your own little landfill, and the things in it are supposed to disappear. But some of them will take longer than others.

Compare what happens in an outside garden with what happened in the "landfill" jars.

Here's what you need:

A bit of land

Trash or garbage to "plant": remains of food (but not meat or grease), old bits of cloth, plastic food packaging, paper food packaging, foil, a piece of newspaper

A shovel or spade

Sticks or stones to use as markers

Water

Your science notebook and pen

Here's what you do:

1. Keep a list of the trash or garbage you are going to "plant." Record what the refuse is made up of, as well as the date you "plant" it.

2. With the shovel or spade, dig a hole about 6 inches (15 cm) deep for each of your items. Cover each item with soil.

Use sticks or stones to mark the location of all the items.

3. Thoroughly water your backwards garden.

4. After a month, go back and dig up the items. Record what's happened to each. You may not be able to find some of them.

5. Go back each month after that, and see if anything else has disappeared.

6. Compare your results with the results from the "landfill" jars. An outside garden has sunlight, rain, and a whole variety of organisms to help break down refuse.

: **NOW YOU KNOW WHAT**
: **HAPPENS—AND DOESN'T**
: **HAPPEN—TO THE TRASH**
: **WE LEAVE BEHIND.**

SET UP A RECYCLING CENTER

Ask your adult associates to help you set up places to separate trash at home or school. Perhaps you can talk them into taking the trash to a central recycling location.

This is an excellent project for a school or family group. Often, adults want to recycle, but they aren't sure how to go about it. You can teach them.

Here's what you need:

Separate bins or trash cans for each type of material you can recycle

Plenty of trash

Here's what you do:

1. Call the trash-disposal people in your town, and find out how you can sort out trash for recycling. They probably have strict rules about how to separate different sorts of trash, but you can figure out those rules.

2. Separate piles of newspapers first. Almost every town has places to recycle newspapers. If you can recycle a pile of newspapers 3 feet high, congratulate yourself. You've saved one tree.

3. Separate glass. The trash-disposal people will probably want you to separate glass by color: clear, green, and brown glass. You will probably need to remove caps and lids. Rinse out glass jars and bottles.

4. Separate aluminum cans. You may be able to return some cans for money. Rinse out the cans. Some recycling centers require you to remove the labels.

In some places, you can recycle aluminum foil and other sorts of aluminum food packaging.

5. Separate toxic waste. Toxic waste sounds like something you'd never have around the house, but everybody does. The trash-disposal people in your town will tell you what needs to be separated. They will probably list things like batteries, old paint, and old motor oil. These are common useful things, but they're poison to the environment.

> YOU CAN BE PROUD OF YOURSELF. A RECYCLING CENTER IS AN IMPORTANT ACHIEVEMENT.

If your town doesn't have a central recycling location, you could write to town officials. And write a letter to the editor of your local newspaper.

········

RECYCLE NEWSPAPER IN A MOST ARTISTIC FASHION

·································

Do you want to have fun recycling newspaper? Then create a papier-mâché bowl, with plenty of papier-mâché fruit to go in it. (*Papier-mâché is a French word, meaning chewed paper. You can pronounce it as "paper mashay."*)

This is a good project for an artistic sort of person who is concerned about the environment.

Here's what you need:

Old newspaper

A bowl (of the right size for your papier-mâché bowl)

Plastic wrap

A large mixing bowl and spoon

Flour

Salt

Water

Cellophane tape

A very fine grade of sandpaper

Poster paints or acrylic paints

A spray-on clear, permanent coating such as Chartpak

Here's what you do:

1. Tear many pages of the old newspaper into strips.

Hint: You will find there is a right and a wrong way to tear newspaper. If you pull in the right direction, the paper will tear into reasonably straight strips.

2. Cover the outside of the bowl with plastic wrap. Get the plastic wrap as smooth as you can.

3. In the large mixing bowl, prepare a mixture of 2 cups of flour, 1 tablespoon of salt, and 1 cup of water. Beat until smooth.

4. Soak about 10 newspaper strips in the mixture. Remove one strip at a time, sliding your fingers down the strip to remove excess flour. As you remove each strip, place it around the bowl. Smooth it down and fold back any overhanging edge. Continue to add strips until all of the plastic on the bowl is covered. Then set aside to dry.

5. Crumple a dry piece of newspaper to form a base for a piece of fruit. Make the shape round for apples and oranges, smaller at one end for pears, small for cherries or grapes, long and curved with pointed ends for bananas. Scrunch it in your hand to get an approximate shape, and use tape to hold it.

6. Soak more newspaper strips in the flour mixture to make the fruit. Carefully create a layer of floured newspaper strips on each of the fruit forms. Set aside to dry.

7. Clean up the mess!

8. After the first layer on the bowl and on the fruit has dried, repeat the process with a second layer, then a third, fourth, and so on. Keep on adding newspaper strips until your bowl is as thick as you want it and your fruit is shaped and firm.

9. Using a very fine grade of sandpaper, sand your bowl and fruit smooth. Remove the original bowl so that your papier-mâché bowl stands on its own.

10. Paint the fruit with either poster paints or acrylic paints. Paint black or brown lines on a yellow banana. Paint a green

and a red apple, an orange orange, green and red grapes, red cherries, and so on.

11. Paint the bowl a bright color. You can paint on your own designs, or glue on cut-outs from magazines.
Or take dried leaves from your "Notebook of Leaves," and glue them on as decorations for your bowl.

12. After the paint dries, spray it with clear protective coating. You should have an adult assist you with this part of the project. Work in a well ventilated room.

NOW YOU'VE ACHIEVED TWO GOOD THINGS. YOU'VE RECYCLED NEWSPAPER, AND YOU'VE CREATED A WORK OF ART. YOUR PAPIER-MÂCHÉ BOWL OF FRUIT WOULD MAKE A WONDERFUL GIFT FOR SOMEONE SPECIAL.

DESIGN BOXES FOR JUICE, CANDY, AND TOYS

If you're a creative sort of person, you'll like this project.

Sketch your designs on paper, and show with labels the kinds of materials you'll use.

This is a good school project.

Here's what you do:

1. Design a juice box. You don't want the juice to leak or spill. On the other hand, you don't want too much packaging or packaging you can't recycle.

2. Design a candy kit. You don't want the fragile candies to break apart. Also, since candy is a special treat, you want the packaging to look very attractive. But the environment doesn't need layers and layers of packaging, especially plastic that won't break down.

3. Design packaging for a toy. You don't want the toy to break. Also, a store needs to display toys so that people can see them. But toys often come with unnecessary packaging. Sometimes there is so much packaging that a child can't get the toy out to play with it. (Remember that some toys don't need any packaging at all.)

4. Write to manufacturers, and tell them what you've designed. They may listen to one of your ideas. You can find the manufacturer's address on the original packages.

    SEE WHAT YOU CAN DO TO
    HELP WITH CREATIVE
    PACKAGES.

GROW SOMETHING GOOD TO EAT
WITHOUT USING SOIL OR PESTICIDES

One way to save the environment is to figure out new, better ways to grow food.

Hydroponics is the science of growing plants with water but without soil or pesticides. The word hydroponics is "water" combined with "work." Water does the work.

With hydroponics, people can grow vegetables in places where the soil is infertile or poisoned.

And they can grow food in places where the weather is bad. People use hydroponics to grow crops in torrid deserts or in icy climates.

You may think this is odd, but hydroponics also works good in places without a lot of fresh water. Growing a plant in water doesn't take much water. Hydroponics farmers can recycle about 90% of the water they need.

Here is a simple way to try hydroponics. Grow your own delicious bean sprouts in just 2 to 4 days.

Here's what you need:

A 1-quart or 1 liter glass jar

¹/₃ cup (80 ml) bean seeds (You might like mung beans or lentils. Or try wheat berries or dried whole peas. Buy fresh, untreated seeds.)

Water

A small piece of clean cotton cheesecloth

A large rubber band

Here's what you do:

1. Measure the seeds into the jar. Fill the jar with warm water, and let the seeds soak overnight.

2. The next day, pour off the water. Cover the top of the jar with the cheesecloth, and hold it in place with the rubber band. Rinse the seeds with warm water through the cheesecloth. Then pour off all the water.

3. Lay the jar on its side in a dark place, such as under the sink or in a cupboard.

4. Every day, rinse the beans with warm water through the cheesecloth. Then pour off all the water.

5. Your sprouts will be ready in 3 to 4 days. Do not wait until they grow roots. Wash the tiny sprouts in cold water, and then drain. Take out any unsprouted seeds.

6. Let the bean sprouts sit in the sun for 2 to 3 hours. The sun will give them a better color.

7. Your tiny bean sprouts are ready to eat. Eat them with Oriental foods or in salads or sandwiches. Refrigerate them until you use them.

: NOW YOU HAVE YOUR OWN
: DELICIOUS BEAN SPROUTS. IN
: THE FUTURE, PEOPLE MAY LIVE
: OFF PLANTS THAT GROW IN
: SMALL AMOUNTS OF WATER
: INSTEAD OF LARGE AMOUNTS
: OF SOIL.

Maybe some day you'll invent another new way to feed hungry people in the world.

ENJOY THE WATERFRONT

*T*hree-quarters of our planet, Earth, is covered with water, so you probably don't have to go far to find a waterfront. Visit an ocean beach or a lake beach. Or look at life on the edge of a pond or by the bank of a river.

Whatever water you choose, you can see wonderful things. And you might bring a few back with you.

TIME THE TIDES

If you could visit every beach in the world, you'd find a different sort of tide on each one of them.

Even if you stayed on your own favorite strip of beach, you'd find different sorts of tides every day of the year. (And because of tides, you might find a different sort of beach each year. Tides help form the seashore, with all its sandbars, sea caves, and sea cliffs.)

Scientists had such a hard time predicting tides that they invented machines to calculate the times and patterns.

Why are tides so complicated?

Tides form a moving bulge in the ocean. They're like a long, slow wave of water lifting from the bottom of the ocean.

Gravity from the moon pulls on the ocean water. The sun pulls, too, but not as much as the moon.

The moon is too small, and its gravity is too light, to lift the water off Earth entirely. But its gravity is strong enough to pull the water from side to side. That pull makes the tides.

When the moon is closest and pulling hardest, that strong pull brings a high tide. (The other name is flood tide.) You may be walking on dry breach, and within an hour, that same strip of beach is covered with rushing water.

As the moon moves away from one part of the ocean, the weaker pull brings a low tide. (The other name is ebb tide.) The ocean is still bulging toward the moon, but the moon is on the other side of Earth. So the water rushes away from the beach.

The name of the moment when the tide turns (either in or out) is slack water.

Here's how to figure the tides:

1. Look in the newspaper. When you're near an ocean (or a large lake or tidal river), you can find times for the tides listed in the local newspaper. High and low tides arrive once or twice a day. The newspaper will mark a low tide with a minus number.
   Or before you leave on a beach vacation, look at an almanac that tells about tides. Then you'll know what to look for.

2. Watch for the tide to turn. Just at the time you expect the tide to change, watch and see what happens. The change will be particularly dramatic on a windy day or just after a storm—and on some special beaches.
   On a hot, sunny day, you can tell if the tide is coming in because the beach and rocks will be dry. If the tide is going out, a strip of beach will still be wet.

3. Study the beach. Low tide is a good time to find live ocean creatures. As the tide goes out, it leaves them stranded on the beach. And low tide is the best time to find newly arrived shells, driftwood, and ocean glass.

It's the safest time to explore, too. Often you can climb on rocks that just hours ago were under the ocean water. But be careful about sudden changes in the tide. You don't want to get stranded or caught in an undertow.

If you were a sailor, you'd like high tide. High tides help in launching ships. High tides also help ships float into port safely, even when they're traveling over shoals, reefs, and sandbars.

MAKE WAVES

If you've ever played with a slinky toy, you know something about how waves move.

The strange thing about a wave is that the water is not moving along its surface. Instead, the water just moves up and down as the wave passes by.

Waves can travel thousands of miles, but the particles of water that the waves travel through hardly move at all. The water just moves in circles.

To prove that's true, make waves in the bathtub.

Here's what you do:

1. Float your rubber duckie (or some other bathtub toy) at one end of the tub.

2. Make waves at the other end by moving your hands up and down just under the surface of the water. Don't splash!

3. You'll see the rubber duckie bounce up and down. It may turn around in circles. But it won't move from its own end of the tub.

YOU MIGHT FIND OUT ABOUT WAVES IF YOU TRY FLOATING IN THEM AT THE BEACH. And maybe some time you'll have a chance to learn surfing.

FIND THE SALT IN THE SEA

You can determine how much salt is in a quart of ocean water. You'll also find other basic materials, just as you can in water from lakes or ponds.

The next time you visit an ocean beach, remember to bring back an unusual souvenir: a jug of water.

Here's what you need:

1 cup (250 ml) of seawater
A 1-quart or liter measuring cup
A glass or enamel pan

Here's what you do:

1. Measure exactly 1 cup (250 ml) seawater.
2. In the glass or enamel plan, boil the water until most of it has evaporated.
3. Turn down the heat. Simmer the water at very low heat until almost all the water has disappeared. Watch carefully so you don't lose it all.
4. Cool what's left.
5. Measure what's left. That's the amount of salt, chemicals, minerals, and basic nutrients in seawater. You'll also have just a little water left over.
   You won't get the same measure of salt everywhere. The amount of salt in the sea varies, especially near rivers and bays, where fresh water mixes in.
6. Figure what percent of your sea water is salt. Divide the salt measure by the total water measure.

> GO ON TO FIND OUT IF SEA
> SALT IS DIFFERENT FROM
> ORDINARY TABLE SALT.

....
FIND OUT IF SEA SALT IS DIFFERENT FROM TABLE SALT
....

Study your sea salt with a magnifying glass. Then study particles of table salt. You'll see a difference in shapes and colors.

You'll also see a mix in the sea salt that isn't there in the table salt. The mix is natural chemicals and minerals from the sea, along with tiny particles of food material.

You can't just add water again to the sea salt and come up with seawater. The chemistry would be different. The particles of food materials would no longer be right. A salt-water creature could not live in home-made salt water.

: **NOW YOU SEE FOR YOURSELF**
: **THE DIFFERENCE BETWEEN SEA**
: **SALT AND ORDINARY SALT..**

....
START A SAND COLLECTION
....

You'd be surprised how many people have sand collections. Maybe that's due to a legend that says, if you bring back sand, you'll get to visit that same beach again. And people always want to go back to the beach.

Also you'll be surprised when you find out how different sand is between one beach and another.

Keep your samples of sand in small bottles. (Pill bottles or camera-film canisters are perfect.) Label the bottles to show where and when you found the sand. And keep a record in your science notebook.

When you study sand with a magnifying glass, you'll see different colors. You'll probably see sparkles. And you'll see the different sizes and shapes of the sand grains. You'll feel different textures, from coarse to very fine.

MAYBE SOME DAY YOU'LL HAVE SAND FROM BEACHES ALL AROUND THE WORLD.

BUILD A SAND CASTLE

You may have seen contests of elaborate sand castles, mansions, pyramids, forts, and even faces. How do the sand sculptors hold the sand together?

Here's a hint. They don't have a secret ingredient. All they have is sand and water.

But professional sand sculptors bring in a particular muddy kind of sand. It looks more like black clay than like the sparkly, golden beach sand that people love most. A sand sculptor can work this other sort of sand almost like modeling clay.

Then the professionals pour just the right amount of water on each layer.

That's one important trick to sand building. If the sand is too dry, the grains don't stick together. You can hardly even build a decent pile out of dry sand, much less a castle.

On the other hand, if the sand is too wet, it drips and oozes. You can make a pile, but you can't make a definite shape.,

If the sand and water mix just right, though, you can build just about anything.

What makes sand and water stick together that well?

The peculiar answer may be electricity. Here's how it works:

1. A grain of sand becomes wet, just wet enough.

2. The moisture causes the surface of the grain of sand to become electrically charged. The electrical charge is very slight, but remember that there are millions of grains of sand together.)

3. This very slight electrical charge changes how the water molecules react. The water no longer flows easily. It almost seems thick.

4. The result is that the grains of sand don't move much either. They all stick together. But that happens only if you have exactly the right amount of water.

REMEMBER TO EXPERIMENT WITH JUST HOW MUCH WATER YOU NEED FOR YOUR NEXT SAND CASTLE. AND DON'T BE DISAPPOINTED IF YOUR CASTLE DOESN'T LAST LONG.

EXPLORE THE BEACH

If you're lucky enough to have a day at the beach, make the most of it.

Here are suggestions for exploring the beach:

1. Wear sunglasses, and be extremely careful about sunburn. Put on lots of sunscreen, and bring clothes that will protect your skin.

2. Don't go into the water without an adult.

3. Be careful climbing wet, slippery rocks. Bring old sneakers so you can climb without slipping or cutting your feet.

4. Watch out for the tide coming in. You don't want to get stuck on a rock that suddenly seems to be in the middle of the ocean. And watch out for the tide going out. That's when you can get caught in an undertow.

5. In the northern ocean or icy spring-fed lakes, don't stay in the water too long.

6. Don't walk on sand dunes or sand cliffs unless there are boardwalks or marked paths.

7. Don't take home live sea creatures or a shell that somebody's already living in.

8. Collect just one of each type of shell. Sea creatures find homes inside old shells. They need them.

9. As a rule, don't collect whole plants. Use blunt scissors so you can cut off parts of a plant without injuring the whole plant.

10. Do collect trash. Leave the beach as you found it—or even cleaner.

· · · · · · · · · · ·
BUILD A WATER'S-EDGE AQUARIUM
· ·

Build an on-the-beach aquarium to study water creatures just for the day.

A temporary aquarium is especially a good idea for ocean beaches. Salt-water creatures probably will not survive if you take them home.

Remember to bring a gallon jar to the beach with you. (Plastic is best.)

Put sand in the bottom, along with some rocks, seaweed, or parts of plants. Then fill the jar with sea water or lake water.

Catch small water creatures for your on-the-spot aquarium. They'll feel right at home, because they are right at home.

Don't catch jellyfish or other beach creatures that could sting you. It's smart to have someone help you identify creatures that can hurt you.

Study them all you want, and then at the end of the day let them go. When you get home, you can consult an encyclopedia or an identification book to see what sort of creatures stayed with you for the day.

AN AQUARIUM FOR THE DAY LETS YOU ENJOY WATER CREATURES WITH-OUT WORRYING THAT YOU'LL HURT THEM.

· · · · · · · · · · ·

DISPLAY A COLLECTION OF SEASHELLS AND OTHER BEACH TREASURES

· ·

Look for shells to take home from the beach.

But look inside the shell first to make sure you're not stealing an animal's home. Collect just one shell of each type. A sea creature may be planning to move in.

Here's what to do with your shells and other sea treasures:

1. When you get home, mix water and bleach, half and half. Soak the shells for a few hours.

2. Scrub the shells with cotton swabs or with an old toothbrush.

3. If you want to keep the beautiful colors of a seashell from fading, store the shell in a dark place.

4. If you don't have a set of small shelves for your collection, make some.
Cut the lid off an egg carton, or set up a cardboard box with dividers. You can always paint or wrap your containers to make an attractive background for your sea collection.

5. Be sure to identify and label each item in your collection. You'll want to remember where and when you found it.

YOU CAN ADD TO YOUR COLLECTION EVERY TIME YOU VISIT A BEACH. MAYBE SOMEDAY YOU'LL HAVE BEACH TREASURES FROM ALL OVER THE WORLD.

··········
COLLECT SEAWEED
·······························

Seaweed comes in a variety of colors. You can find green, blue-green, red, and brown seaweed.

And you can find two kinds of seaweed plants, flat and three-dimensional.

Here's how to collect seaweed samples:

1. Be careful when you wade into water to collect a seaweed sample. You might want to wear old sneakers that you don't mind getting wet. This is a good time to have an adult to help.

2. Use blunt scissors to cut off a piece of floating seaweed. Or use a small spade to scrape a seaweed plant off its base. (Just take one sample of each type. You don't want to disturb beach life too much.)

3. Take your samples home in a bucket of seawater.

4. Look in an encyclopedia or an identification book to name your seaweed.

LOOK FOR A TINT OF GREEN IN ALL YOUR SEAWEED SAMPLES. SEAWEED HAS GREEN CHLOROPHYLL, JUST LIKE OTHER PLANTS. YOU CAN PROBABLY SEE A GREEN TINT IN BROWN OR RED SEAWEED.

· · · · · · · · · · ·
DISPLAY A SEAWEED COLLECTION
· ·

If you want to keep flat seaweed, you'll need to dry it. If you can, take this job outside. At least, keep the wettest parts over a sink.

You'll need a place to dry the seaweed for several days. A covered porch, garage, or storage room would be just right.

Here's what you need:

A spray attachment or watering can

A shallow pan of water

Toothpicks

Old newspapers

Paper towels

A weight such as a board or a large book

Plastic wrap or plastic pages in a photograph album

Labels

Here's what you do:

1. Gently wash off sand and dirt from your seaweed samples. Use a spray attachment or watering can. You don't want to damage your samples.

2. Float the seaweed in the shallow pan of water. Use the toothpicks to arrange the seaweed so that all the leaves are floating separately.

3. Slide an old newspaper under the wet seaweed. Carefully lift the seaweed out of the water. Lay it on a thick layer of other old newspapers.

4. Use toothpicks to arrange the seaweed. Be careful. The seaweed will probably stick to the newspaper.

5. Cover with paper towels. Then flatten the seaweed with something heavy, such as the board or large book.

6. Every day change the newspapers. The seaweed will gradually dry over several days.

7. If you have several samples, you can dry them in layers. Put old newspapers and paper towels between each layer, with the board on top.

8. Display your dry seaweed samples between the plastic pages of a photograph album. Or cover them in plastic wrap. Be sure to label where and when you found the seaweed and what type it is.

> NOW YOU HAVE A SEAWEED COLLECTION. TRY TO GET SAMPLES OF EVERY COLOR.

· · · · · · · · · · ·
GO PONDING

· ·

Even if you can't visit an ocean beach any time you want, you can usually find a pond nearby. And a pond is teeming with interesting life.

You might want to catch some pond creatures for study.

Here's what you need:

A wide-mouthed jar or two (clear plastic is best since it won't break.)

A kitchen strainer

A yardstick, broom handle, or dowel rod

Masking tape or light wire

Here's what you do:

1. Fill the jar with pond water. If you plan to keep your creatures for any length of time, take home an extra jar of pond water.

2. Attach the kitchen strainer to the yardstick, broom handle, or dowel rod. Use the masking tape or wire to attach it securely. Or use a combination of tape and wire.

3. Hold your strainer in the water, and be very patient. Wait for just the right creature to swim inside.

4. Put the creatures you catch into the jar. Study the creatures in the jar. Watch to see if your creatures behave as friends or enemies. You may be surprised to see them start eating one another. But that is the way of nature.

5. Then, unless you are sure you can provide the right habitat, put your creatures back in the pond. They'll like it better there.

6. Even if you decide to take the creatures home, keep the lid off the jar as long as possible. You may need to put on the lid to transport the creatures in a car or on a bicycle. If so, punch air holes in the lid. It's very important that oxygen reach the water from the air. The oxygen dissolves in the water so the water creatures can breathe it.

GOING PONDING IS FUN. BUT DON'T TAKE A POND CREATURE HOME UNLESS YOU KNOW YOU CAN TAKE CARE OF IT.

SEND A MESSAGE IN A BOTTLE

Send a message in a bottle, and chances are about one in ten that you'll get a message back again. In other words, if you really want a message back, you'd better send out at least ten bottles.

This is a good project for a group of friends or a class.

You won't be the only one sending messages in bottles. Scientists often send them as a way of tracking ocean currents.

Here's what you need:

Plastic soft-drink bottles, preferably clear, with screw tops

Dry sand

Cards and stamps

Modeling clay, Play-Doh®, or candle wax

Your science notebook and pen

Here's what you do:

1. If you want to increase your chances of a reply, use clear bottles. People on a beach somewhere will have an extra chance to see that there's a message inside.

2. Fill each bottle with an inch (2 cm) or so of dry sand. That will make the bottle float. If people spot the bottle floating, there's an extra chance that they'll pick it up.

3. Write a message to the person who finds your bottle. If you want an extra chance of reply, put in a stamped postcard addressed to yourself.

4. Put the lid on tight. Help to waterproof the bottle by molding clay all around the lid. Or seal it with melted candle wax.

5. Send the bottle on its way. You don't want it to float right back to the same shore, so if you can, release it away from the shore. Release it from out on a boat or at least from the end of a dock or from a bridge.

6. Keep a record of when and where you release your bottles.

: THEN WAIT FOR A REPLY.

Figure Out Plants

*P*lants are all around us for a reason. They know how to survive.

You can use plant survival power to knock off bottle caps. You can watch plants defend themselves against their enemies. You can tell the life story of a tree.

You can figure out plant power.

FIGURE OUT PLANT POWER ALL AROUND YOU

Notice the many places you see plants growing. They can grow through cracks in the sidewalk. They can grow high in a tree or even in a tree stump. They can grow by the seashore, in the desert, or on a mountain.

The courthouse in Greensburg, Indiana, has a tree growing directly out of its roof.

What is the strangest place you've ever seen a plant growing?

Here are ways to look at plants:

1. What kind of plant is it? If you don't know, draw a picture and also describe the plant: its colors, the shape of its leaves, its size, the size of its stem. Then you can consult an encyclopedia or a field guide to find out the name of the plant.

2. Where is the plant growing? You can find out a lot about a plant by looking at its environment, whether it is growing in deep, rich soil or on rock, in the sun or in dark woods, on a mountain or near the ocean.

Notice how plants change as you go up a hill or into a forest or away from water. You can learn where a certain kind of plant does best by seeing where it grows with the deepest color and largest leaves or flowers.

USE PLANT POWER TO KNOCK OFF BOTTLE CAPS

You'll believe in the strength of plants when you see what they can do.

Here's what you need:

Fresh beans (from a seed packet or from the grocery store)

Water

Two small plastic bottles with pop-on caps

Here's what you do:

1. Soak the beans in the water overnight.

2. Fill one bottle with beans. Fill the other with beans and water. Put the caps on the bottles. (If you are using pill bottles, don't use the childproof lock on the caps.)

3. Wait a few days, and watch what the beans do. They might knock off the cap. They might even make the bottle split apart.

4. Make a comparison. Which beans are more powerful, the beans with water, or the beans without water?

NOW YOU KNOW ABOUT THE GROWTH POWER OF PLANTS.

· · · · · · · · · · ·
LOOK AT SEEDS IN ACTION
· ·

You'll like watching these powerful seeds grow. You may want to make sketches in your science notebook so you can remember how the seeds change day by day.

Here's what you need:

Several paper cups

Scissors or a knife

Plastic wrap

Tape

Rubber bands

Soil

Fresh beans (from a seed packet or from a grocery store)

Water

A plastic tray

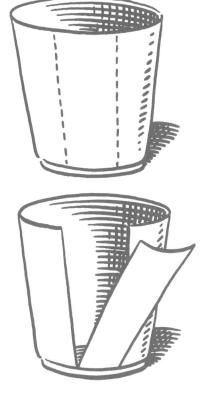

Here's what you do:

1. Punch several small holes in the bottom of each paper cup to allow water to drain.

2. With the knife or scissors, cut two slits down the side of each paper cup, so that you can pull down a section whenever you want to look at the beans. Caution: You need adult help with cutting.

3. Tape plastic wrap over the opening of each cup (not over the top of the cup). Then fold the cut side back up again, and secure it with a rubber band. (You'll need rubber bands that fit the cups tightly without collapsing them.)

4. Fill each cup with soil and three or four beans and set on the plastic tray. Keep the soil moist in each cup.

5. Take off the rubber band each day, and look through the plastic wrap to see how your seeds are doing.

: **NOW YOU CAN WATCH SEED**
: **POWER IN ACTION**

These see-in cups are a good way to do comparisons. You can do experiments to see how plants grow in different conditions.

REALLY SEE A SEED

As the bean seeds grow, occasionally take one out of its paper cup. Cut the bean open, and look at how it sprouts from inside.

Use your magnifying glass.

At first, you'll see the seed coat. The embryo is inside the bean, waiting to grow.

Then you'll see the root. The root is usually the first part to grow since it can absorb water and help the rest of the plant get started.

After that you'll see the beginnings of the stem. Then look for the seed leaves, called cotyledons.

HERE'S ANOTHER WAY TO UNDERSTAND SEED POWER.

Go all around your backyard, a playground, or a section of woods. Count how many different sorts of seeds you can spot in just that one area. You may be surprised.

FIGURE OUT INVISIBLE SEED POWER

If you look around, you can find seeds everywhere. You may even find invisible seeds.

Try this experiment with a sample of soil from your garden, yard, or just about anywhere. You may find hidden seeds in your soil sample.

Here's what you need:

Soil sample
Small pot, can, or empty milk carton
Water

Here's what you do:

1. Put the soil sample into the pot, can, or carton.

2. Water it regularly, and see what happens.

YOU MAY BE IN FOR A SEED SURPRISE.

LOOK FOR ROOT POWER

This job is not as easy as it seems.

Try to pull up a dandelion. See if you can get all the roots.

You'll see how roots hang on. Root power is one way the plant protects itself. Dandelions push a "tap root" deep into the soil. Even if you pull up most of a root, the plant can often grow again from just a little bit of root you didn't get.

That's why you probably see dandelions all over every spring.

Look at a root with your magnifying glass. You can see the root branching into smaller roots. Then those roots branch into even smaller roots. You can probably even see the tiniest root hairs.

· · · · · · · · · · ·
WATCH HOW PLANTS DEFEND THEMSELVES
· ·

Plants defend themselves with roots that hang on hard. And plants have plenty of other ways to beat off attack.

Look around your yard, a garden, or a section of woods. See if you can find plants that defend themselves in any of these ways:

1. Look for thorns and spines. You can get cut on plants like thistles and roses.
   We may be sorry that roses have thorns, but roses aren't sorry. They need the thorns for protection.

2. Look for poison ivy. That's the most common of the poison plants. But don't touch.
   You never want to get an itchy poison ivy rash.

3. Smell for bad odors. What animal would be dumb enough to try to eat a skunk cabbage? (A sweet smell has a purpose, too. A flower's sweet aroma attracts bees and other insects that can pollinate the flower and help it grow.)

4. Look for tough, woody stems on plants. These plants won't hurt you, but they are very hard to pick.

5. Look for milkweed. That's one plant that has a very bad taste, so animals leave it alone.
   Other plants, like some sorts of mushrooms, are poisonous to eat.

6. Go into the kitchen to find one more way that plants defend themselves. Try cutting an onion, and see what the onion does to your eyes.

To make your eyes sting and water, the onion uses a special amino acid that contains a few molecules of sulfur. If the sulfur reaches your eyes, it mixes with the natural fluids of your eyes and creates sulfuric acid. Fortunately, this is a weak type of sulfuric acid. It doesn't do any real harm.

Think of it as the onion's attempt to convince you not to chop it up and eat it.

> **NOW YOU KNOW HOW PLANTS TAKE ACTION AGAINST THEIR ENEMIES.**

REALLY SEE A BLADE OF GRASS

Grass is more than the green stuff that grows in your lawn.

Go into a field, a meadow, or your own yard at a spot where the grass grows deepest. If you look in enough places, you will see different types of grasses. Pick one or two of each.

Look at each kind of grass with your magnifying glass. Describe the color, shape, and feel of the leaves. Look for the places where the leaves grow from the stem and the way some leaves wrap around the stem. If you find seeds, look at how they attach to each blade of grass.

The grass family includes a wide variety of plants. Did you know that corn is a grass? And so are rice, wheat, bamboo, and sugarcane.

Here's how you can tell a grass when you see it:

1. All plants in the grass family have leaves that are longer than they are wide.
2. Parts of the leaves wrap around the stem.
3. All plants in the grass family have stems with solid joints. At each joint, a leaf grows in an opposite direction from the leaf above and the leaf below.

> NOW YOU CAN SEE HOW
> CORN, BAMBOO, AND YOUR
> LAWN ARE ALIKE.

THE LEAF GAME

To play this game, first rake up a small pile of leaves. Then collect a group of friends to play the leaf game with you.

Each player chooses a leaf from the pile and studies it carefully. If you wish, you can let everyone use a magnifying glass. But don't let the players make drawings or take notes.

Now scramble the leaves together.

See how many can pick out their own special leaves. At first glance, one leaf may look like all the others. But that's only at first glance.

> PERHAPS EVERYONE CAN WIN
> AT THIS GAME.

MAKE A NOTEBOOK OF LEAVES

You can make a collection of all sorts of leaves. Leaves are good souvenirs to keep when you travel. You can get different leaves from everywhere you go.

You might want to collect evergreen needles in the same way.

Here's what you need:

A fine collection of leaves for mounting

Old newspapers

Heavy books

Waxed paper

A warm iron

Household paste or glue

Cards or a photo album with plastic pages

Here's what you do:

1. Press your leaves between the old newspapers. Weight them down with heavy books until they're flat.

2. Now put each leaf between two pieces of the waxed paper. Press with the warm iron for just about 10 seconds.

3. Paste or glue your leaves on the cards. Or lay them between the plastic pages of the photo album.

4. Identify each leaf. Include on the label the type (oak, maple, sycamore, etc.), the date, and the place where you found the leaf.

NOW SEE HOW MANY TYPES OF LEAVES YOU CAN COLLECT.

COUNT HOW OLD A TREE IS

Count the age of a tree. And determine what sort of growth season the tree had each year.

Here's what you do:

1. Look at the stump of a tree. Or find a place on a live tree where a branch has fallen or been cut off.
2. Count the rings in the wood. Now you know the age of the tree or the age of the branch. (The branch is probably a lot younger than the tree.)
3. Notice how wide each ring is. A wide ring means that the tree had a good growing season, with enough sunshine and plenty of rain. A narrow ring shows a hard year.

4. What was happening in the world when the tree began its life? Can you think of any events in history that took place as the tree grew?

Did you know that trees can live longer than most any other kind of life? A few of the giant sequoia trees in California are more than 2,000 years old. The oldest tree in the world is a bristlecone pine in California, believed to be nearly 5,000 years old. It would have been pushing up its first sprouts back when the ancient Egyptians were building the pyramids. (Its name, of course, is Methuselah.)

: **NOW YOU CAN COUNT THE**
: **AGE OF A TREE.**

Tell a Tree's Life Story

You can look at a tree, and learn something about its life.

Here's what you do:

1. Look for places where the tree lost branches long ago. You can tell by scars on the bark. The bark may grow in a ring around an old injury or in some other, different pattern.

2. Look at how the tree has twisted and turned as it grew. It may have been avoiding obstacles (such as a fence or other trees) as it grew toward the sun.
   A tree on a steep hillside or in swampy soil may have shifted as it tried to dig in its roots.

3. Look at the way the trunk of the tree grows. An extra trunk or two probably mean that, when the tree was just a sprout, a porcupine nibbled off the top.

4. Look at the shape of the tree limbs. If the tree is tall and narrow, you can guess that the tree once stood by itself. Perhaps at one time the land was a meadow or a pasture. The tree may have once provided shade to farm animals.

5. Look at the condition of the leaves. Drooping, curly leaves show that the tree is trying to survive in bad soil or without enough water.
   If you see that the ends of some of the branches look nibbled, you can guess that a deer has been by and eaten low-hanging leaves.

6. Look for life in the tree. If you're lucky, you'll see bird nests. And look for squirrel nests, clumps of dried leaves high in the branches. If you include insects as well as birds and squirrels, you may find quite a high life count in just one tree.

7. If you find a dead tree, see if you can tell what killed it.
   When lightning strikes a tree, it can stand for years afterwards. It will probably be the only injured tree among a group of healthy trees. But if a fire has hit, you'll see fire scars on all the trees around.
   If you find trees blown down, you may be able to tell from the way they are lying the path of the storm that hit.
   You may find a hole in the ground with a mound next to it. Then you can guess that a tree fell, with its whole root system ripping out of the ground. The remains will be there long after the tree itself is gone.

Now You Know Something About The Life Story Of A Tree.

GROW PLANT POWER

*F*ind out all about plant power. With these experiments, you can find out everything plants need.

You can start new plants from roots, stems, or just one leaf.

You can figure out if plants like music or the human touch. You can even find out if plants like you.

· · · · · · · · · ·

EXPERIMENT TO SEE HOW PLANTS GROW IN DIFFERENT SOILS

· ·

You can compare how plants grow in different kinds of soil. Then you'll be able to decide what's best for your plants.

For this experiment, you will grow seven plants, all the same, under all the same conditions—except one. Only the soil will be different.

Spread old newspapers over your work space, or else do this job outside. It can get messy.

Here's what you need:

Gardening gloves

A small trowel or large spoon

Labels

Seven 4-inch (10 cm) plant pots, cans, or empty milk cartons, all the same

Seeds (Choose any kind you like. But if you're in a hurry, use a seed packet of beans, marigolds, or sweet peas. They grow rapidly.)

Water

Seven white cards or pieces of paper

Scissors

Your science notebook and pen

Here are the seven kinds of soil you need:

Potting soil

Peat moss

Vermiculite

Garden soil

Compost from a compost pile

Sand

Clay soil

Here's what you do:

1. Sterilize any soils you didn't buy from a store. Bake them in the oven for 20 minutes at 350 degrees. The heat will kill grubs and spores that might damage your plants. (Soils that you buy, such as potting soil, vermiculite, and peat moss, have already been sterilized.)

2. Use your gardening gloves and the trowel or spoon to fill each of the seven pots, cans, or cartons with the same amount of soil. Put a different kind of soil in each container. (If you are using cans or cartons, be sure to punch small holes in the bottom of each for drainage.) Label each with the kind of soil it contains.

3. Now plant three or four seeds in each pot. Plant each seed about $3/4$ inch deep, or follow the instructions on the seed packet. Tiny seeds may need only a sprinkling of soil over them.

4. Measure out $1/3$ cup (80 ml) of water to pour into each pot. Make sure that each plant has exactly the same amount of water.

5. Put the pots together in the same place. Cover each with a white card or piece of paper.

6. Every third day, water your plants. Use exactly $1/3$ cup (80 ml) of water for each.

7. When the seeds begin to poke out of the soil, remove the covers.

8. When the plants grow their first real leaves, snip off plants so that each pot has only two.

9. In your science notebook, note how the plants are different after a week:
- The date on which each plant sprouted
- The number of seeds that sprouted in each type of soil
- The size of each plant
- The color of each plant
- The number and condition of the leaves and flowers
- The strength of the stems

10. Look again after 2, 3, and 4 weeks. Now you're ready to draw conclusions. Which soils are best for growing these particular plants? (The soil best for seeds is not necessarily the soil best for full-grown plants.) You might want to re-do the experiment with other kinds of seeds.

11. Here's one more comparison. How do your plants compare with the same sort of plants growing outdoors?

: **NOW YOU KNOW HOW SEEDS**
: **GROW IN DIFFERENT SOILS.**

EXPERIMENT TO SEE HOW PLANTS USE SUNLIGHT

Of course, you already know that plants need sunlight. But you can experiment to see just what happens to a plant without sun. And you can find out how long it takes a plant to recover from lack of sunlight.

If you wish, use plants from other experiments. You need two plants that are exactly the same. The only difference will be the amount of sunlight you give them.

Here's what you need:

Two identical potted plants
Water
Your science notebook and pen

Here's what you do:

1. Put one plant in a dark closet, or close it up in a box. Set the other plant in sunlight.

2. Water the two plants with equal amounts of water. Give them water as soon as the soil is dry.

3. After a week, look at the two plants. They have had the same soil, the same amount of water, the same food reserve. The only differences you see must be due to the difference in sunlight. Note particularly:
   • The size of each plant
   • The color of each plant
   • The number and condition of the leaves and flowers
   • The strength of the stems

4. Now put both plants in the sunlight. Note how long it takes for the deprived plant to return to health.

> **NOW YOU KNOW WHAT HAPPENS TO PLANTS WITHOUT SUNSHINE.**

· · · · · · · · · ·
GROW A SMART PLANT
· ·

Plants have a powerful urge to turn toward sunlight. You can find this out by creating a plant maze.

The easy way to see a plant reach out for sunlight is just to turn a plant pot on its side. You'll see the plant turn and start growing upward toward the sun.

But you'll enjoy creating a plant maze.

Here's what you need:

Seeds (Beans are perfect since they grow fast. Buy them in seed packets or at the grocery store.)

Water

Scissors

A box with cardboard dividers and a cover

A small plant pot

Soil

Your science notebook and pen

Here's what you do:

1. Soak the seeds in the water overnight.

2. With the scissors, cut holes in the dividers of the cardboard box. You are creating a maze to see if your plant can find its way through. Cut a final hole in the outside of the box.

3. Fill a small pot with the soil and seeds. Set it at a far end of the divided carton.

4. Put the cover on the divided carton. Place the box in a sunny place, with the outside hole facing the source of sunlight.

5. Remove the lid about twice a week, and water your plant.

6. As seeds sprout, they grow toward sunlight. Yours will twist and turn around the cardboard obstacles. Finally, you'll see leaves poking through the outside hole. Then you'll know you have a smart plant.

7. Keep notes on how smart your plant is. Note how long the plant took to reach sunlight.

NOW YOU KNOW THAT PLANTS TURN TOWARD SUNLIGHT.

Watch a sunflower some day. Its head follows the sun from sunrise to sunset.

· · · · · · · · · ·
EXPERIMENT WITH GREENHOUSE PLANTS
· ·

Experiment to see why gardeners often grow plants under glass. Make your own temporary greenhouse.

Here's what you need:

Two small plant pots, cans, or empty milk cartons

Pebbles, if you wish

Soil

Flower seeds

Water

Your science notebook and pen

Here's what you can use for your "greenhouse":

A large, wide-mouthed glass jar

or

A large plastic bag with a tie

or

A large plastic "bubble" from food packaging

Here's what you do:

1. If you want to keep these plants, put a layer of pebbles in the bottom of each pot, can, or carton. Then fill each pot with soil. Plant the same number of seeds in each pot.

2. Set the two pots in sunlight.

3. Create a temporary greenhouse. Put the wide-mouthed glass jar upside down over one of the pots. Or tie the pot in the large plastic bag. Or put the large plastic "bubble" over the plant. If the bag or bubble is not large enough, you may be able to prop it up with sticks so it fits over the plant.

4. Every day, remove the jar or plastic for a few minutes to let in fresh air. When the soil looks dry, water each plant with the same amount of water.

5. The two plants have the same soil, the same amount of water, the same plant nutrients. But the "greenhouse" makes three big differences:
   - The temperature inside the jar or bag is higher.
   - The humidity is higher, so that plant gets more moisture from the air.
   - The circulation of air is more limited.

6. Keep a record of how each plant grows. Note particularly:
   - The dates of first sprouting
   - The number of seeds sprouted
   - The color of the plant
   - The number and condition of the leaves and flowers
   - The strength of the stems

COMPARE THE TWO PLANTS, AND DECIDE WHETHER A GREENHOUSE IS GOOD FOR PLANTS. Also consider when a greenhouse is not good.

··········
EXPERIMENT TO SEE HOW MUCH WATER PLANTS NEED
·······························

Of course, you know that plants need water. But plants can get too much water as well as too little. Experiment with watering plants.

Here's what you need:

Three identical potted plants
Labels
Water
Your science notebook and pen

Here's what you do:

1. Set the plants in a sunny place and label them as 1, 2, and 3. Every other day, water plant 1 with 2 cups (500 ml) of water, and water plant 2 with 1/3 cup (80 ml) of water. Once a week, water plant 3 with 1/3 cup (80 ml) of water.

2. After a week, look at each plant. The plants have had the same soil, the same amount of sunshine, the same food reserve. The only differences must be due to the difference in the amount of water.

Note particularly:
- The size of each plant
- The color of each plant
- The number and condition of the leaves and flowers
- The strength of the stems

3. Take notes again after 2, 3, and 4 weeks.

4. Now begin giving plants 1 and 3, as well as plant 2, 1/3 cup (80 ml) of water every other day. Note how long it takes for the overwatered and the underwatered plant to return to health.

> **NOW YOU KNOW WHAT HAPPENS WHEN PLANTS GET TOO MUCH OR TOO LITTLE WATER.**

What would happen if you used cactus plants for this experiment?

MAKE A FLOWER CHANGE COLOR

You can see how a plant takes up water. Just put the stem of a cut flower in colored water. When the water reaches the flower, the flower changes color.

Here's what you need:

Food coloring

A vase or jar

Water

A light-colored flower, such as a carnation or daisy

Here's what you do:

1. Mix several drops of the food coloring into the vase or jar of water.

2. Put the cut flower into the vase of colored water. Before you know it, your flower will change color. If you cut the stem or leaves, you will see colored water there, too.

NOW YOU KNOW HOW PLANTS TAKE UP WATER.

GROW A STEM OR A ROOT INTO A PLANT

Begin with just the stem or just the root from a plant. Use the part of a plant to grow a whole plant.

Spread old newspapers over your work surface, or else do this job outside.

Here's what you need:

A healthy "parent" plant (If you want to grow a plant from just a stem, choose a geranium, coleus, petunia, or fuchsia. If you want to grow a plant from a root, choose a dahlia, a Jerusalem artichoke, a ginger plant, a sweet potato, or a hydrangea.)

A sharp knife

A 6-inch (15 cm) or 8-inch (20 cm) plant pot with an underdish

Pebbles

Potting soil

Water

Your science notebook and pen

Here's what you do:

1. From the healthy plant, "borrow" part of the stem or root. Use the knife to cut off a section of the stem or root with a branch on it. Cut at a slant. If you are cutting a stem, cut off leaves near the cut end, but leave them on at the tip end.

   : *Caution: Get an adult to help*
   : *you with the cutting:*

2. Cover the bottom of the pot with the pebbles. Then fill the pot about halfway with the potting soil. Plant the root or stem with the cut-off end down. Cover lightly with soil, gently packing the soil all around the root or stem.

3. Water, and set in a windowsill or other warm place.

4. Water again every couple of days. Pinch back the growing tip whenever your plant threatens to become too tall and scraggly.

5. Watch your plant grow. Sketch or describe it in your science notebook so that you can remember how it developed day by day.

: **NOW YOU KNOW HOW TO**
: **GROW A PLANT FROM A STEM**
: **OR A ROOT. AND YOU HAVE**
: **YOUR OWN WHOLE PLANT**
: **THAT YOU GREW.**

··········
GROW LEAVES INTO A PLANT
·······························

Begin with just leaves. Use them to grow your own ivy plant.

Here's what you need:

A sharp knife
A healthy "parent" ivy plant
A glass or jar
Water
A 4-inch (10 cm) or 6-inch (15 cm) hanging plant pot
Pebbles
Potting soil
Your science notebook and pen

Here's what you do:

1. Using the knife, cut off a small branch of leaves from the healthy ivy.

   Caution: Get an adult to help you with the cutting.

2. Put the leaves in a glass or jar of water for a few days until they begin to grow roots.

3. Cover the bottom of the pot with pebbles. Then fill it about halfway with potting soil. Plant the branch of leaves. Cover the roots and about half the branch with soil, firming the soil all around them.

4. Water, and hang in a sunny window.

5. Water again every couple of days.

6. Watch the ivy grow. Sketch or describe it in your science notebook so that you can remember how it developed day by day.

: **NOW YOU KNOW HOW TO**
: **GROW PLANTS FROM LEAVES.**
: **AND YOU HAVE YOUR OWN**
: **HANGING IVY THAT YOU GREW.**

GROW JUST ONE LEAF INTO A PLANT

You can rescue a leaf that fell off a plant, or cut off just one leaf, to start your own full-sized plant.

Try this with an African violet. If you want a full-grown violet for Mother's Day, begin some time in the fall.

Here's what you need:

A sharp knife

A mature leaf from an African violet plant

A 4-inch (10 cm) or 6-inch (15 cm) plant pot

Pebbles

Potting soil

Water

Your science notebook and pen

Here's what you do:

1. Use the sharp knife to cut a leaf, along with about 1 inch of the leaf stem, from the African violet plant. Cut on a slant. If you are using a leaf that fell off, make a fresh, slanted cut. (Don't use scissors. You could crush the fragile stem.)

   Caution: Get an adult to help you with the cutting.

2. Let your leaf sit for a few hours.

3. Cover the bottom of the plant pot with pebbles. Fill about halfway with the potting soil, and plant your leaf. Cover the leaf stem with the soil.

4. Water, and set on a windowsill or in another warm place.

5. Water again every couple of days.

6. Watch the African violet leaf grow. Sketch or describe it in your science notebook so you can remember how it grew week by week. Be patient.

   NOW YOU KNOW HOW TO GROW AN AFRICAN VIOLET FROM JUST A SINGLE LEAF.

· · · · · · · · · · ·
GROW YOUR OWN POTATO PLANT
· ·

Begin with just the eye of a potato, and use it to grow your own potato plant. If you leave a sack of potatoes in a cupboard for too long, the eyes all begin to grow without any help.

Spread old newspapers over your work space, or else do this job outside.

Here's what you need:

A knife
A potato
A 6-inch (15 cm) plant pot
Pebbles
Potting soil
Water

Here's what you do:

1. With the knife, cut out an eye from the potato, leaving plenty of potato around it.

   : *Caution: Get an adult to help*
   : *you with the cutting.*

2. Cover the bottom of the pot with the pebbles. Then fill the pot about halfway with the potting soil. Plant the potato eye, and cover lightly with soil. Pack the soil all around it.

3. Water, and set on a windowsill or in another warm place.

4. Water again every couple of days.

5. Watch the potato plant grow. Keep track of its growth in your science notebook.

6. In the spring you may want to transfer your potato plant outside. If so, dig a hole in the garden, and tip the pot so that the plant and soil come out in one piece. Set the potato plant in the hole, and gently pack soil all around it. Water thoroughly. Or you may just want to transfer your potato plant to a larger pot.

: **BY FALL, YOU WILL PROBABLY**
: **HAVE YOUR OWN POTATOES**
: **TO EAT.**

TALK TO PLANTS

You know that plants need good soil, water, and sunlight. But do they need YOU? Are plants happier if you talk to them or touch them? Try this experiment, and find out.

Because it is time-consuming, this experiment is a good project for a group of friends or family.

Here's what you need:

Two identical potted plants
Labels
Water
Your science notebook and pen

Here's what you do:

1. Select one plant for talking to and one control plant for the silent treatment. Label the two plants.

2. Set both plants on a sunny windowsill or in another warm place. Be sure that the room is very quiet most of the time.

3. Whenever the soil looks dry, water the plants with equal amounts of water.

4. Once a day, take the control plant out of the room. Then talk quietly to the other plant. You don't need to tell it any special secrets. Just keep talking for at least 15 minutes. Very gently stroke the plant's leaves as you talk. You might want to play soft music for another 15 minutes or so.

5. After a week, look at each plant. The two plants have had the same soil, the same amount of water, the same degree of sunshine. Any differences must be due to sound or touch.
   Note particularly:
   • The size of each plant
   • The color of each plant
   • The number and condition of the leaves and flowers
   • The strength of the stems

6. Take notes again after 2, 3, and 4 weeks.

: **NOW YOU KNOW IF PLANTS**
: **RESPOND TO SOUNDS AND**
: **TOUCH THAT FOR PEOPLE**
: **MEAN LOVE AND AFFECTION.**

Talk to the Animals, Help Out the Animals

*W*ould you like to communicate with animals? Communicating is not just talking. You can learn the signals that animals send out to you. Maybe you can even send a reply.

You know you can play with a puppy or a kitten. Would you like to play a game with an ant or with fireflies? You might enjoy their company.

You might even be able to figure out what animals are thinking or feeling.

And would you like to help your fellow creatures? In their own ways they're probably helping you. After all, you're part of their habitat, and they're part of your habitat.

TRACK AN ANT

Ants always seem very busy. But maybe an ant will stop long enough to play a game with you. Here's a game you can play with an ant. You'll like it, and the ant will, too.

Here's what you need:

A bright sunny day
A crumbly cookie

Here's what you do:

1. Go outside and find an ant. If there are several, be sure to keep track of the one that is "your" ant.
2. Make a trail of cookie crumbs, with no gaps. Watch your ant, and see if it can find the trail and then stay on it. And see if the ant appears to communicate with other ants about the cookies.
3. Run your finger across the path of crumbs, and see what happens.

THIS IS A GOOD GAME FOR BOTH YOU AND THE ANT. The ant likes the cookie crumbs, and you get to watch how ants operate.

But don't take up too much of the ant's valuable time. Each ant has a job to do, and each job is important to the whole community of ants.

LOOK AT A LADYBUG

Not all of the beetles we call ladybugs are ladies. Half of them are male.

But they all seem to be friends to people, mostly because of what they like to eat. They eat plant lice (also called aphids) and scale insects, the sort of insects that can destroy farmers' crops. A ladybug can eat 50 to 100 aphids a day.

Naturally, the farmers want to keep ladybugs around.

If you pick up a ladybug (carefully!) in your hand, it will happily walk back and forth from one hand to the other. The ladybug seems friendly, and you can see why people think of these insects as bringing good luck.

People also like ladybugs because they're cute. Look for the different colors:
- Yellow with black spots
- Red with black spots
- Black with white spots
- Black with yellow spots
- Black with red spots

And count the spots. On each ladybug, you'll find 2, 9, or 15 spots.

Did you ever hear the verse about ladybugs?

Ladybug, ladybug! Fly away home!

Your house is on fire,

And your children will burn!

Farmers used to burn fields. Fire was a good way to clear the fields and get them ready for the next planting. But they didn't like to burn the ladybug larvae, the ladybug "children." In fact, Christian farmers liked these beetles so much that they gave them a religious sort of name, "beetles of the Blessed Lady."

THAT'S WHY WE STILL CALL THEM LADYBUGS.

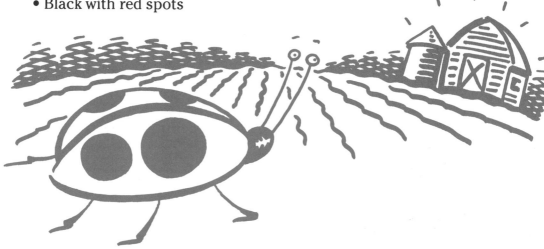

. . . .
"TALK" TO FIREFLIES

. . . .

You really can communicate with fireflies. They'll gather around to "talk" with you.

Each type of firefly has its own light pattern. They flash on and off in distinctive ways. That's how males and females identify others of their own species.

Fireflies also light up in different colors: yellow, pale blue, or pale blue-green.

Here's all you need:

A summer night full of fireflies
A pen-sized flashlight

Here's what you do:

1. Sit outside and wait for a firefly to flash. Hold your penlight close to the ground. Wait a second or two, and then send a reply. Flash your penlight in the same pattern.
2. When you get a response from a firefly, try to match its signal. Give the same number and length of flashes.
You'll see the fireflies gathering around. One may even land on your hand.

The best way to catch fireflies is with your hands. If you decide to put them in a jar for a while, be sure the lid has holes in it for air. You can put the jar in your room to light it up overnight. But after you've studied the fireflies, set them free outside where they belong.

If you put a thermometer in your jar, you'll find no change in temperature. The "fire" of a firefly is cold. A chemical in the firefly reacts with oxygen molecules to create the glow.

So a firefly doesn't possess real fire, and it isn't really a fly either.

REMEMBER; YOU DON'T NEED TO CATCH FIREFLIES TO HAVE AN INTERESTING "TALK" WITH THEM.

FIGURE OUT HOW AN INSECT DEFENDS ITSELF

When you look at an insect, try to discover how it protects itself. You'll find that insects have a multitude of defenses:

1. The insect often has a hard covering. The skeletons of insects are usually on the outside and are called exoskeletons. The word insect means "cut in," or divided into several different parts. Usually, the hard parts consist of a head, a thorax, and an abdomen.

2. The insect may make noises to frighten off creatures that want to eat it.

3. The insect may smell bad. Some insects give off evil-smelling fluids. No other creature wants to come close.

4. The insect may taste bad. A monarch butterfly is a good, bad-tasting example.

5. Sometimes an insect just looks like another type of insect that smells bad or tastes bad.

6. The insect may sting. Some insects have poisonous spines.

7. Ants can fight off danger with their powerful jaws.

8. Most insects blend into the background. The creature who wants to eat them has trouble finding them. The insect may be colored like a flower, leaf, or twig. Some may look just like leaves or twigs. Just try to find the insect called a walking stick. It looks exactly like a stick with eyes.

9. Insects like bees, ants, and termites work together in groups. They have ways to warn one another of danger, and each works to protect the whole group.

10. Fireflies give off a cold light. That's one way males call to females. But the light may also be a defense. Birds and bats seem not to like the light. They stay away from fireflies. (But frogs don't mind a bit. A frog can eat so many fireflies at once that you can see light glowing through the frog's skin.)

YOU CAN LOOK AT INSECTS A LONG TIME BEFORE YOU FIND ALL THE WAYS THEY HAVE TO PROTECT THEMSELVES.

· · · · · · · · · ·

PARACHUTE WITH A DADDY LONGLEGS

· ·

The next time you're out in a field, find a daddy longlegs.

A daddy longlegs looks a bit like a spider. It's in the spider—or arachnid—family because it has eight legs. (Insects have only six legs.) But spiders have two body segments, and a daddy longlegs has only one.

Most important, a daddy longlegs doesn't bite. It's safe to pick up.

Bend down, and coax the daddy longlegs onto your hand. Now stand up, and tap the back of your hand.

WATCH THE DADDY LONGLEGS PARACHUTE GRACEFULLY TO EARTH.

· · · · · · · · · ·

FEED A SPIDER

· ·

Spiders don't need your help to find flies to eat. But you might like to watch how a spider stalks its prey. You can see the spider wrap a fly in its web. And some spiders inject a chemical that makes it impossible for the fly to move.

Just pick up a dormant or dead fly with a pair of tweezers (A dormant fly is one who doesn't move and appears to be sleeping.) Put it on the edges of a spider's web. The web will shake a little, so the spider will know something is there.

Look to see if the spider has other insects in the web. If spiders want a late snack, they just wrap their catch in silk and store it. Or the spider may already have eaten the juicy parts of the insect. A spider sucks the juices out of its prey, leaving only the outer skeleton. When you're done, wash your hands.

AREN'T YOU GLAD YOU'RE NOT A FLY?

STUDY THE DIFFERENCES BETWEEN A MOTH AND A BUTTERFLY

You can catch moths easily by shining a light. The moths will helplessly fly toward the light.

Here are the differences between moths and butterflies:

1. Moths fly by night. Butterflies fly by day.
2. A moth rests with its wings spread out. A butterfly rests with its wings upright.
3. Most types of moths have feathery antennae. Butterflies have thin antennae that end in a club shape.
4. The body of a moth is larger and thicker than the body of a butterfly.

LIKE BUTTERFLIES, MOTHS CAN SOMETIMES BE VERY BEAUTIFUL. For instance, look for a light green lunar moth some time.

GET A CRICKET TO TELL YOU THE TEMPERATURE

Crickets sing faster in warm weather. Count the chirps, and you may come close to learning the temperature.

Here's what you do:

1. Count the number of cricket chirps per minute.
2. Subtract 40. Divide that number by 4. Add 50.

SUPPOSEDLY, YOU GET THE NUMBER OF DEGREES FAHRENHEIT. FOR CELSIUS TAKE THE FAHRENHEIT NUMBER, SUBTRACT 32, AND DIVIDE IN HALF. BUT DON'T WORRY IF YOUR RESULT IS NOT ACCURATE. This is just for fun.

TELL THE AGE OF A FISH

Next time you're having fish for dinner, figure out how old the fish was. Or find a dead fish on the beach. A live fish just won't stay around long enough for you to study it.

Here's what you need:

Fish scales
A magnifying glass

Here's what you do:

1. Study the fish scales with the magnifying glass. If you can study more than one kind of fish, you'll see that the design on each kind is different.

2. On each scale, look for a pattern. You'll see wide, light-colored bands, along with narrow, dark-colored bands. The wide, light bands show the growth of the fish during each summer of its life. The narrow, dark bands show the growth during each winter of its life.

3. To find the age of the fish, just count the sets of dark and light bands.

IN THIS ONE WAY, FISH GROW LIKE TREES. THEY ADD MARKS OF THEIR OWN GROWTH EVERY SEASON.

TELL THE AGE OF A TURTLE

Like a fish or a tree, a turtle records each year of its growth. Use a magnifying glass to count the number of rims or rings on the turtle's shell plates.

TELL WHETHER A TURTLE IS MYRTLE OR YERTLE

You can tell whether a turtle is a male or female by looking at the shape of its plastron. That's the undershell of the turtle.

(The carapace is the upper shell. Two bridges connect the carapace and the plastron. The two bridges hold the top and bottom shells apart, so that the turtle's soft body is safe inside.)

On a female turtle, the plastron is curved outward.

On a male turtle, the plastron is curved slightly inward.

RECOGNIZE FROG CALLS

On a spring or summer night, you may hear frogs calling. Usually, the male frogs are calling the female frogs. You can tell what species of frog (or toad) is calling just by listening:

1. If you hear nighttime quacking, that's not ducks. Wood frogs are calling for their mates.
2. If you hear long trills, the callers are American toads.
3. If you hear whistles or bells, the callers are spring peepers.
4. If you hear a chorus of dull twangs, the callers are green frogs.
5. If you hear snoring, the callers are pickerel frogs.

KEEP AWAY FROM MOSQUITOES

If you can't keep hundreds of bats as mosquito-eating pets, then try other ways to keep away from mosquitoes.

Did you know that only female mosquitoes try to suck your blood? Mosquitoes don't bite for food. Instead, the female mosquito needs blood for protein to produce her eggs. When she bites, she can take in up to three times her own weight in blood.

When a mosquito bites you, she imparts a substance that makes you itchy, uncomfortable, and annoyed. She might even be spreading a disease such as encephalitis.

And then she can fly off, loaded with your blood, and use it to produce as many as 500 eggs for 500 more mosquitoes!

Here are some ways to protect yourself against mosquitoes:

1. Mosquitoes are most eager to bite you at twilight and at dawn. Stay inside at those times, or if you go outside, wear long sleeves and pants.

2. Mosquitoes breed in standing water. Any time you see standing water, even if it's just an old jar left outside, see what you can do to get rid of it. Look for standing water in wading pools or toys, in gutters, wheelbarrows, or watering cans, and in the gardens.

3. Stay away from swamps and wooded places, especially at night. If you're camping overnight, use mosquito netting.

4. Use insect repellent that contains a chemical with the short name of "DEET." You can put it on your skin or clothes.

5. Don't wear perfume outside. Mosquitoes like nice smells.

CAST A TRACK

You can start a collection of animal tracks, all cast in plaster.

When you hunt for animal tracks, be prepared with track-casting equipment. A track doesn't last long. As soon as it rains or people walk over the track, it's gone.

Here's what you need:

Plastic wrap

An empty can

A jug of water (or a handy source of clean water)

Plaster of paris

A stick

A box

Paint, if you wish

Here's what you do:

1. Find a clear animal track on bare, dry ground. Clean off the debris.

2. Line the track with the plastic wrap. Leave some sticking up around the edge of the track.

3. For a small or medium track, fill the empty can with about 1 cup (250 ml) of water. Sprinkle on about 1 1/2 cups (360 ml) of plaster of paris. Use the stick to mix until you have a thick sort of soup. Add more water or plaster as you wish.

4. Pour the mixture into the plastic-lined track until the track is filled. Let the mixture set for 30 minutes or so, until the plaster hardens.

5. Now carefully remove the plaster cast (with the plastic wrap still on it). Put it in the box and take it home.

6. Let the plaster continue to harden overnight.

7. The next day, peel off the plastic wrap. Use a stick or knife to remove any bubbles or rough edges. After you clean the cast, you may want to smooth it with fine sandpaper.

8. Of course, you'll want to find out what sort of animal made the track. When you do, scratch the name on the plaster cast. And you might like to paint the cast. You can use water colors if you wish.

: **NOW YOU HAVE A FINE**
: **PLASTER CAST TO START**
: **YOUR COLLECTION OF ANIMAL**
: **TRACKS.**

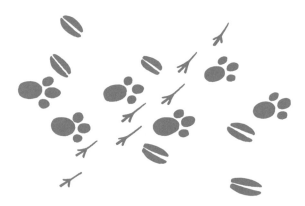

FIND OUT IF A DOG OR CAT CAN SEE COLORS

For a long time, people have believed that dogs and cats see only in black and white. But now scientists are beginning to think differently.

Human beings see color with three sets of cones in their eyes. Dogs and cats have only two sets. So they don't see color the same way as we do.

But dogs and cats sometimes seem able to tell the difference between very different colors, such as red and blue.

Test your pet to find out:

Here's what you need:

A red light and a blue light
Treats

Here's what you do:

1. Set up a "good" red light and a "bad" blue light. When your dog or cat nudges the red light, regard your pet with a treat and praise. But tell your pet it's bad to nudge the blue light.

2. Then switch the position of the lights. See if your pet can still recognize the "good" red light.

BUT DON'T EXPECT YOUR PET TO KNOW THE DIFFERENCE BETWEEN SIMILAR COLORS LIKE BLUE AND VIOLET.

············
TRACK AN IMAGINARY ANIMAL
·····························

Design an animal from your own imagination. Then ask a friend to figure out how to track it to its home.

This is a good project for a school group or a group of friends.

Try to design a really peculiar animal.

Consider:

- The look and size of your own private animal
- How it gets around and the speed at which it travels
- The sort of shelter it prefers
- The food it likes best
- How it takes care of its babies
- Its friends and enemies
- Its temper—Is it shy or aggressive?

Draw a picture or map, and list other clues for your friend to track by. Perhaps your animal leaves behind bits of fur or feathers, food leftovers, or scraps of the stuff it uses to build a home. Probably your animal leaves a few good tracks. Maybe it leaves behind a few really unusual clues.

YOU CAN TRACK AN ANIMAL ANY-WHERE IN YOUR IMAGINATION. AND YOUR FRIEND CAN PUT TOGETHER THE CLUES TO AN ANIMAL THAT DOESN'T EXIST.

. . . .
MAKE A CREATURE HAPPY
. . . .

Here are some small ways to help other creatures. They'll probably help you in some way. They're part of your habitat.

1. If you're out watering the garden and you see a toad, give it a little shower with the watering can. Toads help people. One toad can eat 10,000 annoying insects per summer.

2. If you find a worm marooned out on the street, scoop it up with a bit of leaf or twig. Save the worm's life by moving it to your garden. In turn, worms make better gardens. They tunnel through soil so that the soil stays light and airy. They help get rid of garbage by eating it, and then their waste provides good fertilizer. (Gardeners and farmers often buy worms by the pound.)

3. De-paint a turtle. If someone makes the mistake of buying a turtle with a painted shell, help the turtle. The paint can injure the shell or make the turtle sick. Remove the paint with nail polish remover. Then wash the shell clean.

4. If you find a bat in your house or garage, don't kill it. Instead, throw a blanket over it, and help it to go outside.

    Caution: Don't touch a bat. Bats are not as bad in real life as they are in legends. But a distressed bat could bite you and might even carry a disease like rabies.

Most likely, though, the bat was just out to spend the night eating mosquitoes. And you'll probably agree that's a very good idea.

5. Birds sometimes fly into large windows and get badly hurt. They don't see the glass, or they may be upset by their own reflection in the glass. If your house has a big window, put up stickers (perhaps pictures of owls or other enemies) or tape. Then the bird will be able to see that something is in its way.

6. Help a bird build a nest next spring. Put brightly colored yarn in bushes. You'll be able to spot the nest faster when you can look for the yarn colors.

FEED BIRDS THEIR FAVORITE FOODS

Birds eat 80 percent of their own weight every day. (If you weighed 100 pounds (about 40 kg), you could keep up with a bird by eating 80 pounds (32 kg) of food every day.) So, of course, birds are almost always hungry.

When you buy bird food, look for the kinds that birds like best:

- Berries, raisins, and other dried fruits
- Orange peels
- Peanuts (unsalted, shelled)
- Suet

  (Suet is beef fat. You can buy a chunk from a butcher. Or there may be beef fat left over when your family has had steak or roast beef for dinner.)

- Safflower seeds
- Sunflower seeds
- Thistle seeds

You may particularly want to try safflower seeds because squirrels don't like them. If you use other kinds of seeds, greedy squirrels will do their best to steal them away from the birds.

FEED A BIRD THE EASY WAY

You don't need an expensive bird feeder. Just find a board or a piece of plywood about 1 foot square. Nail the board to a tree stump or branch. Or just set it on the ground.

> *Caution: Don't set up a ground feeder if there are cats around. A low tree stump may be risky too. Birds absorbed in feeding can be easy prey.*

Pile on seeds, berries, or bits of dried fruit.

Or tie a chunk of suet in plastic netting. Hang the netting from a tree or bush.

GIVE THE BIRDS A SPECIAL WINTER TREAT

A Christmas tradition is to be kind to our fellow creatures. Whether you celebrate Christmas or not, winter is an especially good time to feed the birds. And it's a good time to find pine cones.

Spread suet over a large pine cone. Then stick a few seeds into the suet.

Now tie the pine cone in a tree. You could even make a sort of Christmas decoration with red and green ribbons.

Or hammer a nail into a branch or other piece of wood. Stick the pine cone upright on the nail.

YOU'LL GIVE THE BIRDS A MID-WINTER TREAT JUST WHEN THEY NEED EXTRA FOOD THE MOST.

BUILD A BIRD FEEDER

This bird feeder is easy to make, and it will last all year round.

Here's what you need:

A one-gallon (4 liter) plastic bottle, with a screw cap, such as a bleach bottle
Scissors
A piece of rope or twine

Here's what you do:

1. Wash out the bottle. Rinse until you can't smell bleach anymore.
2. With the scissors, cut an opening in the side of the bottle opposite the handle. Start the cut about 1¼ inches (3 cm) from the bottom of the bottle. The opening ought to measure about 5" by 4" (13 cm × 10 cm).
   : *Caution: You need an adult to help you with cutting.*
3. Tie a piece of rope or heavy twine around the neck of the bottle just below the bottle cap.
4. Hang the bottle from a limb of a tree, and KEEP IT FULL OF SEEDS.

THE BIRDS WILL LOVE THEIR BOT-TLE FEEDER.

INSTALL A BIRD BATH

A bird bath needs a rim that the bird can stand on to take a drink. And it ought to be made of something that is not metal. Metal gets too cold in the winter and too hot in the summer.

Here are bird bath ideas:

The lid of a plastic trash can

The underdish of a plastic or ceramic plant pot

Here's how to install a bird bath:

1. Dig a small hole, just deep enough to hold the bath even with the ground. The best spot is at the edge of woods or near a grove of trees.
2. Fill the bath with no more than 2 inches (5 cm) of water.
3. Attract birds to the new bath by cutting a very small hole in a plastic bottle, just big enough to allow a continual dripping of water. Fill the bottle with water, and hang it from a tree over the bath. The dripping water will let the birds know their bath is ready.
4. Birds naturally drink from puddles, so they're used to keeping an eye out for danger. But do what you can to keep cats away from your bird bath.

BE SURE TO PUT IN FRESH, CLEAN WATER EVERY FEW DAYS.

TAKE CARE OF AN ANIMAL IN TROUBLE

What can you do to help an animal in trouble? Here are some ideas:

- In some cases, the best way to help is to leave the animal alone.

Don't be too quick to pick up a baby bird or baby mammal, for instance. The parents are probably nearby. They rarely leave a baby alone for long. And they will be anxious to find a missing baby. The parents know more about how to take care of their baby than you do. If you touch the baby or stay too close, you could scare off the parents.

- For your own sake, it's sometimes wise to leave the animal alone. Some states have laws against taking in wildlife. And everyone fears the spread of diseases like rabies.
- How can you help a baby bird that seems to be in danger? Put on heavy gloves (such as gardening gloves) and pick up the bird very gently. Put it in a shrub or bush out of the reach of cats.

(Putting a baby bird back in its own nest is more difficult than you might think. It's hard to find and reach the right nest.)

- If you find an injured bird, call the Audubon Society or a bird sanctuary. The people there will know what to do.
- If you find a fawn or another, larger animal, call a game warden or a wildlife sanctuary. If you find a very large animal out of its place (like a deer walking down a city street), you probably ought to call the police immediately.

HELP AN ANIMAL IN TROUBLE. BUT BE SURE YOU DON'T DO MORE HARM THAN GOOD.

DESIGN A WILDLIFE SANCTUARY IN YOUR OWN BACKYARD

You can plant a garden or create a backyard that is kind to animals. Here are some ways to attract and help particular kinds of creatures:

1. To help mosquito-eating bats, plant sweet-smelling white flowers.

2. To help butterflies and bees, plant brightly colored flowers.

3. To help hummingbirds, plant red salvia, clematis, hollyhocks, or phlox.

4. To help birds, plant asters, sunflowers, zinnias, shrubs with red berries, elderberry bushes, vibrunum, or high-bush cranberries and cherry trees.

5. To help small animals, leave one section of the yard uncultivated. Uncut grass and underbrush provide shelter and food.

THE NATIONAL WILDLIFE FEDERATION OPERATES A BACKYARD WILDLIFE HABITAT PROGRAM. WRITE TO IT AT 1400 16TH STREET N.W., WASHINGTON, DC 20036-2266.

DESIGN A HABITAT, ADOPT A CREATURE

*W*ould you like to create a terrarium or an underwater garden? Or would you like to adopt a turtle, build an ant farm, watch tadpoles grow into frogs? You can even design your own rain forest.

Every creature has its own habitat, the place where it fits in best. You can create a small world with everything a creature or plant needs, its own special foods and climbing or growing places.

But remember: once you adopt a living creature, it becomes your responsibility. You must take care of it and not forget about it. And, of course, you want to create the best possible habitat.

· · · · · · · · · · ·
DESIGN A TERRARIUM
· ·

A terrarium is a small world, complete inside its own bowl. You might even invite some small creatures inside this world.

Here's what you need:

A fish bowl or aquarium tank

(Or look for 1-gallon (4 liter) glass food jars. Perhaps a restaurant, school, or nursing home will give you an empty jar.)

A small container

Water

Rocks

Soil

Moss

Small plants

Here's what you do:

1. Wash out the bowl, tank, or jar.
2. Put the small container into the bowl, tank, or jar. If the small container is square or triangular, it may look best in a corner. Fill the container with water. The container of water keeps the air in the terrarium moist.

You can cover the terrarium, and the plants will stay alive for a long time. But you will want to add some other kinds of life.

3. Arrange the rocks, soil, moss, and small plants in the terrarium. You'll want a creative and interesting design.
4. If you wish, put creatures in your world on a short-term basis. Try a yellow and black garden spider, a small snake, a walking stick, or a praying mantis. Of course, you'll have to catch insects for them every day. And soon you'll want to put them back in their own worlds, where they belong.

A TERRARIUM IS A GOOD PROJECT FOR A CREATIVE SORT OF PERSON.

· · · · · · · · · ·
DESIGN A MINI TERRARIUM
· ·

You can create a mini terrarium. It makes a fine gift, and it costs almost nothing.

Here's what you need:

Two 2-liter plastic soft-drink bottles

(One must be clear, uncolored plastic. Both need to have removable colored bottoms.)

A knife

Mosses, small ferns, wintergreen, princess pine, violets, or other tiny plants that grow in damp wooded areas, and perhaps a pretty rock

Here's what you do:

1. Cut the bottoms off the plastic bottlers at the edge of the colored bottoms.

   : *Caution: You need an adult to*
   : *help you with cutting.*

2. Remove the clear-plastic rounded piece from inside one of the colored bottoms.

3. Arrange the mosses and other plants inside the other colored bottom. (Leave the clear plastic inside to give your terrarium double strength.) This is a chance to make a creative and artistic arrangement.

4. Water the plants thoroughly. Let them set for about 5 minutes. Then pour off the excess water.

5. Use the clear-plastic rounded piece from step 2 to make a dome over your terrarium. Slide it under the rim of the bottom half.

   : **NOW YOU HAVE A MINI**
   : **TERRARIUM THAT MAY LAST**
   : **FOR A LONG TIME.**

CARE FOR A COCOON

Look for a cocoon on tree twigs and bushes. You may have to look hard. Cocoons are the same color as twigs, and they blend in well.

Collect a cocoon, along with the twigs and leaves to which it's attached. Be careful not to disturb it.

Put the cocoon in a glass jar, with screening, nylon, or cheese-cloth over it. Keep the jar in a cool place, away from direct sunlight or a heater.

Add a moist sponge or a crumpled-up wet paper towel to keep the air in the jar moist.

YOU MAY NEED TO WAIT ONLY A FEW DAYS TO SEE A BUTTERFLY OR MOTH EMERGE. OR YOU MAY HAVE TO WAIT FROM FALL TO SPRING.

RELEASE THE MOTH OR BUTTERFLY IN A PLACE WHERE OTHERS THRIVE.

BUILD A CRICKET GARDEN

People in Asia keep crickets as pets because they love the songs crickets sing.

Create a garden where your cricket can sing for you.

Catch a cricket in a net or with a paper bag, or just use your own two hands. Try to catch a male cricket since only male crickets sing. They sing partly to call females and partly to warn away other males.

If you wish, catch a female cricket to keep your male company. But don't put two male crickets in the same garden. They will fight and may even kill each other.

You can tell the difference between male and female crickets by looking for the female's long egg-laying "tail."

Here's an odd fact: crickets don't hear the same cricket songs we hear. Instead, they hear ultrasonic sounds that we can't hear at all.

Another oddity is their ears. When you catch your cricket, look for his ear. It's a white spot on his front leg, of all places!

Here's what you need for your cricket garden:

A large glass jar

Sand

A large, flat stone

Twigs and leaves

Water

Screening, nylon, or cheesecloth

A large rubber band

Here's what you do:

1. Find a place for your cricket garden away from direct sun or heat.
2. Line the bottom of the jar with the sand.
3. Put in the large stone. Crickets like to crawl underneath the stone to hide in the shade.
4. Put in the twigs and leaves, and sprinkle with the water.
5. Cover the jar with the screening, nylon, or cheesecloth. Secure it with the large rubber band.

LOOK TO SEE HOW YOUR CRICKETS CHIRP. THEY DRAW ONE WING ACROSS THE OTHER. THE WING VIBRATES WITH SOUND.

Female Showing
Egg Laying Apparatus

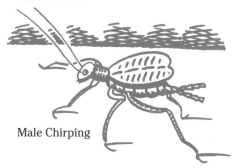

Male Chirping

TAKE CARE OF YOUR CRICKET

Don't forget about your crickets. They need regular care.

Here's what to feed your crickets:

Bits of uncooked potato

Bits of fresh apple

Bits of other fruits and vegetables

Remove any food your crickets don't eat. You don't want spoiled food in their garden.

Every few days, put in a small moist sponge, a crumpled-up wet paper towel, or a moist cotton ball. That will keep the air in the jar moist. Your crickets get the water they need from the juice in the fruits and vegetables you feed them.

LISTEN TO YOUR CRICKETS SING IN THEIR GARDEN.

IF YOU DECIDE TO LET YOUR CRICKET GO, RELEASE THEM WHERE YOU FOUND THEM OR WHERE OTHER CRICKETS THRIVE.

COLLECT ANTS FOR AN ANT FARM

You'll have the best luck collecting ants if the weather is cool. Cool temperatures slow them down.

Here's what you need for your ant hunt:

An old spoon
Several plastic bags
Several rubber bands
Old newspaper
A small spade

Here's how to collect your ants:

1. Begin by looking for ant hills. Then look around rotting logs or under rocks.

2. Use the spoon to put ants (with some soil from their nest) into a plastic bag. Look especially for an extra-large ant, the queen. Secure the bag very tightly with a rubber band.

3. Search for white ant eggs, cocoons, and larvae, which you will also need. Put the eggs, cocoons, and larvae you find into plastic bags. Secure the bags very tightly with rubber bands.

4. Spread out newspaper, and use the spade to put soil from the ant nest onto it. Bring back some soil from the anthill or wood from the rotten log. You want the ants to feel at home.

5. If your parents will let you, put the bag of ants in the refrigerator for half an hour or so. The cool air will slow the ants down before you transfer them to their new home.

BUT YOU'LL UNDERSTAND IF YOUR PARENTS DON'T WANT THEM IN THE REFRIGERATOR, WON'T YOU?

CREATE AN ANT FARM

You can watch a colony of ants go to work in your own ant farm.

Just don't let the ants get loose. You wouldn't like them all over your bed, and you'll be very unpopular if they turn up in the kitchen.

Here's what you need:

A large glass jar or fish bowl

A block of wood or large rock

Soil

Water

Black paper

Large rubber bands

Fine screening, mosquito netting, nylon, or cheesecloth

A large, flat pan

Here's what you do:

1. Find a place for your ant farm away from direct sun or a heater.

2. Put the block of wood or large rock into the jar or fish bowl, so that the ants will have to work at the sides of the jar. You can see them clearly there.

3. Fill the jar with soil.

4. Sprinkle on a few drops of water.

5. Wrap the black paper around the jar, and secure with a large rubber band. The black paper keeps the jar dark, and the ants will feel less upset at their move.

6. TAKE THE ANTS AND THE JAR OUTSIDE. Quickly transfer the ants to the jar. Immediately cover the jar with the screening, nylon, or cheesecloth, and hold it on tight with a large rubber band, Make sure the ants can't get out before you take the jar back inside.

7. Half-fill the flat pan with water. Set the jar into the pan. The ants can't travel across water, so if they escape from the jar, they can't get across the pan.

8. Leave the ants alone for 2 days. Don't take off the black paper or the screening on the lid of the jar.

GIVE THE ANTS TIME TO GET USED TO THEIR NEW FARM.

TAKE CARE OF THE ANT FARM

After about 2 days, the ants will be used to their new home. And they'll be ready for some food.

First put in a small, moist sponge or a crumbled-up wet paper towel. That will help keep the air moist.

Serve the ants their food on a small piece of cardboard. Just lay the cardboard on top of the soil. Then you can remove it quickly before any leftovers spoil.

Here's what to feed the ants:

Bits of uncooked potato

Bread or cereal crumbs

Drops of jam, jelly, or sugar water

A dead, soft-bodied insect or worm

Bits of vegetables or fruits

Now you can take off the black paper, and watch your ants work around their new farm. Use a magnifying glass, and see if you can tell what work different ants are doing.

Ants recognize one another by smell. Watch, and see how that happens.

PUT THE BLACK PAPER BACK ON WHEN YOU'RE NOT WATCHING. ANTS WORK BEST IN THE DARK.

· · · · · · · · · · ·
CATCH TADPOLES
· ·

Adopt a few tadpoles (or polly-wogs, as some people call them), and take them home. You can watch an astounding transformation as they turn into frogs or toads.

If you arrive early enough in the summer, you might find tadpole eggs at the edge of the water. The eggs look like messy jelly. But look closely, and you'll find you can see right through the eggs. They're transparent. You can see a tiny tadpole inside, waiting to be hatched.

Find newly hatched tadpoles in July or August, probably at the nearest pond where water weeds grow. Or look in large puddles in the woods.

Here's how to catch tadpoles:

1. Get two cans, one for catching the tadpoles and one for keeping them. The keeping can needs a lid with holes punched in it.

2. Usually, if you hold the catching can in the stream and stay very quiet, tadpoles will swim right in.

3. Then transfer them to the keeping can. Plan to put the keeping can underwater. The holes in the lid should allow the water to run in and out. The tadpoles will feel cool and comfortable while they wait for you to take them home. You may need to secure the can underwater with stones all around it.

4. When you're ready to take the tadpoles home, cover the can with cool, wet leaves.

5. Bring home an extra jar of water. Add green pond scum and some small water plants.

YOU HAVE AN EXTRA BONUS IF THE TADPOLE POND IS NEARBY. YOU CAN GO BACK OFTEN FOR SCUMMY POND WATER. THAT'S THE KIND TADPOLES LIKE BEST.

MAKE A HOME FOR TADPOLES

Your new tadpoles need a home that's very like their natural environment.

Here's what you need for a tadpole home:

A large glass jar, a fish bowl, or an aquarium tank

Sand or mud

Stones

Water plants

Pond water with scum

Here's how to build a tadpole home:

1. Find a cool place for the tadpole home, away from direct sun or a heater.

2. Line the bottom of the jar, bowl, or tank with the sand or mud.

3. Build an island with the stones. As the tadpoles begin to develop into frogs or toads, they will need a dry place to climb on.

4. Plant the water plants and secure them with stones.

5. Add the pond water, scum and all. Put in a few floating plants.

TAKE CARE OF TADPOLES

Once every few days, replace the water in the tadpole home with new pond water. The tadpoles can eat algae from the pond. And you can give them other food. Or use tap water you have let sit for at least 48 hours.

Don't forget your tadpoles!

Here's what to feed the tadpoles:

Bits of lettuce or spinach
Bits of hard-boiled egg yolks
Soft-bodied insects

WATCH FOR YOUR TADPOLES TO BEGIN CHANGING.

WATCH TADPOLES CHANGE INTO FROGS OR TOADS

Draw pictures for your science notebook. The change of tadpoles into frogs or toads is one of the most amazing happenings in all nature.

You can expect the change to take place over about 2 months. For some types of frogs, though, it takes much longer. Note the dates when you first spot changes.

Here's what to expect:

1. Look at the mouth. When it first hatches, a tadpole breathes by means of outside gills, like a fish. Its mouth is closed. After a few days, its mouth opens, and so does a breathing hole on the left side of the head. Water flows in through the mouth and through the gills, and out through the breathing hole.

2. Look for little suckers on the underside. At first, the tadpole uses them to hold on tight, perhaps to leaves or to the bottom of the pond. After just a few days, the suckers disappear, and the tadpole starts swimming around.

3. Look for bumps growing near the tadpole tail. These will become hind legs.

4. Look for a bump growing at the breathing hole on the left side of the head. That's going to become the left front leg. It's going to grow right out through the breathing hole.

5. Look for a bump growing on the right side of the head. That's going to become the right front leg, and it's going to break right through the skin.
At that point, the tadpole will be breathing water in and out of its mouth. Soon the tadpole will begin climbing out of the water. It's beginning to breathe with lungs instead of gills.

6. Look for the tail to disappear. The tadpole is absorbing its own tail and using it for nutrition. It won't need other food for a while.

SOON IT WILL BE TIME TO RETURN YOUR FROG OR TOAD PETS TO THEIR POND. They'll be happier in the pond. And they'll eat thousands of annoying insects there.

How to Tell Whether Your Tadpole Changed into a Frog or a Toad

Look at the skin.

Frog skin is a bit shiny. Toad skin is dull.

Frog skin is smooth. Toad skin is covered with bumps.

Those toad bumps are glands, and they protect the toad by producing a nasty-tasting liquid. Any creature that thinks about attacking a toad soon thinks instead about leaving.

In a fairy tale, the princess kisses a frog, and he turns into a handsome prince. She would definitely not want to kiss a toad.

Look at Zoo Habitats

When you visit a zoo, think about the animal habitats. No animal wants a habitat of plain concrete. See if the zoo builds habitats that have the right trees or grasses, the right water, or even the right ice and snow.

· · · · · · · · · · ·
DESIGN A RAIN FOREST
· ·

Rain forests are in danger of disappearing. In some places, people cut down the trees or burn the land. They need the land to grow food. Or they want to raise sugar cane or herd cattle on the land.

But often commercial companies destroy the rain forest for less important reasons.

The destruction of rain forests is a problem for the whole world. Rain forests keep nature in balance.

The trees help produce oxygen for the earth. Of course, all trees give off oxygen, so all trees are important. But the rain forest is particularly important because it keeps producing oxygen all year round. (Trees that shed their leaves in winter do not produce oxygen then.)

Rain forests also help keep the earth at the right temperature, with the right sort of weather.

And rain forests are home to thousands of different creatures. If a rain forest is destroyed, those creatures die. More than half the species of animals and plants in the world need the rain forests as a habitat.

Rain forests grow in the tropical regions of South America, Africa, Asia, and Australia. They are found in Brazil, Costa Rica, Puerto Rico, the Congo, Hawaii, and Honduras. They're also called tropical forests or jungles. "Rain forests" is a fitting name, though, because they get a lot of rain, usually more than 80 inches (or more than 2 meters) a year.

Design an artistic rain forest at home or school. The students at the Winn Brook Elementary School in Belmont, Massachusetts, created a rain forest in a corridor of their school. Look at pages 278–280 for some ideas on how to construct your rain forest.

PEOPLE WHO VISIT YOUR DISPLAY CAN GET AN IDEA OF WHAT A RAIN FOREST IS LIKE.

SUGGESTIONS FOR A RAIN FOREST DISPLAY

If you don't have space for a whole rain forest display, make a rain forest collage. A collage can give an idea of the vast variety of the rain forest.

Here's what you might include in your rain forest display:

1. Crepe-paper streamers for the entrance so that people feel they are going into a strange, different world.

2. Green lights to give a feeling for the colors deep in the rain forest. (You can cover ordinary light fixtures or flashlights with green plastic wrap. But don't let the plastic come too close to the light bulbs themselves.)

3. A tape of waterfall or bird sounds to imitate the sounds of the rain forest.

4. Crepe-paper streamers to create a waterfall and a river. (Don't forget to put paper fish in the river.)

5. Paintings of the trees, plants, birds, animals, insects, and fish of the rain forest. (You'll need a large group of artists to produce all the paintings you'll need to represent just some of the thousands of species in the rain forest.)

6. Paper models of the plants and creatures of the rain forest. (Dangle some from the ceiling.)

MAYBE SOME DAY YOU CAN VISIT A RAIN FOREST. YOU MIGHT EVEN DISCOVER A NEW SPECIES OF PLANT OR ANIMAL. Scientists say there are millions of new species waiting to be discovered.

MAKE PALM TREES FOR YOUR RAIN FOREST

If you want big trees, go to a carpet store and ask for a large tube of the sort that carpets come rolled in.

If you want small trees, buy brown butcher paper and roll it into tubes for the tree trunks.

Then construct some palm fronds for your trees.

Here's what you need:

Wire coat hangers
Green crepe paper
Double-faced tape

Here's what you do:

1. Straighten 3 or 4 coat hangers for each tree. Bend an end to fit into the trunk of the tree.

2. Cut a length of green crepe paper long enough to cover the wire. Then make parallel cuts from the edges, leaving a strip about an inch wide in the middle. Now you have palm fronds.

3. Use double-faced tape to attach the palm fronds to the coat hangers, so that the center of the frond covers the wire and the cut edges hang down at the sides.

YOU'LL BE SURPRISED AT HOW REAL YOUR TREES LOOK.

· · · · · · · · · · ·
SUGGESTIONS FOR RAIN FOREST PAINTINGS AND MODELS

· ·

You might make special paintings and models of the rain forest species in danger of disappearing. You'll want to look at pictures so that you will know how these wonderful forms of life look. Then you can get all the details right.

Birds of paradise

Butterflies and moths

Crocodiles and alligators

Fish

Frogs (including poisonous frogs) and tree toads

Hummingbirds

Iguanas

Jaguars, leopards, ocelots

Lianes, woody plants that climb and loop from the ground
to high among the tallest trees

Lizards

Macaws

Monkeys, gorillas, chimpanzees, orangutans

Orchids and other exotic flowers

Parrots and parakeets

Sloths

Snakes

Spiders (including bird-eating spiders)

Scorpions

Tapirs

Tarantulas

Toucans

Trees: banana, cacao, coffee, kapok, mahogany, mangrove,
palm, rosewood, teak

TRICK YOUR OWN EYES

*Y*ou can trick your own eyes with these projects.

You can see optical illusions—or create your own. Like a rabbit pulled out of a hat, these optical illusions are really something else.

Or how would you like to trick a friend's eyes with moving cartoons or with a tricky Halloween feast? You can even try an experiment with shadowy results.

TRICK YOUR EYES IN WHITE AND GRAY

Try this simple trick with two white cards.

Here's what you need:

Two small white index cards
Scissors
A window (in daylight)

Here's what you do:

1. In the middle of one card, cut a hole, 1 inch (2 cm) or so across. The hole can be any shape.

2. Set the other card flat on a windowsill so that daylight falls on it.

3. Hold the card with the hole in it parallel to the card on the windowsill. View the card on the windowsill through the hole. Both cards will appear white.

4. Now tip the card you are holding (the one with the hole) toward you. The card on the windowsill will look white, but the card you are holding will look gray.

5. Now tip the card you are holding away from you. The card on the windowsill will look gray, but the card you are holding will look white.

Why? When you hold the two cards parallel to each other, each receives the same amount of light from the same direction.

When you tip the card you are holding toward you, it receives less light and looks gray in comparison. When you tip that same card toward the window, though, it receives more light and then the card on the windowsill looks gray.

> **NOW YOU KNOW HOW TO TRICK YOUR EYES IN GRAY AND WHITE.**

You can try this trick with color cards, too.

See What the World Is Like Without Color

If you go out in the dark, you can see what the world is like without color.

To see the world without color, though, you need pure moonlight, and sometimes that's hard to find. If any electric lights are nearby, you'll see some color.

Why does color disappear at night?

The reason lies in how the nerve cells in our eyes work. In the retina at the back of our eyes are nerve cells called rods and cones.

The cones see all the beautiful colors of the world. The rods see only black, white, and shades of gray.

(You can remember which is which by noticing that "color" begins with "co," and so does "cone.")

The cones help us see best in the light. The rods take over at night.

And here's another difference in night vision: Odd, as it seems, you can see the stars (or anything else, for that matter) more clearly in the dark if you don't look straight at them.

That's so because the cones that see color are in the center of the retina. The rods that see best in the dark are concentrated at the outer edges of the retina.

So you can see best in the dark if you look out of the corner of your eyes.

Here's how to prove it.

AN ALMOST COLORLESS EYE TRICK

When you catch a glimpse of something out of the corner of your eye, you won't see what color it is.

Here's all you need:

Pens, pencils, crayons, or sticks of different colors

Here's what you do:

1. Sit in a chair, and look straight ahead at a point directly in front of you. Keep your eyes on that point, and don't cheat! If you have a helper, ask your helper to stand slightly behind you and to your side and to slowly move one of the colored pens forward.

2. If you're by yourself, keep your eyes focused on a point directly in front of you, and hold two pens of different colors behind your back. Change them from hand to hand until you don't know which is which. Hold them upright, and slowly bring them forward.

3. Stop when you think you know the color. You probably will see the pen before you can tell the color. Even at that point, you will see that the color is not distinct. (Of course, if the pen is light yellow, you may be able to guess the color right away because of the difference in intensity between light and dark.)

NOW YOU HAVE PROOF THAT YOUR EYES SEE COLOR BETTER WHEN YOU CAN LOOK DIRECTLY THAN WHEN YOU LOOK ONLY FROM THE CORNERS OF YOUR EYE.

. . . .
CONSTRUCT YOUR OWN COLORFUL MAXWELL TOP
. . . .

James Clerk Maxwell was a famous physicist who lived in Scotland more than 100 years ago. Make his colorful top so that you can spin colors to your heart's content.

With a Maxwell top, you can spin blue and red out of white and black. And you can trick your eyes into seeing any number of other color combinations.

Here's what you need to make the basic top:

A piece of heavy cardboard or plastic

A drawing compass

Scissors strong enough to cut the cardboard or plastic

An awl or a punch

A $1/2" \times 1/8"$ (10 mm x 3 mm) machine screw with a nut to fit

Here's how to make the basic top:

1. Use your compass to draw a 4-inch (10 cm) circle on the cardboard or plastic. Cut the circle out with heavy scissors.

2. Use the awl or punch to make a $1/8$-inch (3 mm) hole in the exact center of the circle.

3. Push the screw through the hole. Attach the nut on top, but don't screw it all the way in.

: **NOW MAKE THE COLOR DISKS**
: **FOR YOUR MAXWELL TOP.**

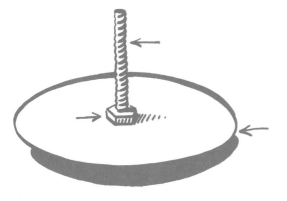

DESIGN SPINNING COLOR DISKS FOR YOUR TOP

For your Maxwell top, you'll want both colored disks and black-and-white disks. (You'll discover that black-and-white disks have some mysterious colors.)

Here's what you need to make the disks:

Colored construction paper

You especially need red, green, blue, and yellow, but use as many colors as you like.

Scissors

A piece of heavy white paper

A black felt-tipped pen

A pencil

Here's what you do to make the colored disks:

1. Cut out a 4-inch (10 cm) disk on each color of the construction paper.

2. Make a ¹/₈-inch (3 mm) hole in the exact center of each disk. Cut a slit from the hole to the edge of the disk.

A.

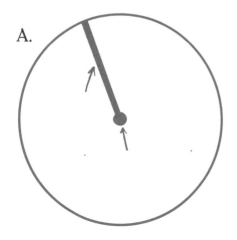

Here's what you do to make the black-and-white disks:

1. On the heavy white paper, draw several 4-inch (10 cm) disks.

2. Cut out the disks.

3. Punch a ¹/₈-inch (3 mm) hole in the center of each.

4. Choose one white disk, and draw a line dividing it in half. Using the black felt-tipped pen, color half of the disk a deep black.

   Divide the white half of the disk into four equal sections. Use a pencil to mark the sections lightly.

   Use the black felt-tipped pen to draw lines in each white section, like this:

B.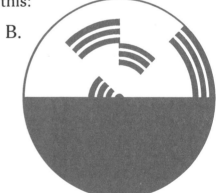

5. Make other black-and-white disks, but vary the ways you draw the parallel lines. Be creative, and see what happens.

: **NOW YOU'RE READY FOR THE**
: **FUN PART, SPINNING THE DISKS.**

SPIN YOUR TOP FOR MYSTERIOUS COLOR CHANGES

Get your top and all the disks ready to spin.

Here's what you do:

1. Slide the first black-and-white disk onto the screw, and screw the nut over it. Spin the disk, and watch for colors as it slows. If you spin the disk clockwise, you ought to see the outer ring look blue and the inner rings look red.

   But if you spin the disk counter-clockwise, the outer rings should look red and the inner rings look blue.

2. Spin the other black-and-white disks, and see what colors you get.

3. Now spin the colored disks for other color changes.

   First, slide a red disk and a blue disk under the nut. Twist them so that the edge of the red disk slides under the edge of the blue disk. Spin the disk, and see how the colors combine.,

   Next, spin the red and yellow disks together. Then try blue and yellow.

   In each case, write down the combination of colors you get.

4. Now try all the other variations you can think of. Slide the disks around so that you vary the amount of each disk showing. And be sure to try three colors at once.

> **NOW YOU KNOW HOW YOUR EYES SEE NEW COLORS INSIDE OLD ONES.**

ALWAYS HAVE SOMETHING COLORFUL TO DO WHEN YOU'RE BORED

When is black white? When is blue yellow? You can find out any time you're bored, wherever you happen to be sitting.

Here's what you do:

1. Turn your face toward a neutral-colored wall or door. (White or off-white is best.) Next, for about 30 seconds, stare hard at a brightly colored object, such as a picture or a book. Then quickly look again at the wall. You will see a phantom image of the colored object—but in a different color.

2. The color you see in an after-image is a complementary color. If you look at a red object, for instance, the after-image will be green. See how many complementary colors you can identify.

3. Sometime when you're feeling artistic, draw a striped design. Stare at it for about a minute. Then quickly look away at a piece of white paper. In a few seconds, you'll see the stripes— but in complementary colors.

A very secret hint: Try looking at a stained glass window, and then look away for the after-image. Some of us know from experience that colors can brighten up a sermon that has gone on too long. Just don't tell anyone what you're doing.

: **NOW YOU ALWAYS HAVE**
: **SOMETHING INTERESTING TO DO**
: **NO MATTER WHERE YOU ARE.**

DRAW YOUR OWN MOVING CARTOONS

You don't have to be a great artist to draw cartoons that seem to move. You may be surprised to find artistic ability you didn't know you possessed.

Here's what you need:

A small pad of paper
A pencil with soft lead
A nickel
A ruler or triangle

Here's what you do:

1. Begin with an idea for something that moves.

2. Starting with the last page of the pad of paper, draw your first picture. Press rather hard with the soft pencil.

3. Turn down the next-to-last page so that you can see your drawing through it. Trace the ground scene just as it is in the first drawing. Then draw a change. Make something move about 1/8 inch (3 mm).

4. Continue in this way, page after page, moving something in your pictures about 1/8 inch (3 mm) with each drawing.

5. Now, flip the pages of your pad, and you see the movement. Your eyes trick you, just as they do when you watch cartoons and movies. The still pictures go by so rapidly that they look as if they're really moving.

NOW YOU KNOW HOW CARTOONISTS WORK.

· · · · · · · · · ·

LIGHT UP YOUR EYES WITH COLORED SHADOWS

· ·

Look for shadows in this experiment. You'll find you can make some spooky color changes. Or are your eyes just tricking you again?

Here's what you need:

Colored lights: red, green, yellow, and violet

(A string of Christmas lights will do. Or cover a lamp that has an ordinary white bulb with colored plastic—but don't put the plastic directly on the light bulb.)

A solid white object, such as a white dish

Here's what you do:

1. In indirect sunlight, shine each light bulb onto the white object, and look for the color of the shadow.
   You may see the shadows best if you cast them onto a white wall, white paper, or a white table-cloth. And you may need to experiment with how far away you hold the lights.
   Here are the opposites we think you'll see:
   - The red light creates a greenish shadow, and the green light casts a reddish shadow.
   - The yellow light casts a violet shadow, and the violet light casts a yellow shadow.
2. Try making shadows with the same light bulbs shining on the same white object—only this time in the dark, with no day-light to change the colors.

Now the shadows are all black.

3. Now try using two lights, one red and one green—again in the dark.
   - The red light casts a bright green shadow, and the green light casts a bright red shadow. But look where the two shadows overlap. There the shadow is black.
   Try mixing a blue light and a green light. Where the two shadows overlap, you'll get a black shadow.
   Try three lights at once to see what happens. This is one way that lighting artists mix stage lights for dramatic effects.
4. Now look at shadows outside, and you'll see some of the same odd color combinations, especially in winter, when you can see them on snow.

SHADOWS ARE SOME OF NATURE'S BEST EYE TRICKS.

LIGHT UP A REALLY GHOULISH HALLOWEEN PARTY

These refreshments will really light up your Halloween party. You'll trick the eyes of your guests in the most delightfully ghoulish fashion.

Here's the menu:

A make-your-own sandwich plate, with sliced roast beef, ham, turkey, cheeses, rolls and bread, mayonnaise, and mustard

A serve-yourself salad bowl, with lettuce, spinach, and cabbage greens, tomatoes, diced apples and raisins, and dressings

Serve-yourself fruits

Red fruit punch, iced with frozen cranberry juice ice cubes

Halloween cookies

Here's what else you need:

A red light
A blue light
A yellow light

Here's what you do:

1. Set up the three lights so that each can be used in turn to light the room. (You'll also want a normal white light to use when your guests actually eat the Halloween feast.)

2. As your guests arrive for the feast, change from the normal white light to the red light.

   Perhaps you'll trick their eyes. The sandwich meats will look great, but the salad will look black and bread will appear bright red.

3. Now change to the blue light.

   The roast beef will look greenish and spoiled, and the bread will take on a moldy color.

4. Now turn on the yellow light.

   The red punch will resemble castor oil, and your guests themselves will suddenly look like zombies.

TURN ON THE WHITE LIGHT BEFORE YOUR GUESTS LOSE THEIR APPETITES ALTOGETHER.

TEST OUT YOUR TASTE BUDS

*W*ould you like to test out your taste buds? Here's how.

Or perhaps you'd like to play tricks on your taste buds. Here's a full set.

. . . .
LOOK FOR MYSTERY TASTE BUDS
. . . .

Look at your tongue, and you'll see small bumps all over the surface. Those are papillae, and every one of them holds hundreds of taste buds.

Scientists think that each tiny taste bud knows only one of four basic tastes: sweet, sour, salty, or bitter.

But since you can't see your taste buds, how can you tell which is which?

Taste buds are in groups, so whole areas of your tongue can taste only sweet, sour, salty, or bitter substances. You can test your own tongue to find the four kinds of taste buds.

Here's what you need:

Room-temperature water
A bit of sugar
Lemon juice or vinegar
A few grains of salt
A few coffee granules
5 cotton swabs or flat toothpicks
Your science notebook and pen

Here's what you do:

1. To test your sweet taste buds, dip a cotton swab or toothpick into the water and then into the sugar. Dot different parts of your tongue, and see where you get a taste bud reaction.
Now rinse out your mouth, so that you don't get tastes confused. Discard the swab or toothpick.

2. To test your sour taste buds, dip a cotton swab or toothpick into the water and then into the lemon juice or vinegar. Write down where you get a taste reaction. Rinse out your mouth before you go on. Discard the swab or toothpick.

3. To test your salt taste buds, dip a cotton swab or toothpick into the water and then into the salt. See where you get a taste reaction. Rinse out your mouth before you go on. Discard the swab or toothpick.

4. To test your bitter taste buds, dip a cotton swab or toothpick into the water and then into the coffee granules. See where you get a taste reaction.

5. Now check out the taste divisions on your tongue. You'll find some overlap, especially at the tip of your tongue.

    NOW YOU'VE FOUND YOUR OWN TASTE BUDS.

You could even draw a map of your tongue.

· · · · · · · · · · ·
CHILL YOUR TASTE BUDS

· ·

What happens to your taste buds when your food is very cold?

Find out by rubbing an ice cube on your tongue. Then once again dot your tongue with the sweet, sour, salty, and bitter tastes.

Your taste buds will probably not work nearly as well. They will be too cold to distinguish basic tastes.

And what if your food is too hot?

Your taste buds can probably deal with that problem. Tiny as they are, taste buds are made of even tinier cells. The cells change every 10 days or so. You get a constant fresh supply. So, if you burn your tongue just a bit on food that's too hot, your taste buds will repair the damage.

But your taste buds have their preferences. Food tastes best to you when it's just the right temperature, between 72° and 105°F (22° and 42°C).

NOW TRY ANOTHER EXPERIMENT ON TEMPERATURE AND TASTE.

· · · · · · · · · · ·
A HALF-DELICIOUS TEMPERATURE-AND-TASTE EXPERIMENT ON HOT ICE CREAM

· ·

Your taste buds react best to familiar food temperatures. Now there's nothing really wrong with hot ice cream. But will hot ice cream taste the same—will it taste as good?

Here's all you need:

Ice cream

Here's what you do:

1. Eat half the ice cream.
2. Melt the other half (30 seconds or less in a microwave oven), or, if you have the courage, make it really hot, 1 minute in the microwave oven.

HOW DO YOU LIKE IT? It tastes the same, and yet it doesn't taste the same. Temperature makes the difference.

THE REAL MYSTERY TASTE BUDS

No one is sure, but your taste buds may be able to distinguish the taste of soap and the taste of metal.

Of course, you don't particularly want to taste soap or metal.

But your taste buds don't exist just to make your food taste good. They also help you survive. A soapy taste warns you against alkaline poison. A metal taste alerts you to rotten food and some sorts of acid poison. (Unless, of course, you're in the habit of chewing on steel bars, but then that's not so good for you either.)

A SMELL-AND-TASTE EXPERIMENT ON VERY DIFFERENT FOODS

You might think that a potato, an onion, and an apple taste very differently. But without the clues of smell, and texture, can you really tell them apart?

Here's what you need:

A potato
An onion
An apple
A blindfold

Here's what you do:

1. Grate small amounts of raw potato, raw onion, and raw apple.

2. Blindfold yourself, and hold your nose. Eat just a bit of each. Make sure you eat very tiny bits so that the textures of the three foods are about the same.

CAN YOU TASTE THE DIFFERENCE WITHOUT THE CLUES OF TEXTURE, SMELL, AND LOOKS OF THE FOOD?

. . . .

TASTE THE DIFFERENCE BETWEEN YOUNG AND OLD

. . . .

Try giving a small child a taste of grapefruit or lemon. Have a camera ready to capture a really funny face.

Small children react more to taste because they have more taste buds than older people.

People lose taste buds as they grow older. A baby has more taste buds than you. You have more taste buds than your parents.

How can you prove that this is true?

Here's what you need:

A 3-ounce (90 ml) can of frozen grapefruit concentrate
Water

Here's what you do:

1. Mix ⅓ of the grapefruit concentrate with 1 cup (250 ml) of water. That's "regular" grapefruit juice.
2. Mix ⅓ of the grapefruit concentrate with ½ cup (120 ml) of water. That will have a very strong grapefruit taste.
3. Mix ⅓ of the grapefruit concentrate with 2 cups (500 ml) of water. That will have a very weak grapefruit taste.
4. Ask people of different ages to do a taste test for you. Ask them to taste each grapefruit drink and to tell you which they like best. Notice which they react to the most.

YOU MAY FIND THAT CHILDREN REACT MOST TO THE STRONG GRAPEFRUIT DRINK. Small children may say they don't like the stronger mixture.

Older people may like the strongest grapefruit taste best.

FIND OUT YOUR OWN SECRETS

*T*est your heart and your lungs. Study your own one-of-a-kind fingerprints. Play tricks on your sense of touch.

Figure out how to survive and how to thrive.
You can find out a lot about yourself.

TEST HOW MUCH AIR IS IN YOUR LUNGS

You can create a device to measure how much air your lungs hold. This is a good project for a school group or a group of friends.

Here's what you need:

A large glass or plastic bottle

A 2-cup (500 ml) measure

Masking or freezer tape

A small piece of cardboard

A large sink

Water

Noncollapsible plastic or rubber tubing, smaller in diameter than the mouth of the bottle

Your science notebook and pen

Here's what you do:

1. First, divide the bottle into 1-pint (500 ml) measures. Put masking or freezer tape up the side of the bottle, and pour in a 1 pint (500 ml) of water. (That's 2 cups.) Mark the tape at that point. Then pour in another pint of water, and mark. Keep going until you've filled the bottle.

2. Fill the sink with water.

3. Cover the bottle with a small piece of cardboard. Turn the water-filled bottle upside down in the sink water. Then slide off the cardboard.

4. Slip the tubing into the opening of the bottle.

5. Now take the deepest breath you can, and blow into the tub. The air from your lungs will push out some of the water.

6. Look at how many pints of water you were able to push out of the bottle.

> NOW YOU KNOW HOW MUCH
> AIR YOUR LUNGS CAN HOLD.
> GET OTHER PEOPLE TO
> MEASURE THE AIR THEIR LUNGS
> HOLD, AND SEE WHAT THE
> DIFFERENCES ARE.

. . . .

TEST YOUR HEARTBEAT

. . . .

Did you know that you can't actually hear a heartbeat? The heartbeat itself is just a contraction of muscle and is perfectly quiet. What you can hear is the sound of heart valves snapping shut.

Here's how to test your heartbeat:

1. Press the first two fingers of one hand over the radial artery in the wrist of your other hand. That's the artery in the depression just below the base of your thumb. Move your fingers until you can feel the pulse of your blood.

2. Use a watch with a second hand, and count the number of beats in 10 seconds.

3. Multiply by 6. Now you know the number of beats per minute.

4. Run or exercise for 10 minutes or so. Take your pulse again, and see how much faster your heart is pumping.

YOUR HEARTBEAT CAN TELL SOMETHING ABOUT YOUR OVERALL HEALTH AND FITNESS.

PLAY THE GENETICS GAME

Nature plays a very serious game with all people (and with all animals and plants, too). Who inherits what?

Will the baby be smart at math like her mother, and musically talented like her father?

Will she have poor eyesight like her father?

Will she be clumsy like her mother or athletic like her father?

We inherit our traits from our mothers and fathers and also from all the grandparents and great-grandparents who lived before them. Genes carry our inherited traits.

The scientific study of how genes work is called genetics.

Play a not-too-serious genetics game.

Imagine a land of odd colors. The mother of a certain family has green ears. The father has purple ears. Figure out what their children may inherit in the way of ear color by drawing what's called a Punnett square.

Genes are not always equal. Some genes are stronger than others (that is, dominant), and a child is more likely to show a dominant trait than another. Other genes are weaker or recessive. A child is less likely to show a recessive trait.

An upper-case G stands for green ears. A lower-case p means purple ears.

Here's how to draw the Punnett square:

This is how the Punnett square would look if green ears are a dominant trait and purple ears are recessive.

Mother

	G	G
p	Gp	Gp
p	Gp	Gp

Father

From this chart we can see that the chances are that all the children will have green ears, the dominant trait. But each child will also carry the gene for purple ears.

THIS IS A SIMPLE EXAMPLE. ACTUALLY, THE SCIENCE OF GENETICS GETS MORE AND MORE COMPLICATED. IT MAKES AN INTERESTING PUZZLE.

KEEP ON PLAYING THE GENETICS GAME

Suppose the parents with all the green-eared children particularly like purple ears. Can they hope to have a grandchild with purple ears?

Suppose one of their daughters marries a man with green ears. He carries no gene for purple ears. The chart for their children looks like this:

Mother

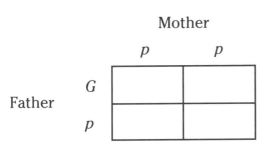

Next, suppose one of their sons marries a woman with purple ears. She carries no gene for green ears. Fill out the chart for their children:

Mother

Father

	p	p
G		
p		

Finally, suppose another son marries a woman with green ears. But, like him, she carries a gene for purple ears. Fill out the chart for their children:

Mother

Are the grandparents likely to have any grandchildren with beautiful purple ears?

LOOK AROUND YOUR FAMILY, AND SEE IF YOU CAN TELL WHAT YOU INHERITED.

HEAR WITH BOTH EARS

Cover one ear, and then try locating a sound. You'll have trouble telling the source of a sound if you can't hear it with both ears.

Why? With two ears, you get a clue to the direction a sound comes from when the sound vibration hits one ear a split second before it hits the other ear. And you get another clue about direction when the sound is very slightly louder in one ear than in the other.

THE PAPER BAG GAME

Test your sense of touch.

Have a friend put some small objects in a paper bag. Here are some that are surprisingly hard to identify:

- A small battery
- A marble
- An unshelled nut
- A grape
- An olive
- A pincushion with no pins in it

Reach into a paper bag, and see if you can tell what is inside without looking.

THIS IS A GOOD GAME TO PLAY WITH FRIENDS.

PROVE YOUR SIXTH SENSE

You have senses of sight, hearing, smell, taste, and touch. You also have another sense, which lets you know where the parts of your body are in space. The name for this sixth sense is the kinesthetic sense.

Just lose your eyes or put on a blindfold. Touch your nose. Reach for your ears. Stand on one foot. Put your hands behind your back.

YOU'LL NEVER MAKE A MISTAKE. YOU ALWAYS KNOW JUST WHERE EACH PART OF YOUR BODY IS, EVEN WHEN YOU'RE NOT LOOKING.

MAKE A MAP OF YOUR NERVES

Try mapping where you are most sensitive and least sensitive. You'll need a friend to help.

Have your friend poke your back (gently, not so it hurts) in different places with one, two, or three pencil points. See if you can tell how many pencil points are touching you at each place.

Close your eyes, and have your friend try again on your fingertips. You'll probably guess better when the pencils touch your fingers than when they touch your back.

Try pencil points at different places on your arm, leg, and feet.

NOW YOU HAVE AN IDEA OF HOW YOUR SENSE OF TOUCH CHANGES IN DIFFERENT PARTS OF YOUR BODY.

TRICK YOUR FINGERTIPS

You may have very sensitive fingertips. But your fingers can't tell what the temperature is.

Here's a temperature test on your fingertips:

1. Get three bowls. Fill one bowl with cold water and ice cubes. Fill the second bowl with hot tap water. Fill the third bowl with room-temperature water.

2. Put the fingers of one hand in the icy-cold water. Put the fingers of the other hand in the hot water.

3. After a few minutes, put both hands in the room-temperature water.

THE WATER FEELS COLD TO THE HOT FINGERS, BUT FEELS HOT TO THE COLD FINGERS. YOU'VE TRICKED YOUR OWN FINGERTIPS.

BE A DETECTIVE WITH YOUR FINGERPRINTS

You have fingerprints that are all your own. Nobody else has fingerprints like yours. The patterns of lines on your fingertips formed before you were born, and they'll be the same all your life.

That's why detectives look at fingerprints as clues. Fingerprints are a good way to tell whodunit.

Here are three ways to see your fingerprints:

1. Rub a soft pencil across a section of paper again and again until the paper is quite dark. Now press your thumb or other fingertip on the dark paper until the pencil transfers to your skin. Sometimes you can make a good fingerprint by pressing directly onto a piece of white paper. Or stick tape across the dark part of your fingertip. Peel off the tape, and you'll see a fingerprint on it.

2. Roll your thumb or other fingertip on an ink pad, then on paper.

3. Rub your thumb or other fingertip on your nose until you pick up a little skin oil. Then press your fingertip on a mirror.

Use a magnifying glass to study your fingerprints. If you can compare them with prints from another person, you'll see how they're different. But the patterns will probably fit into one of these general types:

- Circles inside circles inside circles
- Sharp little hills or ridges
- Circles and hills mixed

WHY DO YOU NEED CIRCLES AND HILLS ON YOUR FINGERTIPS? THEY HELP YOU TO HOLD ONTO THINGS. OTHERWISE, YOUR FINGERS MIGHT BE TOO SLIPPERY.

· · · · · · · · · · ·
SURVIVE AND THRIVE
· ·

Imagine you're an astronaut. You've just landed on the planet Mars, where you plan to spend several weeks exploring.

Put these items in order. What do you need the most, second most, and so on?

Astronauts have actually taken versions of all these things on their spacecraft. And all of them have been useful (or interesting) in one way or another.

- A strong rope
- Radio connection back to your spacecraft
- Radio connection back to Command Central on Earth
- A portable oxygen tank
- Your school flag
- A suit that allows you to escape extreme heat or extreme cold
- A motorized spacecar that can take you safely over sand dunes and up mountains
- Packets of dried food
- A lantern
- A television camera
- Gallons of water
- A first-aid kit
- Instructions on what to do if you meet a Martian animal
- A shovel
- Bags to carry back small discoveries
- A flashlight
- A golf club and golf ball
- Instructions for an experiment on how to grow plants in space

Think what you need to survive on your own planet, Earth. You need air, food, clothes, shelter, and a great number of other things.

WHAT ELSE DO YOU NEED? WHAT COMES FIRST?

REMEMBER: YOU WANT TO SURVIVE, AND YOU ALSO WANT TO THRIVE.

FOR PARENTS AND TEACHERS

*E*veryone seems to agree that young people need to learn science "hands on." Kids need to learn to solve problems by solving problems, not just by reading about how to solve problems. They need to learn the skills of science.

They don't need to concentrate on memorizing information, the "dull data dumps" that kill science interest for many children early in their lives.

In a way, young people need to learn science the old-fashioned way. Children used to learn science on farms and in vacant lots. Perhaps no one called it science. But just about every kid once knew how to chart the phases of the moon, predict a rainstorm, or pick up an insect. Kids spent whole summers collecting fireflies, flying kites, building sand castles, and watching tadpoles turn into frogs.

Young people even used to learn science from time-honored magic tricks and old parlor games. You may remember writing to a friend with invisible ink, or using your beginning knowledge of sound vibrations to spy on your sister.

This is a book to help kids look at the world around them. It's a book to help them learn by doing.

Here are some ways to help:

1. **Encourage kids to keep a science notebook**. Many parents give a child a diary as soon as the child can write. Many English and a few astute science teachers ask students to keep a journal. Encourage young scientists to draw pictures as well as write about what they see.

2. **Go out of your way to encourage girls and minority young people to enjoy science.** They often come to believe too young that science is not for them. Tell them stories of women or minority people who succeeded in scientific discovery. (These stories are often entrancing. Everyone likes the idea of a person who succeeds against the odds, whether it's Cinderella or Underdog.)

3. **With science-phobic kids, don't use the word *science* upfront.** Perhaps they'll love science when they don't know it's science.
   Even kids who think they don't like science, for instance, may like the science behind throwing a curve ball. They might like to design survival clothes or to design their own space alien. They might like to build

something like a kaleidoscope, a kite, or a simple paper airplane. They might enjoy creating a habitat and taking care of live creatures in it.

Just don't tell a science-phobic kid that all this is science.

4. **Introduce science in the kitchen**. Teach young people about mixtures and emulsions, and have them come up with something edible—salad dressing or gelatin dessert. Let them use supercooled ice to make their own ice cream. They might grow a crystal they can eat, or brew some sun tea.

5. **Emphasize the art and creativity of science.** A class or group of creative young people might like to draw models of the solar system or design a crepe paper rain forest. They'd certainly like to grow crystal gardens or construct a color wheel.

   Environmentally concerned artists can put old newspapers to good use by making a papier-mâché bowl full of papier-mâché fruit. Try art work on light-sensitive paper so that the sun finishes the picture.

6. **Provide a little gentle competition**. Hold a floating (and sinking) contest for handmade boats. Have kids grow plants in different ways, and see which plants grow best. See who can be the first to spot the first thrilling sliver of the new moon.

7. **Exploit natural curiosity**. Set up problems to solve. Young chemists like testing for starches, or for acids and bases (especially when they can create invisible ink and perform magic tricks along the way).

8. **Keep an eye on the calendar.** Science can be a holiday event.

   Try having kids magnify and draw snow crystals at Christmas time. Encourage young people to learn about eggs and flowers for Passover and Easter. Start a leaf-growing project when school starts in the fall, and each kid will have a full-grown violet to give on Mother's Day. Teach the eerie science of colors at a Halloween party.

9. **Take science on vacation**. If you visit a waterway, take the opportunity to study water currents together and to send a message in a bottle. If you visit an historic house, let the kids look up the old-fashioned chimney and see the stars during the day.

   Start a collection of rocks or fossils, seashells or beach sand, seaweed or exotic leaves. Make a vacation night magic by looking for planets, satellites, and shooting stars.

10. **Slow down**. If you're always willing to stop and look at the world, you're encouraging scientific observation.

11. **Keep things safe and everybody happy**. Science does not need to seem distant and boring. Science is looking at our own real, immediate world. Young people need to know the thrill of discovery. Then they will grow up loving science.

GLOSSARY

Acid A chemical compound that joins with a base to make a salt. Edible acids give food a tangy or sour taste. Many acids should not be eaten or even touched because they cause burns.

Algae A group of water plants without roots or flowers. Examples are seaweed and pond scum. Some types spread over the surface of polluted water and prevent air from getting to the water creatures.

Alum An astringent aluminum salt (aluminum potassium sulfate) used to stop bleeding and to keep pickles crisp.

Anemometer An instrument that measures the wind speed.

Asteroids Thousands of various-sized rocks that revolve around the sun like planets, mostly in a belt between Mars and Jupiter.

Atom The tiniest particle into which an element can be divided without losing its character. Atoms connect or bond together into molecules.

Barometer An instrument that measures air pressure. A barometer's measurements predict changes in the weather.

Base A chemical compound that joins with an acid to make a salt. Edible bases give food a slightly bitter taste. Many bases are too strong to eat and can cause burns. The other name is alkali.

Boiling point The temperature at which a liquid begins to escape into the air as vapor or gas. The boiling point of water at sea level is 212 degrees Fahrenheit or 100 degrees Celsius.

Buoyancy The power of water (or another liquid) to push an object up toward the surface.

Calibrate To determine or correct the measuring marks on a thermometer.

Carbohydrate Chemical compounds formed by plants from carbon, hydrogen, and oxygen. Starches, sugars, and cellulose are carbohydrates. Both plants and animals use carbohydrates as food.

Cellulose A chemical substance that forms the walls of plant cells. Cellulose makes up the woody part of trees and plants.

Celsius A scale for measuring temperature (also known as Centigrade). On the Celsius scale, the freezing point of water at sea level is zero degrees, and the boiling point is 100 degrees. Anders Celsius designed the scale in 1742.

Centigrade Another name for the Celsius scale for measuring temperatures.

Chlorophyll The chemical in plants that makes them green. Plants use chlorophyll to make food.

Colloidal Mixture A gel, or a combination of two or more substances so that very small particles of each are suspended throughout the others. Examples are gelatin, milk, and varnish.

Color spectrum The band of colors into which white light separates when passed through a prism or other filtering device. A rainbow is a spectrum. The colors of the spectrum are always in the same order: red (with the longest light waves), orange, yellow, green, blue, indigo, and violet (with the shortest light waves).

Compound
A combination of two or more elements that forms a new substance.

Condensation
The change of a gas to a liquid or solid form. Or any change to a denser or more compact form.

Conductivity
The ability of a substance to carry or transmit electricity, heat, or sound.

Cotyledon
The first leaf that the seed of a plant develops.

Crystal
A nonliving substance that has atoms arranged in regular shapes with flat surfaces. Examples are diamonds, ice, salt, and quartz. Or a type of fine high-quality glass.

Dewpoint
The temperature at which water vapor in the air begins to condense into liquid water. The temperature at which raindrops form.

Diameter
The length of a straight line that passes through the center of a circle from one side to the other.

Directional compass
An instrument for showing directions. A directional compass has a needle that points north.

Drawing compass An instrument for drawing circles.

Ecology
The study of how humans, animals, and plants relate to each other and their environment.

Electricity
A basic form of energy carried by electrons and protons. Electricity produces heat and light and is used to run motors, engines, computers, and televisions.

Electromagnetic waves
Waves that travel at the speed of light including electric energy and magnetic energy. Examples are light waves, radio waves, X-rays, and microwaves.

Electron
A tiny particle that constantly moves about the outer surfaces of atoms. An electron has a negative electrical charge.

Element
One of the basic materials from which all things are made. The atoms of an element cannot be broken down by ordinary chemistry. There are more than 100 known elements which are listed in a chart called the "periodic table."

Embryo
A plant, an animal, or a human in the very first stage of its development.

Emulsion
A combination of liquids in which droplets of one liquid are suspended throughout the other liquid.

Evaporation
The change of a liquid or solid into a gas. Boiling water evaporates to become water vapor.

Fahrenheit
A scale for measuring temperatures. On the Fahrenheit scale, the freezing point of water at sea level is 32 degrees, and the boiling point is 212 degrees. Gabriel Daniel Fahrenheit designed this scale more than 200 years ago.

Ferric
Containing or related to iron. Ferric compounds tend to be more stable and less prone to combine with other elements than ferrous compounds. Ferric salts are usually yellow or brown.

Ferrous
Containing or related to iron. Ferrous compounds are usually less stable and more likely to combine with other elements. Ferrous salts are usually light green.

Fossil
The remains or imprint of an animal or plant that lived very long ago.

Freezing point
The temperature at which a liquid turns into a solid. The freezing point of water at sea level is 32 degrees Fahrenheit or zero degrees Celsius.

Fulcrum	The support on which a lever turns in order to lift something.
Genetics	The study of how plants, animals, and people inherit characteristics from parents and ancestors.
Gravity	The force that pulls objects toward the center of the earth. Balls thrown into the air will always fall back to earth because of gravity.
Habitat	The place or type of surroundings where a plant, animal, or human lives or grows.
Homogeneous mixture	A combination of substances that shares the characteristics of the ingredients. For example, when red paint and white paint combine to form pink, this color incorporates both the red and white, and so it's a homogeneous mixture.
Humidity	The amount of water vapor in the air.
Humus	A dark part of the soil made mostly of decayed plants and animals, especially nutritious for growing plants.
Hydroponics	The science of growing plants in water and nutrients, without using soil or pesticides.
Inclined plane	A slanted or sloped surface, such as a board leaning against a platform.
Indicator	A pointer or sign. A substance used to show what's in another substance. An example is a chemical that changes color when exposed to acids or bases.
Infrared	A band of invisible light waves, outside the spectrum of visible light waves at the red end. These light waves are longer and vibrate more slowly than the red light waves in the spectrum of visible colors.
International date line	The theoretical line around the earth from north to south where each new calendar day begins.
Ion	An atom or group of atoms carrying positive or negative electrical charges.
Kaleidoscope	A tube that contains small bits of colored glass and mirrors at one end so that a person looking in at the other end and turning the tube sees changing patterns and colors.
Kinesthetic sense	A person's sensation of body position and movement.
Larva	The often worm-like form of an insect when it first hatches from its egg. A caterpillar is the larva of a butterfly or moth.
Lava	Melted rock that erupts out of a volcano from far beneath the crust of the earth.
Lever	A pole or rod used to lift things.
Loam	The top layer of soil usually made of a mixture of sand, clay, silt, and decayed plants and animals, especially healthy for growing plants.
Luster	A shine or glow. Luster is used to identify rocks.
Magnetism	The power to attract iron, steel, and certain other metals. All electric currents produce magnetism.
Meteor	A small body of metal or stone that floats in space. When a meteor falls into the earth's atmosphere, it may burn and be visible for a moment as a "shooting star."
Meteorite	A meteor that has fallen to the earth's surface.
Meteorologist	A person who studies weather, weather forecasting, and the earth's atmosphere.
Microscope	A device that makes things look larger. Used to look at very small objects.

Microwaves Electromagnetic waves whose wavelengths are waves longer than infrared. Examples are radar, sonar, and radio waves.

Milky Way The thousands of faraway stars visible on earth as a white band of light across the nighttime sky. The sun is a star in the group of stars called the Milky Way Galaxy.

Mineral A substance that is not animal or plant. Mineral atoms form in crystal structures. Examples are salt, gold, and iron.

Molecule A tiny particle made up of two or more atoms connected or bonded together. A molecule may contain atoms of one element or a compound of several.

Neutron A tiny particle that is part of the center, or nucleus, of an atom.

Nutrients The nourishment needed by plants, animals, and people to survive. People and animals get nutrients from their food and water. Plants draw nutrients from water, air, and soil, but some plants eat insects.

Optical illusion A misleading image that tricks you into seeing something differently than it really is.

Organic Related to or coming from living plants or animals. Containing the element carbon.

Organism A living plant or animal.

Papillae Small bumps, such as the small bumps on the tongue that hold the even smaller taste buds.

Pendulum A weight hung so that it can swing back and forth. Often used to tell time.

Pesticide A chemical used to kill pests, usually insects.

Precipitate A solid substance that separates from a solution because of a chemical reaction or a physical change.

Primary colors The basic colors that combine to make all other colors. In paint, the primary colors are yellow, red, and blue.

Prism A transparent object that breaks up a ray of white light into the colors of the color spectrum.

Protractor A device that measures angles and helps people draw angles.

Proton A tiny particle that is part of the center, or nucleus, of an atom. A proton has a positive electric charge.

Pulley A wheel, used with a rope or chain, used to lift heavy weights.

Pumice A type of igneous rock, very light in weight and used as a powder to smooth and polish.

Quartz A type of igneous rock, often translucent, but sometimes clear or brightly colored. Examples are moonstone and amethyst.

Rain forest A tropical jungle that provides habitats for many types of animals and plants. Rain forests receive more than 100 inches of rain per year.

Reflection The return of light from a surface. An image given back by a mirror.

Refraction The bending of light, heat, or sound waves as they pass through one substance into another. An example is light waves passing from air through water or from water into glass and bending so that they form a rainbow. Or the bending of an image given back by an angled or distorted mirror.

Retina The lining at the back of the eyeball. Cells in the retina receive an image from the lens of the eye and then send the image through the optic nerve to the brain.

Rods and cones The nerve cells in the retina of the eye that allow for sight. The cones transmit color images. The rods transmit black, white, and gray images.

Satellite
1. An object people have put into space that orbits the earth. Satellites forecast weather, connect radio and television communications, and help study conditions on earth and in space. 2. A body in space that moves around a larger body. The moon is a satellite of the earth.

Secondary colors
The colors created by mixing two primary colors. In paint the secondary colors are orange, purple, and green.

Smog
Air pollution created by a combination of smoke and fog.

Solar power
Energy from the sun. People sometimes use solar power for heating, electricity, and cooking.

Solar system
The sun and the planets, moons, asteroids, and comets that revolve around it.

Solution
A mixture of one substance scattered evenly throughout another substance, usually a liquid, which does not separate over time.

Starch
A white food substance that most plants make and use as nourishment. Starch is a major type of carbohydrate.

Static electricity
Electrical charges that don't move. Usually in the air.

Subsoil
The layer of soil just under the topsoil, usually formed of clay or sand.

Suet
The hard fat from beef, often used as bird food.

Supercooled
Cooled below its usual freezing point without turning to a solid.

Supersaturated
Containing an amount greater than usual, describes a solution that has dissolved more of a substance than normally possible.

Terrarium
A bowl or bottle enclosing a garden of small plants, without standing water.

Translucent
1. Allowing light but not images to pass through. Frosted glass is translucent. 2. Glowing.

Transparent
Allowing both light and images to pass through. Clear. Window glass is usually transparent.

Ultraviolet
A band of invisible, high frequency light waves outside the spectrum of visible light at the violet end. These light waves are shorter and vibrate faster than the violet light waves in the spectrum of visible colors.

Vapor
Small droplets of mist that can be seen in the air. Vapor rises above a pot of boiling water. However, the gas that makes up water vapor and steam is invisible.

Volcano
An opening in a mountain through which lava, gases, and ashes erupt from deep in the earth.

INDEX